A guide to finding quality information on the internet

About the first edition

'Cooke has produced a valuable work which . . . gives plentiful advice for those undertaking literature searches or using the Internet as an information resource.'
Internet Resources Newsletter

'This book adds a lot of value by bringing together valuable insights, examples and checklists in a highly accessible format.' *UKOLUG Newsletter*

'A recommended companion for any serious web searcher.'
The Web Search Workshop

'A systematically organised handbook with a simple and clear approach to evaluating the quality of information sources on the internet which should be used by librarians, teachers, students – indeed anyone who is looking for information on the internet . . . . Its clear presentation makes this a valuable tool for librarians to use for their own benefit and to enhance their teaching skills.'
Australian Library Journal

'Ideal for library professionals in academic, school, or public libraries; or any information educator who is interested in training users.'
Reference & Users Services Quarterly

'[They] have 'pounced' on this book in our library, declaring that it was just what they were looking for to further their researches. Their views of the text, and its usefulness, on return, were no less enthusiastic in all cases.' *ELG News*

'Using friendly, understandable language, Cooke deftly balances the objectivity and subjectivity necessary for effective quality evaluation, and tackles a complex issue with mastery.' *Online and CD-ROM Review*

'A comprehensive resource . . . equally useful to both instructors who wish to increase classroom Internet usage and to students who wish to efficiently choose sites that are suitable for research.' *InfoTech*

'A worthwhile contribution to the Internet literature, and a particularly useful book for LIS students and Internet trainers, both inexperienced and veterans.'
The Electronic Library

'Cooke writes with wit and ease . . . ' *School Library Journal*

'A very useful book.' *Journal of Youth Services in Libraries*

'An intelligent method for selection . . . recommended.'
Journal of Academic Librarianship

A guide to finding quality information on the internet

Selection and evaluation strategies

Second edition

Alison Cooke

LIBRARY ASSOCIATION PUBLISHING
LONDON

Published by
Library Association Publishing
7 Ridgmount Street
London WC1E 7AE

Library Association Publishing is wholly owned by The Library Association.

First published 1999
This second edition 2001

British Library Cataloguing in Publication Data

A catalogue record for this book is available from the British Library

ISBN 1-85604-379-7

Typeset in 10/13pt Classical Garamond and Verdana by Library Association Publishing.
Printed and made in Great Britain by MPG Books Ltd, Bodmin, Cornwall.

Contents

Acknowledgements

The first edition of this book was based upon the results of doctoral research carried out between October 1994 and July 1998 at the Department of Information and Library Studies, University of Wales, Aberystwyth. Internet users were interviewed concerning a specific case where they had used the internet to look for information, and the interview transcripts were analysed to determine how assessments of quality were made and to identify evaluation criteria. The results were developed into a tool for assessing the quality of internet-based information sources. Chapters 3 and 4 of this book remain based largely upon the results of the research.

I would like to express my gratitude to those involved in arranging the fieldwork (Betsy Anagnostelis, Librarian at the Royal Free Hospital; Frank Norman, Librarian at the National Institute for Medical Research; Sue Welsh, previously also at the National Institute for Medical Research; Bob Parkinson at the Queen's Medical Centre, Nottingham University; and Wendy Roberts at the School of Clinical Medicine, Cambridge University). I would like to thank all those who participated in the fieldwork for their time and co-operation, and all of the information professionals who offered advice and feedback at various stages throughout the research. I would also like to thank the University of Wales for funding the research, and the members of staff at the Department of Information and Library Studies, University of Wales, Aberystwyth, and in particular my PhD supervisors, David Stoker and Su James, for their professional support and advice.

I would also like to thank all those people at Library Association Publishing involved in the production of this book. I am particularly grateful to Helen

Carley, Helen Vaux and Lin Franklin for their continued support and advice during the process of writing the book, and for their involvement in its production.

Thanks also to all of the staff in the Medical Library at the Royal Free Hospital, as well as the staff of the other medical libraries within University College London, for their professional advice and support. Acknowledgement also must go to all those who have attended internet training sessions in the Medical Library at the Royal Free, and who unknowingly have been a source of ideas and inspiration about what quality means in relation to the internet.

Every effort has been made to contact the holders of copyright material reproduced in this text, and thanks are due to them for permission to reproduce the material indicated. If there are any queries please contact the Publishers.

1

Introduction: some questions answered

What's the problem?

In 1969, the beginnings of 'the internet' consisted of four networked computers located in three universities and a research institute in America. By the
early 1980s, the number of 'host' computers connected to this international
network had grown to over 1000. By January 2001 almost 110 million host
computers, distributed throughout almost every continent and country across
the globe, were connected to what is now known as 'the internet'.[1] The number of newsgroups multiplied from three in 1979 to 10,696 in 1994, and the
number of websites from 133 in June 1993 to 2500 in June 1994, rising to
10,000 at the end of 1994.[1] By January 2001, there were almost 28 million
websites[1] providing access to over 2 billion unique pages of information.[2]
Advances in computer networking during this period offered unforeseen
advantages in terms of accessing and disseminating information, and the resulting explosion in the volume and variety of sources could never have been
predicted. However, far from an information utopia, this rapid explosion has
brought with it many problems.

Too much of a good thing

The ease of dissemination of information via the internet has resulted in an
unimaginable quantity and variety of sources of potential interest to any internet user. However, while the more commonly used search tools continue to be
driven by the perceived need to retrieve as much as possible of the available

material, users are constantly faced by information overload – too much information to sift through and utilize in any meaningful way.

For example, a seemingly straightforward search on *Google* (**http://www.google.com/**) for 'vegetarian recipes' results in 133,000 hits, as displayed in Figure 1.1. Adding the term 'casseroles' reduces the number to 19,000. However, this remains a vast amount of material, making it difficult to find what you are looking for. The result? The internet can be an inefficient and time-consuming option when looking for information, particularly when a search result of 19,000 hits does not necessarily mean that any one site will provide what you want.

Useless information

Information overload is not the only problem. Anyone, anywhere with access to the internet can now become an author and their own publisher. Without the constraints previously imposed by commercial and academic publishers, huge volumes of junk are being produced.

Accessing *The Useless Pages* (**http://www.go2net.com/useless/**) provides an insight into the range of resources of questionable usefulness that is currently available. As can be seen in Figure 1.2, the useless site of the week at the time of writing was *Pet Emails* (**http://www.petemails.com/**). Access the site and you can enter your pet's e-mail address, compose a message and select a type of pet. The program translates your message into pet-speak – e.g. 'glub glub splash

Fig. 1.1 *The results of a search for 'vegetarian recipes' on 'Google'*

Fig. 1.2 *'The Useless Pages'*
© 2001 InfoSpace, Inc. All rights reserved. INFOSPACE and its designs and related marks are the intellectual property of InfoSpace, Inc. Used with permission.

glub gurgle blub gurgle glub gurgle gurgle glub gurgle' for a fish. When recipients open their mail, they can follow a link to the original message. A previous site of the week was *Ugly People of the Internet* (**http://www.tqci.net/~tvc15/ugly/main.html**), a collection of images from around the internet of 'ugly people' collated through 'reader submission'. It is difficult to envisage many situations in which such sites could be considered of value.

Further drawbacks relate to personal home pages. These can contain little more than images of 'My friends', 'My cat' and 'Where I live'. Again, it is often difficult to envisage how such sites could appeal to a wide audience. Additional problems arise because individuals develop a personal site while in a particular job, or while at college or university, but after three or four years they move on without removing the information, or without notifying external sites which point to their documents. Following links to these sites subsequently results in the familiar 'file not found' message. Almost without exception, every internet user will have encountered links to pages that no longer exist. Others will have experienced outdated information from a seemingly reputable organization or individual, and sites that look interesting at first glance but in reality lack any useful material.

Inaccurate information

Not only is much of the information available via the internet potentially useless, but it may also be inaccurate or misleading. This has become an area of particular concern with regard to health information, particularly as most

3

readers are likely to have used the internet at one time or another to find information relating to their own health or the health of a friend or relative. This is
supported by statistics of search engine use – the internet search engine *Lycos*
(**http://www.lycos.com/**) maintains an index of the top 50 most frequently used
search terms.[3] While 'sex' topped the charts in 1999 as the most frequently
used term, 'pregnancy' ranked higher than, for example, 'the Simpsons' or
'Austin Powers'.

However, as early as 1996, the *British Medical Journal* (*BMJ*) noted a growth
in the number of unverified health claims being made via the internet. Examples included:

> Advertisements for shark cartilage which 'inhibits tumour growth and can-
> cer' and melatonin which is banned in the United Kingdom but freely
> available in the United States and is claimed to 'strengthen the body's
> immune system'.[4]

More recent studies have attempted to gauge the extent of the problem. A review
of resources on advice to deal with fever in children at home was also published
in the *BMJ*.[5] Over 40 web pages were evaluated and compared to authoritative
medical guidelines and only four provided advice which closely adhered to the
published recommendations. Advice varied for seemingly straightforward procedures, such as taking a child's temperature, and the authors subsequently
recommend 'an urgent need to check public oriented healthcare information on
the internet for accuracy, completeness, and consistency.'

More worrying is the availability of inaccurate and unreliable health information that has the potential to cause harm. Culver, et al. assessed the accuracy
of messages posted to a mailing list for people with painful hand and arm conditions.[6] They found that the advice frequently had little medical basis and
compliance may in some cases have increased risk to an individual or caused
harm. Desai, et al. evaluated information sent to a pharmacy newsgroup and
found that only half of the information was accurate while 19.4% was potentially harmful.[7]

Figure 1.3 displays an image from a site by Dr Hulda R. Clark (**http://
members.aol.com/sidskids1/health/cancerbk.htm**). The site advertises the
author's book containing details of how all cancers can be cured – according
to the author, cancer is caused by a parasite; kill the parasite and the cancer is
cured. This type of wildly inaccurate information is relatively easy to detect
because the site is making 'cure-all' claims (and usually involves the consumer
purchasing a product). However, not all inaccurate information is as easy to
recognize and it is likely that many internet users will have little or no know-

Fig. 1.3 *'Cure-all' claims on the internet*

ledge of healthcare issues in order to make an assessment. Furthermore, people seeking health-related advice are potentially vulnerable to any treatment claims they encounter because either they or a friend or relative may be seriously ill. Thus, users of the internet are faced with the need to detect inaccurate sources of advice, but many of us lack the necessary knowledge and skills to make such an assessment.

Why have these problems arisen?

The above section has highlighted just a few of the problems associated with using the internet to find information. So, why have these problems arisen?

Early development of the internet

Prior to the 1980s, internet users had access to three basic tools: e-mail, telnet, and File Transfer Protocol (FTP). These provided access to vast quantities of information but relied upon prior knowledge of the location and availability of resources, as well as knowledge of the commands to access and use them. Therefore their use was limited to those with some basic knowledge of computer networking and uptake was slow.

In the late 1980s and early 1990s, the development of distributed client-server computing fundamentally altered the way in which information could be accessed via the internet. Distributed client-server computing enables users to access information with their own local computer, the client, handling interaction with a remote computer, the server. Simply, the information is located on a remote machine, while the software for accessing it is located on the user's machine. This enables users to decide how they access information. Gopher was an early example of a distributed client-server tool that offered a menu-based interface to internet sources. The software was friendlier and more helpful than the command-line interfaces used for accessing telnet resources or FTP archives, and individuals could browse through the menus of resources without having to know filenames and locations.

The web and multimedia browsers

The 'world wide web', sometimes known as 'WWW', or more commonly, the 'web', is another example of a distributed client-server tool. The web is built around a standard hypertext language, HyperText Mark-up Language (HTML), which can be read by almost any computer and can be used to define links between different parts of the same document or between different documents. While early versions of web browsers (the software for accessing the web) were text-based, multimedia browsers such as *Mosaic* and *Netscape Navigator* were soon freely distributed. Using these browsers, files could be located, retrieved and displayed easily with the full integration of text, graphics and sound. In addition, browsers provided access to existing information sources, such as newsgroups, Gopher resources and FTP archives, as well as to web information in a hypertext format.

By the mid-1990s, the potential of the internet was beginning to be fully realized. The web quickly became the most heavily used tool for accessing information and there was a rapid explosion in the volume of materials that were being made available. Reasons for this included the ease of using multimedia browsers to access information, as well as the ease of producing documents in HTML format. HTML initially appears confusing to the new user, but the code of existing documents can be captured and amended in order to create new pages both quickly and easily. In addition, during the mid-1990s, a number of software packages were developed which enabled users to create pages without any in-depth knowledge of HTML, including packages with the facility to convert existing materials in an electronic format into HTML. More recently, tools such as Dreamweaver have been developed which can be used to create large-scale sites with integrated graphics, moving images and sound files.

The new millennium

Estimates suggest that in the year 2000, 11 million people in the UK alone were using the internet every month.[8] The continued fall in the price of PCs and computer equipment generally, combined with a price war over offering cheaper and cheaper access to the internet, has contributed to this figure. A web presence is considered essential for any commercial organization, and '.com' companies, such as *amazon.com* and *lastminute.com*, have become household names. Another factor contributing to the rise in usage levels must be the availability of *Internet Explorer* on millions of home and work computers, a web browser included as part of the Microsoft Office suite of software products. The number of potential authors and publishers of information is astounding – any one of these people now has the technology to write and publish whatever they want and to make their views available to literally millions of people all over the world.

What is the purpose of this book?

I have written this book because, although the internet can often prove to be a valuable source of information, it can also be a waste of time, frustrating, and the information which is available is often useless, outdated or difficult to authenticate. The book is a comprehensive manual designed to assist internet users in searching for high-quality information, and in filtering through materials and assessing their quality once they have been found. It has been divided into the following chapters:

- using search facilities to maximize the quality of information retrieval
- assessing the quality of an information source
- evaluating particular types of sources
- using checklists, kitemarks and other quality indicators.

Using search facilities to maximize quality information retrieval

There is an ever-increasing range of different tools that enable you to search for information available via the internet. These range from general search engines such as *Google* or *AltaVista*, through general subject directories such as *Yahoo!*, to services for accessing high-quality materials, such as *SOSIG*. This section provides a guide to the different types of search facilities, some examples and how they work (including those mentioned here), their respective advantages and disadvantages, and what to use when attempting to find high-quality materials. The aim of the section is to introduce the range of search facilities that are available, while focusing on how to find high-quality materials.

Assessing the quality of an information source

The next section of the book focuses on assessing quality. The following ten areas are examined which require consideration in the evaluation of any information source:

- identifying the purpose of a source
- assessing coverage
- assessing authority and reputation
- assessing accuracy
- assessing the currency and maintenance of a source
- considering the accessibility of a source
- evaluating the presentation and arrangement of information
- assessing how easy a source is to use
- making a comparison with other sources
- assessing the overall quality of a source.

Each section contains extensive notes on how to approach the particular aspect of evaluation, drawing on real examples, and there is an easy-to-use checklist of the points that are mentioned in the text.

Evaluating particular types of sources

A wide range of different types of information sources exists via the internet. Examples include personal home pages, organizational sites, newsgroups, electronic journals – the list is almost endless. Different people access and use these different sources for different reasons, and are often interested in different quality issues. For example, a user of a personal home page might simply want an e-mail address, whereas a newsgroup reader may be seeking advice. Therefore this part of the book is concerned with evaluating particular types of information sources. It has been divided as follows:

- organizational sites, personal home pages and other websites
- mailing lists, newsgroups and other forms of communication via the internet
- full-text documents
- databases
- electronic journals and magazines

- sources of news information
- advertising, sponsorship and commercial information
- image-based and multimedia sources
- current awareness and alerting services
- FTP archives

Each section includes criteria specific to each source type, with detailed notes on their application and use, and some worked examples. A checklist for each source type is also included for easy referral.

Using checklists, kitemarks and metadata to indicate 'quality'

Internet resources are generally evaluated using criteria for guidance in critically appraising information . The approach adopted in this book is to describe as many as possible of the available criteria so that you can select those that are relevant to your own needs and the source that you are evaluating. However, additional approaches to indicating resource quality are either currently in use or under development. This section examines checklists and rating tools, kitemarks and other seals of approval, and the potential role of metadata in identifying quality information. Rather than recommending, for example, a particular checklist or seal of approval, the aim of this section is to introduce the range of additional instruments and techniques that are available. If you are interested in using a particular instrument or technique, references and website addresses are included in the text for further information.

And finally . . .

At the end of the book are some additional tools designed to assist readers both in finding their way around the text and in assessing information quality. There is a glossary of technical terms, a compilation of all the checklists from Chapters 2, 3 and 4 of the book, an alphabetical list of all websites mentioned in the text and an index.

Who should use the book?

Anyone, anywhere, anyhow . . .

Ultimately, this book is aimed at any internet user, and the number of potential situations when it might be needed to assess the quality of information is almost infinite. One person might want to find information for a college project and be interested in the best places to start looking. Another might need an answer to a specific health question, have identified some relevant sources, but not know how to establish the accuracy of what they have found. This guide offers indicators of where to start looking for information and how to make a quality assessment when potentially relevant materials have been located. The book will be helpful to those who are new to using the internet, or who are less experienced in evaluating the quality of information, because it provides an introduction to different tools for searching, alongside a thorough grounding in assessing quality. The book will also be of value to experienced internet users because it provides insight into the methods that are currently available for finding quality sources of information. Those who are well versed in evaluation techniques will be able to refresh their skills as well as learn about additional methods for information evaluation.

Information professionals and students

Students and practitioners of librarianship and information science will no doubt be aware of the increasingly important role that information professionals now have to play in filtering information. Therefore, both library students and professionals alike who are likely to be involved, or already are involved, in the selection and evaluation of internet-based information sources will find this guide of particular value. It can be used as a manual for selecting resources for inclusion in library collections. In addition, it might be used for training or advising library users on how to assess the quality of information available via the internet, and in order to increase awareness regarding the need to think critically about sources of information generally.

Developers of internet materials

Any author wants to produce a high-quality product that is of value and use to their intended audience. This is nowhere more important than the internet, where millions of people are competing for the attention of an audience. Despite this, it never ceases to amaze me how regularly I find sites that lack the most basic of signposts – contact details and the date a page was last updated. For these reasons, this guide is equally relevant to information providers and to information consumers. The sections on assessing quality in particular relate to the wide range of factors which affect our perceptions of quality – consideration of these will not only help to improve information sources, but also ensure that the basic signposts are available to assist users in making their judgements. In addition, knowledge of how to find quality information can assist in understanding what is needed to ensure that the discerning internet user finds your site. Furthermore, anyone developing a site is likely to link to other materials – this guide can be used as an aid to selecting sites to link to for further information.

How should the book be used?

Newcomers to the internet and information quality

Newcomers to both the internet and evaluating sources of information are advised to work systematically through the book. You should begin by reading Chapter 2 on 'Using search facilities to maximize quality information retrieval' as it explains the differences between different search facilities and provides numerous tips on how to search the internet more effectively. You are then advised to read Chapter 3 on 'Assessing the quality of an information source' in order to become familiar with source assessment. By reading through this section in its entirety, you will be provided with a thorough grounding in the various factors affecting the quality of any information source that can be accessed via the internet.

When seeking high-quality materials

As already mentioned, Chapter 2 on 'Using search facilities to maximize quality information retrieval' provides a guide to the different types of search facilities which are now available, some examples of each of the different facilities, how they work, their respective advantages and disadvantages, and how they can be used to look for high-quality materials. The chapter provides guidelines on where to start looking, as well as ideas for finding high-quality sources. Therefore, if you are interested in searching for information, this chapter will be the most relevant to you.

When assessing a specific source

Many readers will come to the book with a particular source that they want to evaluate. The most relevant section if you are in this situation is 'Evaluating particular types of sources' (Chapter 4). Firstly, decide what type of information source you have – e.g. is it a personal home page, a newsgroup or an electronic journal? In many cases, this will be immediately obvious from the source itself, but readers may want to examine the definitions that are provided in the sections for the different source types. Once you have decided what type you want to evaluate, examine the detailed notes relating to the evaluation of the source type concerned. If you cannot decide on a particular source type, the general section on assessing quality (Chapter 3) is applicable to the evaluation of any source available via the internet. Indeed, many of the issues discussed in this section are also applicable to the specific source types. In order to prevent repetition, the issues have not been repeated but readers are referred back to the relevant sections where appropriate.

Expert internet users and evaluators

If you are familiar with using the internet, and with evaluating different types of information sources, you may find that you can begin immediately with the checklists provided at the end of each section for assessing quality, at the end of the sections relating to each source type, or the compilation of all of these checklists at the end of the book. These are designed to provide a reminder and prompt for what to look for when assessing quality. Other users may find it beneficial to refer initially to the detailed explanatory notes, but use the checklists as they become more familiar with source assessment.

What is the role of this book in quality assessment?

The term 'quality' is used in a wide range of contexts and its meaning is often assumed rather than clearly defined. It is generally used as an abbreviation to denote 'good quality' or 'high quality'. However, in order to understand the role of this book in information quality assessment, it is important to understand what is meant by 'quality'.

The *Oxford English Dictionary* does not offer a particularly useful definition – 'the degree of excellence of a thing'. This suggests there is a grade of excellence to which all things can aspire. Likewise, the British Standards Institution definition, at first glance, seems equally unhelpful – 'the totality of characteristics of an entity that bear on its ability to satisfy stated and implied needs'.[9] However, this latter definition is perhaps more useful than it at first seems. It suggests there can be no absolute measure of 'quality' because any understanding of, for example, the quality of a product, will depend upon the needs of those using it and the ability of the product to meet their needs. If we interpret quality as the ability of a product to meet the needs of an individual, it would be possible to identify the characteristics of a product that will affect its ability to meet those needs. For example, someone wanting to buy a computer might evaluate those that are available according to cost and the hardware specification because they have a small budget but need high-speed access to the internet.

'Information' can be treated in the same way as any other product when quality is being assessed. There can be no definitive statement of the quality of a source of information, but its quality can be assessed according to its ability to meet the stated or implied needs of a user. Likewise, it is possible to identify the characteristics of information that affect its ability to meet stated or implied needs. For example, people looking for images for a presentation will evaluate the images they find according to whether they portray the correct subject and are in an appropriate format for use.

However, in the electronic environment of the internet, the users and providers of information number in the millions. It might therefore be suggested that there are so many possible variables involved in any assessment of quality that the whole process is entirely subjective and there can be no role for a book on the subject. It is exactly this understanding of the subjectivity of quality assessment that shapes the content and purpose of this book. The book is designed to encapsulate all of the possible criteria and techniques that might be used for selection and evaluation. No single internet user could attempt to utilize all of the criteria that are presented here. Instead, readers will need to consider their own needs, as well as the nature of the source being evaluated, and select the appropriate criteria from those that are described.

Furthermore, quality assessment is not a straightforward procedure involving an identification of the presence or absence of different features or facilities. Instead, quality assessment is a complex process involving consideration of a wide range of interrelated issues that are of varying importance depending upon the nature of the source and the needs of the user. For example, while factual accuracy might be an important issue for one person, another individual might be more interested in the presentation and arrangement of information. Furthermore, it is not always possible to assess accuracy but there are numerous factors that affect our perceptions, such as the expertise of the author or the quality of presentation. Due to the complex nature of quality assessment, it would not be possible to provide a straightforward list of criteria. Instead, the guidelines include detailed explanatory notes and examples highlighting the relationships between different quality issues. Again, readers will need to consider their own needs and what they are evaluating, select the appropriate criteria and apply them as necessary.

References

1 Zakon, R. H., *Hobbe's internet timeline* (Version 5.3), 2000 [online], available at **http://info.isoc.org/zakon/Internet/History/HIT.html** [2001, March 8].

2 Kennon, J. and Johnson, A., Internet exceeds 2 billion pages, *Cyveillance* [online], available at **http://www.cyveillance.com/newsroom/pressr/000710.asp** [2000, November 25].

3 *The Lycos 50 daily report – 1999's hottest topics revealed!*, 1999 [online], available at **http://50.lycos.com/121799.html** [2001, March 8].

4 Bower, H., Internet sees growth in unverified health claims, *BMJ*, **313** (7054), 1996, 381.

5 Impicciatore, P., et al., Reliability of health information for the public on the world wide web: systematic survey of advice on managing fever in children at home, *BMJ*, **314** (7098), 1997, 1875–9.

6 Culver, J. D., Gerr, F. and Frumkin, H., Medical information on the Internet: a study of an electronic bulletin board, *Journal of General Internal Medicine*, **12** (8), 1997, 466–70.

7 Desai, N. S., et al., Evaluation of drug information in an Internet newsgroup, *Journal of the American Pharmaceutical Association*, **NS37** (4), 1997, 391–4.

8 Green, L. and Addison, D., *11 million people in the UK now use the internet every month*, 2000 [online], available at **http://www.mmxieurope.com/press/releases/20001114.jsp** [2001, March 8].

9 British Standards Institution, *Quality management and quality assurance: vocabulary*, British Standards Institution, 1995.

2 Using search facilities to maximize quality information retrieval

The first step to finding high-quality sources of information is looking for them, which is what this chapter is about. Many internet users begin their explorations by opening either *Netscape Navigator* or *Internet Explorer* – whichever is loaded on the computer that they are using – and then clicking on the 'search' button. Either a preselected search tool or a selection of tools is displayed with a blank space for users to type their query. At this point, many people type a single word, click on 'go', and find they are presented with literally hundreds of thousands of results. There is often little descriptive detail about each site and they are faced with the laborious task of sifting through the lists of links to locate some relevant material.

Generally the type of search tool that is used in this scenario is a *search engine*. Search engines are automatically generated databases of web-based materials. They have become by far the most popular type of tool for searching the internet – partly because they are located using the method described above, but also because they claim comprehensive coverage of the internet, and because the interfaces are friendly and easy to navigate. However, there are several problems with using search engines, particularly for users concerned about the quality of the information they are seeking. As mentioned in Chapter 1, anyone can disseminate information via the internet, and search engines index potentially any of the available information. Other types of search facilities are available which provide access to preselected materials and can offer a more effective approach to searching. In addition, each search tool works in a slightly different way – by understanding how a specific tool works, it is possible to utilize its features to maximum effect, and in some cases, find higher-quality materials.

This chapter examines the different tools that are now available for searching the internet. While there are many more types than discussed here, the following are looked at in detail:

- search engines
- gateways and virtual libraries
- subject catalogues and directory services.

A detailed example is discussed for each type of tool, and their respective advantages and disadvantages are considered. Additional types of search tools are also briefly described. Towards the end of the chapter, tips are provided on where to start searching and when to use which facilities. Lastly, a checklist is provided of what to look for in a search tool when seeking high-quality materials.

This chapter is not intended as a general guide to searching the internet, as this is outside the scope of the book. The aim of the chapter is to introduce the range of search facilities that are available, while focusing on how to find high-quality materials. If you are interested in searching generally, many valuable guides are available on the subject, such as the *Netskills* web page *Resources for searching*,[1] the *Search Engine Watch* site,[2] or the materials available from Phil Bradley's home page.[3]

Search engines

As mentioned above, search engines are the most commonly used type of tool for finding information on the internet. Search engines utilize software to automatically generate a database of websites and pages – the software continuously visits web pages to create the database. Because they run automatically and index so many pages, search engines often contain information not listed in the tools described later in this section. However, search engines are problematic because they do not discriminate between the quality of the materials that are indexed. This section examines an example of a search engine to explore how they work. Other search engines are also described briefly. The advantages and disadvantages of search engines are considered, particularly in relation to finding high-quality internet materials.

Example   *Northern Light*

Suppose that you have just been diagnosed with an illness, such as diabetes. After returning home from your doctor, you would probably think of numerous questions that you wish you had asked – you would want additional information, and where better to look than the internet?

Northern Light (**http://www.northernlight.com/**) is one example of a search engine. As displayed in Figure 2.1, entering the term 'diabetes' in the search box results in 1,334,650 hits – an almost unbelievable volume of information. The immense number of results can be explained by examining how search engines work. Search engines generally consist of three major parts: firstly, the 'spider' or 'crawler', the software which visits web pages, reads them and indexes them; secondly, the database, also sometimes called the catalogue or index, which contains a copy of every web page that the spider finds; and thirdly, the search engine, the program which sifts through the millions of pages in the database to find matches to a user's query. The spider returns to

Fig. 2.1   *Search results for 'diabetes' in 'Northern Light'*

Reprinted with permission from Northern Light Technology, Inc.

sites regularly (e.g. every week) to look for changes and to update the database, ensuring that its coverage of the web is current and extensive. This results in an enormous number of results for almost any search. Not only is this potentially problematic in itself, but the automatic generation of search engine databases means that there is no discrimination in terms of the quality of the information that is retrieved. Anyone, anywhere can publish information via the internet. The lack of quality control of internet resources generally, and the lack of discrimination by search engines of the available material, means that the vast quantities of retrieved information can range from potentially high-quality and relevant materials to highly dubious information.

Relevance ranking and resource descriptions

The results in Figure 2.1 are listed with those considered most relevant first. The percentage displayed next to each site is the relevance ranking – the higher the figure, the more relevant a site is deemed to be. Pages are assumed to be more relevant where your search terms appear in the title of a page, where the terms appear near the top of a page, and where the terms appear frequently in the text. However, you should not assume that relevance ranking is always successful. As can be seen in Figure 2.1, the first site is entitled 'health conditions, herpe... lice, headache'. Non-relevant pages are sometimes listed among the first results from search engines on account of the enormous amount of material that is indexed. In addition, one method that has been used to increase site relevance is 'spamming'. This involves repeating a word many times on a page so that the engine assumes its increased relevance. However, many engines now penalize pages if they detect spamming by ranking them lower than they might otherwise appear in the results or by excluding them altogether.

One problem with using search engines is that the descriptions about each site are generated automatically by the software and they therefore often provide little meaningful information. For example, the first site displayed in Figure 2.1 reads:

> . . . health conditions,herpe... color=blue>diabe... lice,headache, Conditions and Diseases. Categories for Conditions and Diseases. Search for "Conditions and Diseases" on:... Date Not Available.

It is unclear why this site has been retrieved and how the information relates to our search on 'diabetes', other than the abbreviated 'diabe'. Likewise, the second and third sites sound more appropriate to our search – the 'National Institute for Diabetes and Digestive and Kidney Diseases' and the 'American

Diabetes Association'. However, the descriptions offer little insight into their content and users would need to link to each site separately and browse the content to assess its appropriateness.

Narrowing searches down

Different search engines offer different options to assist in focusing your searches. *Northern Light* generates a list of 'custom search folders' – these are designed to 'make looking for information easier and faster by dynamically grouping your results into meaningful categories'. For example, a search on 'diabetes' includes the following folders:

- diabetes
- hypoglycemia
- diabetic diet
- movies
- juvenile diabetes.

It is therefore possible to select the aspect of diabetes that you are interested in. However, as can be seen in Figure 2.2, selecting a custom search folder does not necessarily alter the search results effectively – the 'diabetes' folder has been selected, reducing the result from over a million sites to 74,127. While this is a significant reduction in size, it remains an unmanageable amount of information, particularly as there is no guarantee of the quality or relevance of the information.

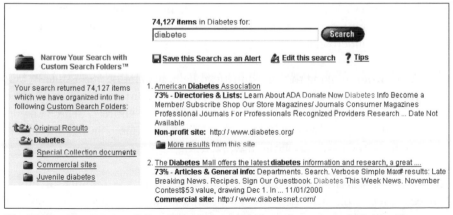

Fig. 2.2 *Contents of the 'Northern Light' custom search folder for 'diabetes'*

Reprinted with permission from Northern Light Technology, Inc.

Other search engines offer different options. *Google* (**http://www.google. com/**), for example, has a link to 'similar pages' from each hit in your search results. When you click on the 'similar pages' link, the search engine, *GoogleScout*, automatically looks for web pages that are related to the result. The theory is:

> If you like a particular site's content, but wish it had more to say, Google-Scout can find sites with similar content that you may not be familiar with. If you are looking for product information, GoogleScout can find competitive information for you, so that you can get the best deal. If you are interested in researching a particular field, GoogleScout can help you find a large number of resources very quickly, without spending time worrying about which keywords might be used on those sites.[4]

Selecting this option has a major impact on the number of search results – 'diabetes' retrieves over two million pages and the first hit is the *American Diabetes Association* home page; selecting the 'similar pages' link results in only 19 sites. However, the results include the *American Heart Association*, the *American Cancer Society* and the *American Lung Association* – it appears that the determining factors for retrieving similar pages are the word 'American' and the fact that this is an organizational home page.

A simple method for narrowing searches down when using search engines is to add more terms. Most people simply type one word or an individual's name – this is illustrated by a visit to the *Excite* 'search voyeur' (**http://www. excite.com/search/voyeur/**). At the time of writing, searches being conducted included 'puzzles', 'e-mail', 'browsers' and 'vitamins'. However, Phil Bradley compares this approach to searching with someone walking into a library and simply saying 'underpants':

> Apart from thinking they need medical help, it's almost impossible to help them. Do they want a history of underwear, or a list of suppliers, or references to underpants in the news, or something else entirely? Search engines have the same problem; unless users put their requests into some sort of context they have very little to work with.[5]

For example, searching for 'diabetes insulin' reduces the number of hits in *Northern Light* from 1,334,650 to 157,002, and 'diabetes insulin dependent' restricts the results to 51,769 items. *Northern Light* automatically 'ANDs' any additional terms together so that only those pages are retrieved which contain all of the terms. This is illustrated in Figure 2.3 – the shaded areas represent the retrieved pages for each search. The reduction in the number of results illustrates the potential effectiveness of this technique. However, the problem remains that 51,769 is an unmanageable amount of information and we still have no assurance of its quality or usefulness.

Additional options for searching

Northern Light provides a link from the opening screen to 'tips' (**http://www.northernlight.com/docs/search_help_optimize.html**). Several options are described which can be used to refine searches and ensure more effective retrieval. For example, you can use Boolean operators 'AND', 'OR' and 'NOT' to combine two or more different words. 'AND' will retrieve only those sites which contain your search terms, 'OR' will retrieve sites which mention one or other or both words, and 'NOT' excludes sites mentioning a particular word – this is illustrated in Figure 2.4. Using double quotes around two or more terms specifies that you only want to retrieve items where they appear as a phrase – "insulin dependent" will only retrieve pages where these

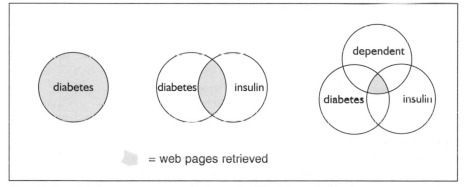

Fig. 2.3 *Adding more search terms in 'Northern Light'*

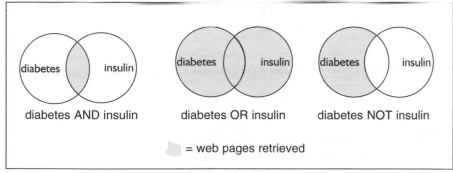

Fig. 2.4 *Combining search terms using 'AND', 'OR' and 'NOT'*

21

two words appear as they are typed here. A '*' can be used as a truncation symbol to replace multiple variations of a word ending – diabet* will retrieve pages which mention diabetic, diabetics or diabetes. Therefore, our earlier search could be retyped as "insulin dependent" AND diabet*' – this retrieves 42,241 hits. These options, as well as many others, are commonly available in search engines. It is therefore often worth consulting any help information to determine what options can be used in each tool to improve the effectiveness of your searches.

Furthermore, many search engines offer an 'advanced' search screen. Selecting 'power search' from the opening screen in *Northern Light* **(http://www.northernlight.com/power.html)** leads to the additional search options displayed in Figure 2.5.

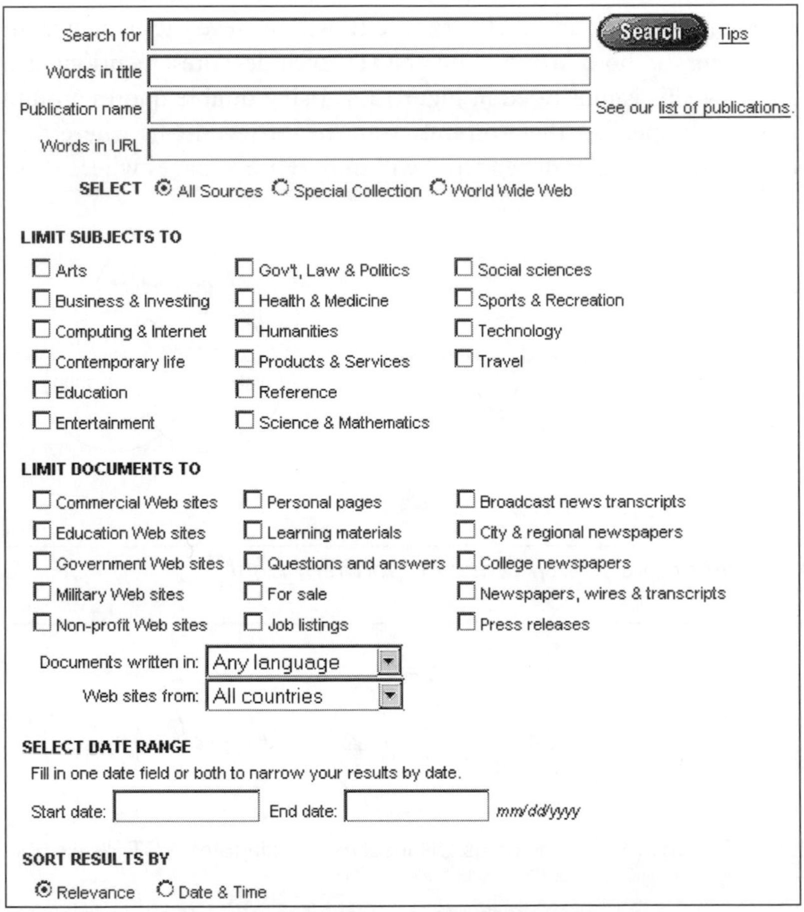

Fig. 2.5 *'Power Search' options in 'Northern Light'*
Reprinted with permission from Northern Light Technology, Inc.

As displayed, these options mean:

- you can search for words that appear only in web page titles (this would be a useful method for restricting your searches to a few highly relevant sites)
- you can search for characters that only appear in the URL (the web page address) – this would be useful if you remembered only part of an address but knew a site existed
- you can limit your search by subject area, type of document, language, date range or sites from specific countries.

Searching for "insulin dependent" AND diabet*' in the titles of web pages, and restricting by subject to health and medicine, and by language to English, results in only 529 hits. However, while this is a much more manageable amount of information than was retrieved in our previous searches, the problem remains that we have no assurance of the likely usefulness or quality of any of the material.

Web citation searching – finding quality using search engines?

Researchers have been using citation searching as a method for finding potentially high-quality papers for a number of years. At the end of each published research article, authors list any references mentioned in the text. The *Science Citation Index*, the *Social Sciences Citation Index* and the *Arts and Humanities Citation Index* are databases that have been built around the references listed at the end of each article. It is possible to search one of these databases and establish how many times a particular paper has been cited elsewhere, as well as to examine the papers which have cited the original article. The theory is that the more times a paper has been cited by other authors, the higher its quality. However, there are obvious limitations to this approach to assessing quality: a paper might be cited to refute its arguments, or it might be highly controversial (and therefore frequently cited), without necessarily being a high-quality paper.

Options are now available for searching the web which draw upon the same principles of citation searching. The web is built around the use of hypertext links, which connect different documents in different locations. Web citation searching involves using these links to indicate quality. For example, *Google* uses the number of links to a site to rank web pages in its search results:

> *Google* interprets a link from page A to page B as a vote, by page A, for page B. But, *Google* looks at more than the sheer volume of votes, or links a page receives; it also analyses the page that casts the vote. Votes cast by pages that are themselves 'important' weigh more heavily and help to make other pages 'important'.[6]

It is also possible to search for pages that link to a particular site. For example, you can type 'link:www.soccerage.com' into the search box in *Google* to find other sites which link to this site. The theory here might be that you consider *SoccerAge* (**http://www.soccerage.com/**) to be an authoritative source of information about football and that therefore, by conducting this search, you might locate other similar sites because they have chosen to link to *SoccerAge*. Alternatively, you may be unsure of the authority of *SoccerAge* – by conducting the same search, you can assess how many other people have linked to the site, assuming that the more people linking to it, the greater the likelihood of its authority. In addition, you may be familiar with some of the other sites that link to the original page, again providing a potential indicator of authority.

Using metadata to improve resource descriptions and retrieve quality sites

Metadata is information about a web page that is written into the HTML of the page itself but is not displayed automatically to the user. Authors can include descriptive information about their pages as metadata that is then detected by search engines and displayed in any search results. For example, a search using *AltaVista* for 'Chelsea football scores' results in 1,340,781 hits, the first of which is from *SoccerAge*. *AltaVista* uses the following description for the site: 'The best international Soccer coverage including stats scores standings transactions schedules rosters odds and analysis.' If you access this site and view the HTML code for the page (choose 'source' from the view menu in *Internet Explorer* or *Netscape Navigator*), you will see that there is a 'description' tag containing this information. There is also a 'keywords' tag containing keywords which are used by some search engines to retrieve this site. Furthermore, certain search engines rank sites more highly in the search results if your search terms appear in the meta-keywords used by a site. In addition to improving the meaningfulness of resource descriptions and the relevance of search results, the potential for using metadata to indicate the quality of information has been considered. This is discussed in Chapter 5.

Browsing search engine directories

Northern Light is one of the few search engines which does not include the option to browse for information from its opening screen. Alternatively, *Excite* (http://www.excite.com/) provides a list of browsable headings (displayed in Figure 2.6). Selecting, for example, 'Health' leads to additional headings, including 'Diseases and Conditions'. After selecting 'Conditions A-Z', 'Conditions D' and 'Diabetes', you are eventually presented with ten websites about diabetes. These range from the *American Diabetes Association* to *Camp Sweney*, 'a national youth summer camp for kids with diabetes'. This is a manually created directory of selected resources identified by those based at *Excite*. The advantages and disadvantages of using this approach to information retrieval are discussed below under 'Subject catalogues and directory services' (page 42).

Other search engines

Northern Light is just one example of a search engine. Many more exist, and below is an overview of some of the more commonly used tools. Each internet

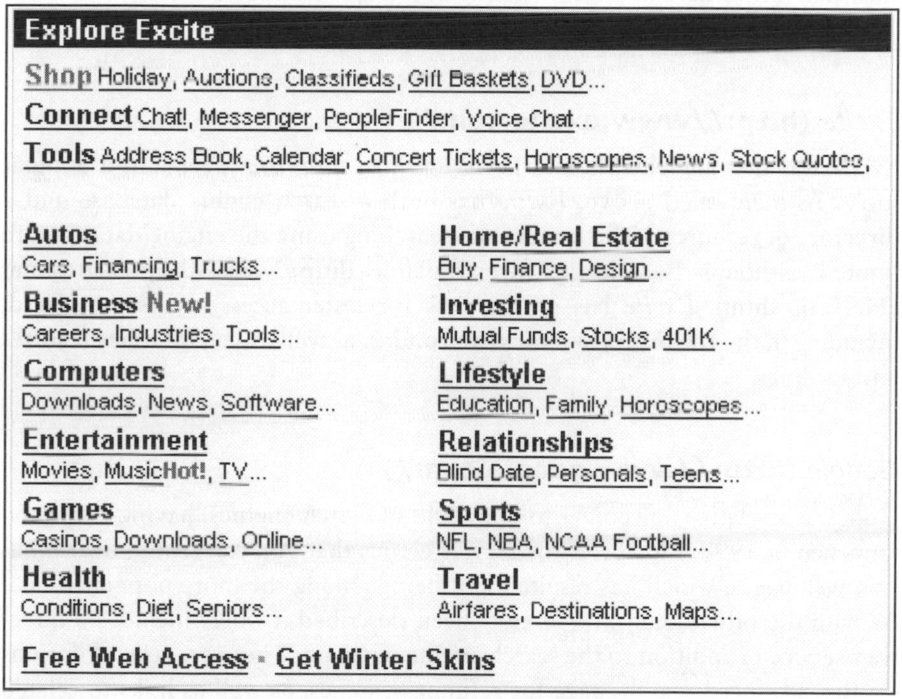

Explore Excite

Shop Holiday, Auctions, Classifieds, Gift Baskets, DVD...

Connect Chat!, Messenger, PeopleFinder, Voice Chat...

Tools Address Book, Calendar, Concert Tickets, Horoscopes, News, Stock Quotes,

Autos Cars, Financing, Trucks...	**Home/Real Estate** Buy, Finance, Design...
Business New! Careers, Industries, Tools...	**Investing** Mutual Funds, Stocks, 401K...
Computers Downloads, News, Software...	**Lifestyle** Education, Family, Horoscopes...
Entertainment Movies, MusicHot!, TV...	**Relationships** Blind Date, Personals, Teens...
Games Casinos, Downloads, Online...	**Sports** NFL, NBA, NCAA Football...
Health Conditions, Diet, Seniors...	**Travel** Airfares, Destinations, Maps...

Free Web Access ▪ **Get Winter Skins**

Fig. 2.6 *Browsable subject headings in 'Excite'*

Excite, and Excite Search, Logo are trademarks of Excite, Inc. and may be registered in various jurisdictions. Excite screen display copyright 1995–1999 Excite, Inc.

search facility works slightly differently, using different techniques to create a database and retrieve information. However, the principles are generally the same as those described in relation to *Northern Light*.

AltaVista (**http://www.altavista.com/**)

AltaVista is one of the more popular search engines.[7] Digital Equipment Corporation first developed the tool in 1995, and in January 1999 it became a subsidiary of Compaq. *AltaVista* offers several options for searching that can be located using the help information, or by following the link from the opening screen to 'more search options'. There are also browsable subject headings displayed on the opening screen. *AltaVista* was the first search engine to offer multilingual searching capabilities, including the option to search in Chinese, Japanese, Korean and Russian, as well as European languages such as French, German, Italian and English. Additional services include a language translation service and the option to customize your 'view' of *AltaVista*. It also has a number of mirror sites to enable faster searching outside the USA. These include Australia (**http://au.altavista.com/**), the UK (**http://uk.altavista.com/**) and India (**http://in.altavista.com/**).

Excite (**http://www.excite.com/**)

Excite was first launched in late 1995, and like *AltaVista* it remains a popular tool.[7] As mentioned above, *Excite* has both a search engine database and a directory of resources. The options for searching using the engine database are limited, although 'search tips' are available (**http://webselfhelp.excite.com/eHNC/tips.htm**). *Excite* has mirror sites for faster access across the world, including in the UK (**http://www.excite.co.uk/**), as well as several other features and facilities.

Google (**http://www.google.com/**)

Google is a relative newcomer to the world of search engines, having only been launched in 1999. However, the service claims that you can search over a billion web pages, which has resulted in it being among the more popular tools.[7] As with the others that have already been described, *Google* includes a directory service in addition to the search engine database. There are several options on the 'advanced search' page for refining searches, as well as links to related information once you have completed a search (discussed earlier).

Lycos (**http://www.lycos.com/**)

Lycos has been available since 1994, and is one of the oldest of the major search engines. At the time of writing, it was the most popular search engine of those mentioned here.[7] The service provides access to resources via two routes: the general search engine and its directory. As with the other search engines, numerous additional features and facilities are available from *Lycos*, including advanced search options and mirror sites around the world.

Advantages and disadvantages of search engines

The size of it all

The major advantage of search engines has already been mentioned, namely their comprehensive coverage of the web. Crawlers or spiders search and index the web regularly and update the databases with any new sites, as well as with any changes to existing pages. At the time of writing, estimates suggest that *AltaVista* indexes 350 million pages, *Northern Light* 330 million pages, and *Excite* 250 million pages.[8] Other plus points include the use of relevance ranking and of different features to facilitate retrieval, such as those described for *Northern Light*. For these reasons, search engines can seem invaluable if you are interested in comprehensive coverage of the web. However, the major advantage of search engines can also be disadvantageous. The huge number of hits for any one search requires time to sift through the results, and this problem is compounded by the lack of meaningful explanatory information about the materials that are retrieved.

A lack of discrimination

Within the context of this book, the most significant disadvantage of search engines is that they do not discriminate between materials included in their databases in terms of quality. Anyone anywhere can disseminate information via the web provided they have access to the required hardware and software. Because search engine databases are generated automatically, any search will result in material from potentially any source, whether it is authoritative and reliable, or highly biased and misleading. Therefore a site may include subject terms of interest to you, but the information may be outdated, inaccurate or lacking authority, or a site may be little more than a front page with no detailed information.

A related problem with search engines is that there is no discrimination in terms of the subjects covered and they search every word of every page in response to a query. Therefore, a search on 'virus' would retrieve material on both computer viruses and medical viruses, and a search for 'corn' would retrieve material about corns on your feet as well as corn which grows in fields. The mechanism for ranking the relevance of sites simply lists those results where the terms appear more frequently and/or prominently, irrespective of the subject. While different search engines offer an increasing range of options for refining searches, such as through 'advanced' or 'power' search pages, it remains that the results are automatically generated and therefore once again there is no guarantee of their quality or relevance.

Inclusion of materials

Further problems with using search engines relate to the inclusion of materials in their databases. Although search engines claim coverage of vast quantities of web pages, they are in reality only covering a small proportion of the potentially useful material that is now available via the internet.

Search engines are usually restricted to web-based materials – they are generated automatically using software which 'crawls' around the web – so that if the material is not contained within a web page, the software will not be able to gain access and index it. In order to locate, for example, messages from newsgroups, a separate search facility is generally required (this is discussed later). Likewise, if a full-text report or paper is in a format other than HTML, search engines are less likely to include it. For example, many journal articles are produced in Portable Document Format (PDF). This enables documents to be printed in a format which is identical to the original paper-based publication, allowing the use of more sophisticated text and graphics than is possible using HTML. A separate piece of software, Adobe Acrobat, is required to access material in this format. Consequently, most search engines are unable to index the information and a separate tool is required (also discussed later). This is with the exception of *Google*, which includes PDF documents in its search results.

In addition, search engines are restricted to the 'publicly indexable web'. The 'invisible web' refers to information that search engines cannot index because it is hidden behind a search interface, such as in a database, or behind a login screen, such as papers in electronic journals. Estimates suggest that the 'invisible web' is 500 times the size of the 'publicly indexable web'[9] – if *AltaVista* claims to index 350 million pages, this means that at least 175 billion pages are not included in its database. For academic users of the internet in particular, exclusion of information from databases and electronic journals means potential exclusion of precisely the high-quality information that is likely to be of most interest to them. Again, separate search tools are being developed to enable access to this type of material (these are discussed later).

Further information on search engines

The above is only a rough guide to search engines and how they work. All search engines are slightly different, and each will often return different results for the same search. For more information on search engines and how they work, as well as further information on which search engines are available and how to use them, *Search Engine Watch* (**http://www.searchenginewatch.com/**) is an invaluable guide.[2] *Search Engine Watch* is designed for both webmasters and end-users, and provides a comprehensive and frequently updated guide.

Gateways and virtual libraries

The availability of large quantities of information of variable quality via the internet has resulted in several initiatives for providing more effective access to information. In particular, *gateways* or *virtual libraries* are collections of high-quality resources within a particular subject area that are of interest to a specified audience. It is difficult to differentiate concisely between internet search tools because each works in a slightly different way, but generally what is being referred to here are guides to quality materials. The defining attribute is that there are predefined criteria for the selection and evaluation of materials. In addition, subject specialists, usually those within the library profession, have developed these guides.

The major benefit of using a gateway or virtual library is that someone with knowledge of the area has searched the internet and attempted to filter the useful from the not-so-useful. Hence, using a gateway or virtual library as a starting point can save you a lot of time and effort because you need not sift through thousands of outdated or useless sites. This section examines an example of one such guide to illustrate how they work. In addition, an overview is provided of other gateways and virtual libraries, with some suggestions for finding other guides. The advantages and disadvantages of gateways and virtual libraries are also considered.

....

Example   *The Social Science Information Gateway (SOSIG)*

Background to *SOSIG* – the eLib subject-based information gateways

In 1993, an investigation was undertaken in the UK into how to deal with pressures on library resources caused by the rapid expansion of student numbers and the worldwide explosion in academic knowledge and information. This led to the *Electronic Libraries Programme*, *eLib* (**http://ukoln.ac.uk/services/elib/**), a centrally funded national programme of research into the role and development of the 'electronic library'. There were various strands within *eLib*, one of which was 'access to networked resources'. As part of this strand, several subject-based information gateways were developed, including *SOSIG*, the *Social Science Information Gateway*.

Each of the gateways was slightly different, but generally they shared the same characteristics:

- a searchable and browsable database of internet resource descriptions within a particular subject area
- clearly defined criteria for evaluating the quality of materials prior to inclusion within the gateway
- the involvement of library professionals and subject experts in the development of the service
- manual creation of records to ensure meaningful and informative resource descriptions
- cataloguing and classification of materials using traditional library methods to enable more effective retrieval.

These services were generally aimed at the UK higher education community and were developed by a consortium of partners, usually within the academic arena.

The Resource Discovery Network (RDN)

Recognition of the important contribution of the *eLib* gateways in providing effective access to high quality internet materials resulted in additional funding from the UK government for the *RDN*, the *Resource Discovery Network* (**http://www.rdn.ac.uk/**). The *RDN* was established in January 1999 as a free internet service 'dedicated to providing access to high-quality internet resources for the learning, teaching and research community'. The *RDN* built on the foundations laid by *eLib* – each of the *eLib* gateways submitted a proposal for the development of their service into a subject 'hub'. The plan was that each hub would have a wider scope than the original gateways, and all areas relevant to the higher education community within the UK would be covered by the collection of hubs.

At the time of writing, the following hubs had been launched or were under development:

- computing (under development)
- engineering (http://www.eevl.ac.uk/)
- health and medicine (http://omni.ac.uk/)
- humanities (http://www.humbul.ac.uk)
- life sciences (http://biome.ac.uk/)
- mathematics (under development)
- physical sciences (http://www.psigate.ac.uk/)
- reference resources (http://www.rdn.ac.uk/findit/)
- social sciences, including business and law (http://www.sosig.ac.uk/).

While each hub has a unique 'identity', it is possible to search across several hubs simultaneously and there is now an overall collection development policy. The ethos of the original gateways has remained the same – a catalogue of descriptions of selected and evaluated internet materials within a specified area.

SOSIG (http://www.sosig.ac.uk/)

SOSIG, the *Social Science Information Gateway*, was one of the gateway services originally developed under *eLib*, which later secured funding from the *RDN* to expand its coverage and become the hub for the social sciences. The service is aimed at social scientists in higher education and research, and covers a wide range of subjects, including business, education, geography, law, philosophy, politics, psychology and sociology.

As can be seen in Figure 2.7, *SOSIG* offers two main options for accessing information – browsing the subject headings or entering keywords to search the database.

Selecting the 'Economics' heading from the opening screen (see Figure 2.7) leads to further headings within this area (see Figure 2.8). As displayed in Figure 2.8, examples include 'Economic Systems and Theories' and 'Insurance'. Selecting the latter leads to a list of resource titles, also displayed in Figure 2.8. Resources are categorized by type, e.g. 'Data', 'Government Publications' and 'Organisations/Societies'. Clicking on a title leads to a description about the individual item – the full details for the 'Lloyd's List' can be seen in Figure 2.9.

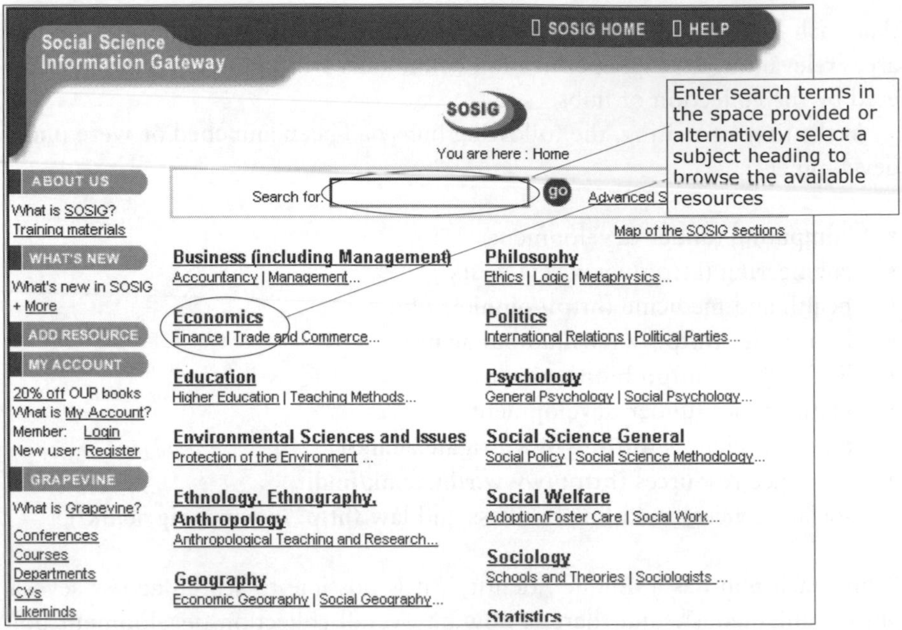

Fig. 2.7 *Accessing information in 'SOSIG'*

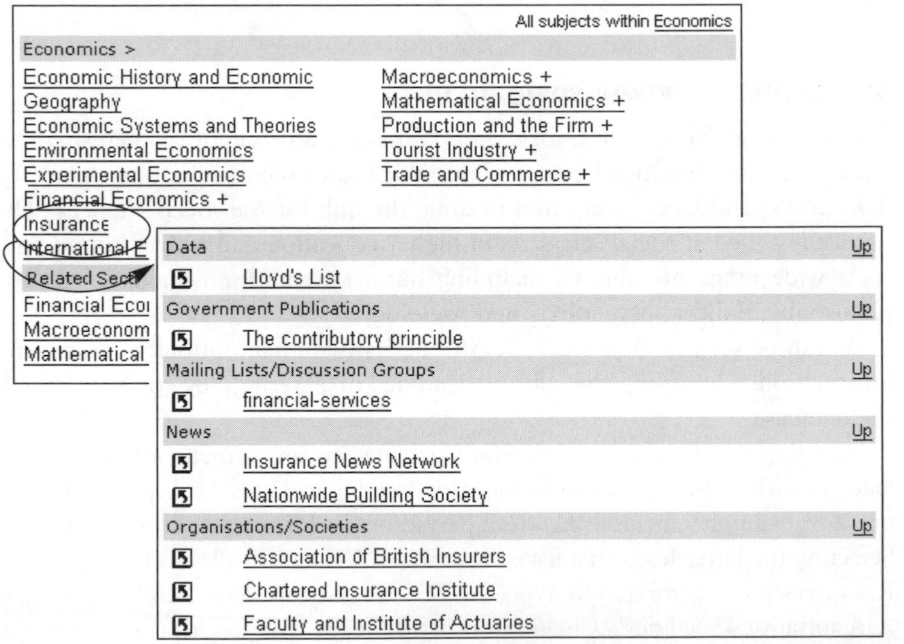

Fig. 2.8 *Browsing subject headings in 'SOSIG'*

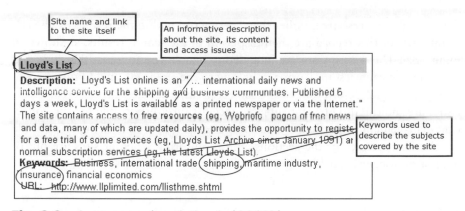

Fig. 2.9 *A resource description in 'SOSIG'*

on the opening screen (displayed in Figure 2.7). For example, typing 'gender studies' results in 111 hits. The full details for each resource are displayed in the format shown in Figure 2.9. An 'advanced search' option is also available from the opening screen – this offers the option to define where users want their search terms to appear (e.g. in the resource title, description or key-words), and to define the type of resource they would like to retrieve (e.g. data, government publications and organizations/societies). An additional feature allows a word stem to be entered to retrieve any variations of the stem – entering 'econ' will retrieve sites mentioning 'economy', 'economics', etc. An example of an advanced search might be for 'Mailing Lists/Discussion Groups' mentioning variations of 'gender stud' – this results in eight hits only.

Resource selection, evaluation and description

A key characteristic of *SOSIG*, as with other gateways and virtual libraries, is that it only provides access to the descriptions of high-quality resources. Prior to inclusion in the database, every resource has been evaluated using explicit criteria (**http://sosig.ac.uk/desire/ecrit.html**). These criteria relate not only to the presentation of information, but also to subject coverage, currency and accuracy. The availability of the criteria online means that individuals are able to assess whether the criteria used by *SOSIG* equate with their own views about what a quality resource entails.

The *SOSIG* librarians complete a template for each of the resources selected for inclusion in the database. The template is similar to any record in a standard library system and contains information such as title, description, keywords and internet address. The records are added to the database, and when you undertake a search, you are searching the information held in the database about a resource, rather than every word within the resource. The relevant parts of this record are then displayed in the search results, as shown in Figure 2.9. The descriptions are intended to enable you to assess the value and usefulness of each resource prior to linking to the site itself. In addition to providing a detailed description of the subject areas and materials covered, access issues are indicated. Different subject specialists are responsible for the collection management of particular areas of the service, as well as being responsible for the maintenance of the sections, and monitoring whether sites are out of date or no longer available.

Cataloguing

In addition to the descriptions about each resource, many gateways and virtual libraries use traditional methods of cataloguing and classification to categorize resources and ensure their effective retrieval. The keywords in *SOSIG* are controlled terms used to describe the subject areas covered by a resource. The rationale for using controlled keywords is that different authors use different words to describe the same subject, but if predefined keywords are adopted, you can find which keyword is used to describe your subject and therefore retrieve all relevant records. A traditional scheme of keywords is used – this is a standard scheme used in libraries throughout the world to describe materials.

When you browse the headings in *SOSIG*, in reality you are browsing the controlled keywords – in Figure 2.8, the heading 'insurance' was selected and the 'Lloyd's List' displayed in the set of search results. The full description for the 'Lloyd's List' in *SOSIG* includes the keyword 'insurance' (Figure 2.9). The keywords can be grouped by area and arranged into a hierarchy according to whether one term is more or less specific than another, as well as according to whether one term is as specific as another but has a related (rather than the same) meaning. For example, if you select 'accountancy' from the opening screen, the broader heading 'business' is displayed, as well as the narrower term 'auditing', and the related terms 'economics' and 'management'.

In addition to the subject headings, resources in *SOSIG* are also categorized according to the type of document. This therefore means that when the catalogue is browsed, resources are categorized according to their type (see Figure 2.8). Likewise, it is possible in the advanced search screen to limit a search according to a specific type of information.

Expanding coverage: social science search engine

Due to the high level of manual input involved in selecting, evaluating and describing resources, gateways and virtual libraries are limited in terms of the volume of materials that they can cover, particularly in comparison to search engines. For this reason, many gateways and virtual libraries now connect users to a search engine to expand their searches automatically. *SOSIG* connects to a database of 50,000 social science web pages that have been identified using software called a 'harvester' (**http://sosig.ac.uk/harvester.html**). However, there is no quality-filtering of the materials contained in this section of *SOSIG* and the resource descriptions are generated automatically. The pros and cons of this approach to searching have been considered already under 'Search engines' (page 16).

Other gateways and virtual libraries

The *RDN* gateways now cover a wide range of subject areas, and the ability to search across them is a useful feature. However, the gateways remain focused on resources of interest to internet users within the UK higher education sector, although they are likely to be of interest to a much wider audience. Many more gateways exist, each covering a different 'subset' of the internet – below is a selection of some that are likely to be of interest to readers of this book.

BUBL Link / 5:15 (**http://bubl.ac.uk/link/**)

BUBL, the *Bulletin Board for Libraries*, is a centrally funded national information service for the higher education community in the UK. *BUBL Link / 5:15*, originally the *BUBL Subject Tree*, was established in 1993 by the UK Office for Library Networking (UKOLN). Now funded by the UK Higher Education Council's Joint Information Systems Committee (JISC), *BUBL Link / 5:15* is a searchable and browsable catalogue of 12,000 selected internet resources. A team of library and information professionals is involved in the selection and evaluation of resources, which are then described and categorized. The broad subject categories include: general reference, creative arts, humanities, language, literature and culture. It is possible to browse using these broad headings, to browse an alphabetical listing of topics, to browse by type of resource (e.g. mailing list, journal, institution), or to search the catalogue.

Infomine: scholarly internet resource collections (**http://infomine.ucr.edu/**)

Infomine began in January 1994 as a service provided by the library of the University of California, Riverside, in the USA. The service is now developed collaboratively by librarians at over 20 University of California, California State University, and other university and college libraries. It receives funding from the USA Fund for the Improvement of Post Secondary Education and the USA Institute of Museum and Library Services. It is intended for use by faculty, students and research staff at 'university level' and has been developed as 'a showcase, virtual library and reference tool containing highly useful internet/web resources including databases, electronic journals, electronic books, bulletin boards, listservs, online library card catalogs, articles and directories of researchers'. *Infomine* provides access to resources within a range of areas (medical sciences, government information, instructional resources, physical sciences, engineering, computing, maths, regional and general interest, social sciences, humanities, and visual and performing arts). Within each area, a searchable and browsable database of resource descriptions is available.

The Internet Public Library (**http://www.ipl.org/**)

The *Internet Public Library* is a browsable guide for the types of resources which might be found in a public library, including reference materials, exhibitions, newspapers and magazines, full-text materials, and sources for 'teen' and 'youth' audiences – the 'teen' section, for example, contains information on dating, health, career and college. All materials have been evaluated, catalogued and described, and at the time of writing, the *Internet Public Library* described 33,905 items in total. The idea for the service arose from a seminar held in the School of Information and Library Studies at the University of Michigan in 1995, and it was launched in March 1995. It is now well established with three full-time members of staff, and receives external funding from the W. K. Kellogg Foundation and corporate sponsorship from Bell and Howell Information and Learning.

Librarians' Index to the Internet (**http://lii.org/**)

The *Librarians' Index to the Internet* is a directory of more than 7100 internet resource descriptions. The resources have all been selected and evaluated by librarians 'for their usefulness to users of public libraries'. The service was started in 1990 as a reference librarian's Gopher bookmark file, but later moved to Berkeley Public Library and became the *Berkeley Public Library*

Index to the Internet. In March 1997, the service became the *Librarians' Index to the Internet.* The *Index* is both browsable and searchable. Each resource is categorized under subject headings, and there is a detailed and informative description offering insight into the content of the resource and its potential value to users. Topics covered are as diverse as the topics covered by any public library, ranging from computers to religion and philosophy. The service is supported in part by the USA Institute of Museum and Library Services and the Library of California.

The SCOUT Report Signpost (**http://www.signpost.org/**)

The *SCOUT Report Signpost* was first launched in 1995 as an e-mail-based service that provided 'a fast, convenient way to stay informed of valuable resources on the internet'. It is now web-based but the ethos remains the same: it contains 'only the best internet resources' and is 'designed to guide US higher education to quality electronic resources'. Library professionals and subject experts identify, evaluate and describe valuable resources. It is possible to search the descriptions of the 3720 catalogued resources or browse them using the broad subject headings displayed on the opening screen. The project is located at the Department of Computer Sciences at the University of Wisconsin–Madison, and is funded by a grant from the National Science Foundation in the USA.

Locating gateways and virtual libraries

Each gateway or virtual library is relatively small in size compared to a search engine. For example, while the *Librarians' Index to the Internet* described 7000 resources at the time of writing, it was possible to search 1,326,920,000 web pages using the *Google* search engine. Thousands of gateways and virtual libraries now exist around the world, and as can be seen from the brief overview above, each covers a slightly different subject area or has a different target audience. However, there has been little co-ordination to date of the development of different guides in terms of ensuring comprehensive coverage across disciplines and user groups. As a result, locating an appropriate gateway or virtual library can be problematic. This section provides an overview of how to locate a guide covering a topic that you are interested in.

The Argus Clearinghouse (**http://www.clearinghouse.net/**)

The *Argus Clearinghouse* is a gateway to other gateways. It is the most obvious starting place for users embarking on a quest for quality internet materials, because it provides a gateway to other services that seek to enable access to high-quality resources. *Clearinghouse* staff evaluate, categorize and describe 'value-added topical guides which identify, describe, and evaluate internet-based information resources'. The *Clearinghouse* contains descriptions of gateways and virtual libraries in a wide range of subject areas, including the arts and humanities, business, government and law, health and medicine, recreation, the sciences and the social sciences.

The *Clearinghouse* is both searchable and browsable. Clicking on the heading 'Arts & Humanities' from the opening screen leads to the narrower categories displayed in Figure 2.10. Selecting 'history' followed by 'American history' results in the list of guides, also displayed in Figure 2.10. The titles are displayed, with keywords indicating the coverage of each guide, and an over-

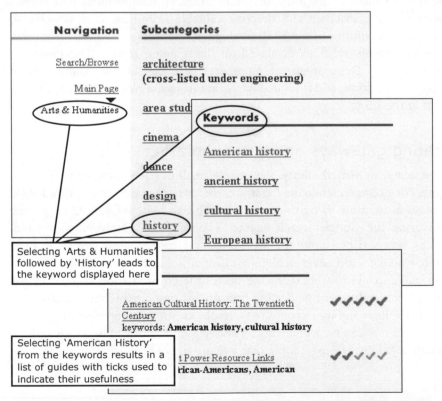

Fig. 2.10 *Browsing the 'Argus Clearinghouse' for guides to 'American history'*

all rating of between one and five ticks, which is designed to indicate the quality of each guide at a glance.

Guides are submitted to the *Clearinghouse* by their authors and evaluated by *Clearinghouse* staff. The *Clearinghouse* describes itself as 'extremely selective' – of the guides that are submitted for inclusion, between 5% and 10% meet the minimum quality standards that are required. Once a guide has been defined as suitable for inclusion, it is then evaluated according to the following criteria:[10]

- level of resource description
- level of resource evaluation
- guide design
- guide organizational schemes
- guide meta-information.

Each criterion is rated on a scale of one to five, and an average score is calculated. The average score is presented graphically to the user as the series of red ticks (see Figure 2.10).

Clicking on a link from the list in Figure 2.10 leads to more detailed information about a specific guide (see Figure 2.11). This includes a breakdown of the scores for each of the evaluation criteria. Additional information includes details of the organization or individual responsible for the guide, the date the *Clearinghouse* last checked the site, and a link to the site itself.

Additional guides to gateways and virtual libraries

The *Argus Clearinghouse* is an excellent starting point for finding gateways and virtual libraries, but as with any other evaluative guide, it cannot cover everything. Some of the guides to internet searching mentioned earlier also consider virtual libraries.[1,3] In addition, *PIER, the Sussex University Guide to the Internet* (**http://www.sussex.ac.uk/library/pier/subjects/general/gateways.html**) contains a list of gateways, and *PINAKES* (**http://www.hw.ac.uk/libWWW/irn/pinakes/pinakes.html**), based at the Heriot-Watt University in Scotland, is 'a subject launchpad' to gateways and virtual libraries.

Advantages and disadvantages of gateways and virtual libraries

Quality not quantity

The principal advantage of gateways and virtual libraries is that they provide

---

Guide Information

`http://www.nhmccd.edu/contracts/lrc/kc/decades.html`

Keywords

American history, cultural history

Compiled by

Peggy Whitley (peggy.whitley@nhmccd.edu)
Library Reference Coordinator
Kingwood College

Rating

Overall: ✔✔✔✔✔
Resource Description: **5**
Resource Evaluation: **4**
Guide Design: **5**
Organization Schemes: **5**
Guide Meta-information: **5**
(Rated 02/2000)

Last Checked by Argus Clearinghouse

January 13, 2001

Fig. 2.11 *Detailed guide information in the 'Argus Clearinghouse'*

access to the descriptions of only high quality resources. They are developed and maintained by information professionals and subject experts, and you can access these services assured in the knowledge that an individual working in the field has already identified and evaluated high-quality resources. This relieves you of much of the work in filtering potentially useful sources from the vast quantities of dross that are currently available via the internet. In addition, as indicated by the example from *SOSIG*, the descriptions are intended to provide an accurate, concise and meaningful indication of the value and usefulness of each resource, saving you from linking to irrelevant, outdated or inaccurate sites.

Narrow audience focus

One of the problems of generic search tools is their undefined audience – such services are aimed at any internet user and therefore it would be difficult for all of the resources that are included in them to be relevant to any one individual. The services included in this section have an identified audience. For example, *SOSIG* is aimed primarily at social science users based in higher education or research. Quality is a subjective issue, and one individual's source of quality information is likely to be another's dross. Therefore, the more clearly and narrowly defined the audience focus of a service, the easier it is to decide whether the material that it covers is likely to be of interest to you.

Explicit evaluation criteria

Another advantage is that the criteria used by these services for evaluation are explicit: there is usually a document describing the criteria or a collection development policy. For example, the following criteria can be accessed online:

* evaluating internet resources for *SOSIG*
  http://sosig.ac.uk/desire/ccrit.html
* selection criteria for the *Librarians' Index to the Internet*
  http://lii.org/search/file/pubcriteria
* *SCOUT Report* selection criteria
  http://scout.cs.wisc.edu/report/sr/criteria.html
* the *Argus Clearinghouse* ratings system
  http://www.clearinghouse.net/ratings.html

The criteria are generally designed to assess a range of factors which affect the quality of an information source, including accuracy, currency and coverage. Consequently, you can examine the criteria in order to determine whether they match the aspects of quality assessment that you are interested in.

Types of material covered

A further advantage of gateways and virtual libraries is that they cover the full range of internet materials. As discussed earlier, search engines are usually restricted to web-based materials and to the 'publicly indexable web'. In order to locate, for example, discussion lists or information in a format other than HTML, a separate search facility is generally required. Gateways and virtual libraries do not discriminate between materials according to their format –

those involved in their development use the full range of search tools to identify any material that may be suitable for inclusion. It is therefore possible to locate all types of materials using one tool – if additional software is required to access material, or if you need to pay or register, the resource description will tell you.

Retrieval

A further advantage of gateways and virtual libraries is the use of traditional cataloguing and classification techniques. These are used to ensure accurate subject description and facilitate the retrieval of resources. In addition, there tends to be less repetition in the search results from a gateway because resources are evaluated and described at the individual resource level. Search engines index materials at the individual page level – however, one resource may be made up of many pages, thereby causing repetition in the search results.

Limitations

Gateways and virtual libraries have their disadvantages. The high level of human input involved in developing and maintaining these services means they cover a much smaller number of materials compared to search engines. In addition, the narrow audience and subject focus means that they are limited in terms of their appeal. Furthermore, as mentioned earlier, there has been little co-ordination to date of the development of different guides, and locating an appropriate gateway or virtual library can be problematic. For this reason, you may need to supplement your use of gateways by using search engines and the other types of search tools discussed below.

Subject catalogues and directory services

Like gateways and virtual libraries, subject catalogues or directories are created manually. Sites are submitted by their authors or identified by the site developers, and then assigned to an appropriate subject category or categories by the catalogue maintainers. However, unlike gateways and virtual libraries, there is no selection and evaluation of the information to assess its quality prior to inclusion in the catalogue. To confuse matters, many search engines also include a subject catalogue element (as mentioned earlier), and many catalogues connect users automatically to a search engine to expand their search results. In addition, some catalogues claim to evaluate and/or rate the 'quality' of the sites that are included. An example of a catalogue, and its advantages and disadvantages, is discussed below.

Example   *Yahoo!*

One reason for using a subject directory might be to look for information for a school child working on a project about the ancient Egyptians. Inputting a search in *Yahoo!* (**http://www.yahoo.com/**) for 'ancient Egyptians' results in 127 website matches. The results are displayed according to the appropriate subject categories, with a link to each site and a brief description (see Figure 2.12).

Yahoo! was launched in 1994, and claims to be the oldest and largest directory, listing approximately 1.5 million websites. Users suggest most of the sites, and each suggestion is examined by a member of the *Yahoo!* staff 'whose job it is to decide where the site best belongs'. When submitting sites, authors are asked for details about the site, including its name as it will appear in *Yahoo!*, the site address, and a paragraph of up to 25 words describing its contents. Figure 2.12 displays the site name and descriptive information in the search results. The subject categories are recommended by site authors and then verified by staff involved in developing and maintaining the directory. Within the first few hits, one site, 'Ancient Egyptian Information', sounds particularly relevant to our search from the description provided: 'Egyptian interactive activities, books, magazines, egyptologists e-mail addresses, archeological digs'.

Fig. 2.12 *Search results for 'ancient Egyptians' in 'Yahoo!'*

43

Subject catalogues and directories are generally both browsable and searchable. From the opening screen of *Yahoo!*, various broad categories are displayed, including arts and humanities, business and economy, computers and internet, education, entertainment, government, health, recreation and sports, regional, science, social science, and society and culture. A user interested in information about the ancient Egyptians would need to select from a range of potentially relevant categories – regional, arts and humanities, social science, society and culture, or perhaps education. Browsing under 'regional', followed by 'countries', 'Egypt', 'society and culture', and 'mythology and folklore', leads to 24 potentially useful-sounding sites. Browsing under 'arts and humanities', followed by 'cultures and groups' and 'Egyptian' also leads to potentially relevant resources.

Retrieval

Authors are required to provide information about their resources when submitting material for inclusion in *Yahoo!*. When you search *Yahoo!*, the tool searches for your terms in the website title and description, as well as in the category headings. This is the same approach adopted by gateways and virtual libraries but not search engines (search engines search for your terms in every word of every page in their database). *Yahoo!* lists results by relevance which is assessed by the number of times your terms appear in the site or category description – sites or categories with more matches are ranked higher, and sites and categories with matches found in the title are ranked higher than those where matches are found in the description.

Expanding coverage: using the *Google* search engine within *Yahoo*!

Figure 2.12 displays the *Yahoo!* 'category' matches and 'site' matches for a search on 'ancient Egyptians'. In addition, at the top of the page, there is a link to 'web pages'. Selecting this link results in 30,800 hits – *Yahoo!* searches are automatically expanded by connecting to the *Google* search engine. In addition, if no sites or categories are found in response to any search within *Yahoo!*, the search is automatically conducted on *Google*. The pros and cons of using search engines have already been considered earlier in this chapter.

Quality control in catalogues and directories – *Britannica.com*

During the mid-1990s, there was a trend towards providing more effective access to internet materials through the development of catalogues or directories which claimed to evaluate the quality of the materials they provided access to. Many of these services were developed, which were of varying value and usefulness, and most have now disappeared. However, some catalogues continue to claim that they evaluate materials – for example, *Yahoo!* claims it is 'created by a staff of editors who visit and evaluate websites, and then organize them into subject-based categories and sub-categories.' However, there is no indication of the quality of the sites that are included in *Yahoo!*, and there are no details about who evaluates the sites and on what basis.

Britannica.com (**http://www.britannica.com/**) is another example of a directory. Selecting the link to 'arts and entertainment' from the opening screen of *Britannica.com*, followed by 'internet guide' leads to the results shown in Figure 2.13. As displayed, the results include a brief description about each resource and a star rating designed to indicate the quality of each resource – sites are awarded five stars for 'best of the web', four for 'superior', three for 'excellent', two for 'recommended', and one for 'noteworthy'. Authors can only recommend sites for inclusion in this guide. When sites have been recommended, they are then examined and evaluated by Britannica staff to determine whether they are appropriate for inclusion in the service. According to the help information, sites are judged according to: accuracy, usefulness, depth and breadth of information; credentials and authority of the author or publisher; quality of design, graphics and multimedia; ease of navigation; and timeliness of revision. They are then awarded a star rating designed to indicate at a glance to users the quality of each resource. However, there is no indica-

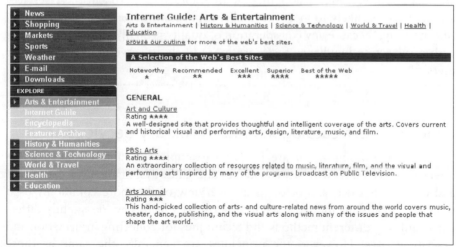

Fig. 2.13 *Rated sites in the internet guide on 'Britannica.com'*

tion of who the quality ratings are aimed at, and beyond the brief details provided here, there is no further indication of how the evaluations are undertaken.

A number of rating services were developed during the mid-1990s. In 1997, *Internet World* voted one such service, *Lycos Top 5%*, 'best' of a range of reviewing services, and argued that the service saves the user time in 'pursuit of quality information' (*Lycos Top 5%* was no longer available at the time of writing).[11] Likewise, the use of star ratings in *Britannica.com* is designed to indicate the quality of sites at a glance – it is easy to identify the most highly rated materials from the results in Figure 2.13 by glancing at the number of stars allocated. However, it is questionable whether such services truly provide any useful indication of quality. Authors within the library profession compared a range of different services in order to examine the approaches used for evaluating and describing resources, and also to consider their effectiveness in guiding users towards quality materials.[12-15] The general conclusions are that rating and reviewing services offer little indication of site quality. Indeed, one argument is that the 'criteria for inclusion and the rating scale are highly impressionistic and descriptive notes on each site are minimalist'.[12] Furthermore, 'the impressionistic "cool" counts for a great deal' and the 'ratings are useless except to those who hold the same subjective preconceptions'.[12] One of the major problems of such services is that they have no clearly defined audience, but appear to be designed for popular appeal, i.e. any internet user. As discussed previously, quality is subjective. The potential users of the internet are vast and therefore, by adopting an all-embracing approach, these services are perhaps less likely to meet the quality aspirations of particular individuals. Alternatively, 'because any consideration of quality is highly subjective, services with a subject and audience focus are more likely to serve the needs of their users'.[16]

Other subject catalogues and directory services

Yahoo! and *Britannica.com* are just two examples of subject catalogues or directory services. As with search engines and gateways, many more catalogues and directories exist, and below is an overview of the more commonly used tools. As already mentioned, each internet search facility works slightly differently, utilizing different methods and techniques for collecting information and describing sites. However, the principles are generally the same as those described in relation to *Yahoo!* and *Britannica.com*.

Galaxy (**http://www.galaxy.com/**)

Galaxy was first developed in 1993 and went live in early 1994, and claims to be the oldest internet directory service. *Galaxy* is similar to *Yahoo!* as it is both browsable by broad subject headings and searchable. Again, authors submit their resources for examination by a member of the *Galaxy* staff. The resources are then allocated to an appropriate subject category or categories.

LookSmart (**http://www.looksmart.com/**)

Founded in 1995, *LookSmart* claims to be the 'global leader' in web directories. There are 31 directories in total, spanning 28 countries and 13 languages – *LookSmart* provides the directory component of, for example, the *AltaVista*, *Excite* and *Lycos* search engines. The service also claims that its directories are used by 83% of internet users in the USA. At the time of writing, there were over two million sites organized into more than 200,000 categories. Like *Galaxy* and *Yahoo!*, the directories are both browsable and searchable. *LookSmart* has an 'express submit' option – website authors can pay $199 to guarantee that their material is reviewed for inclusion in the directory within two working days. There is also a 'basic submit' option – for $99, sites are reviewed within approximately eight weeks.

NBCi.com (**http://www.nbci.com/**)

NBCi.com claims to be a directory of the 'best' websites. Like the other directories and catalogues that have already been described, *NBCi.com* is both browsable by broad subject headings and searchable. *NBCi.com* directory listings are selected, described and categorized by its editorial team. In addition, some sites are denoted 'top sites' and are marked with a tick to indicate that 'they're among the best sites on the web'. Like *LookSmart*, *NBCi.com* charges $199 for those who want a quick response on whether their sites have been selected for inclusion in the directory.

Major advantages and disadvantages of subject catalogues and directories

Subject directories and catalogues can provide more meaningful search results than search engines. Authors are generally responsible for describing their own materials and therefore the descriptions are often more helpful than those which are generated automatically by search engines. However, there are drawbacks to human maintenance. In particular, subject catalogues and directories are not as extensive in their coverage as search engines – *Yahoo!* only covers 1.5 million websites in comparison to *AltaVista*, which claims to index 350 million pages. However, they are generally significantly larger than gateways or virtual libraries where extensive manual effort is required to select, evaluate, describe and catalogue resources. Another drawback is that directories are not automatically updated, and therefore when sites or pages change, the directory is not necessarily updated as regularly as a search engine. This is a problem that applies equally to gateways and virtual libraries.

Indications of quality?

A disadvantage of particular interest here is that catalogues and directories do not necessarily discriminate between sites in terms of their quality. Those involved in developing and maintaining the databases are concerned with the subject relevance of materials. This contrasts with gateways and virtual libraries, where the emphasis is on selecting not only potentially relevant resources, but also high-quality materials for a target audience. Some catalogues or directory services claim to evaluate sites, but the limited usefulness of any quality assessments has already been highlighted.

Further information about subject catalogues and directories

The general references on searching mentioned already include further information about catalogues and directories.[1-3] In addition, further information about rating and reviewing services is available.[12-16] In particular, readers are recommended to examine Cooke, McNab and Anagnostelis,[14] which compares the facilities offered by various popular services.

Other search tools

As mentioned earlier, this section is not intended as a general guide to searching the internet as this is outside the scope of the book. However, the options for searching the internet are far more extensive than those described above, and some additional tools have implications for finding 'quality' information. There are specialist services for finding specific types of resources (e.g. PDF files and images), databases covering the 'invisible web', and tools for searching across several databases simultaneously. It is also possible to search for regional or subject-specific information. A brief overview and some examples are provided below.

Metasearch engines

Metasearch engines, also sometimes called meta-crawlers or multi-search engines, enable you to search several search tools at once rather than searching a single database. The results are then presented together, generally on one page.

The BigHub.com (**http://www.isleuth.com/**)

The *BigHub.com* is one example of a metasearch engine. Formerly known as *iSleuth.com*, the *BigHub.com* allows you to search several search engines, web directories and news databases simultaneously and receive one summary of results. The service claims it offers users 'a more convenient, efficient search than is available with traditional single-database search engines.' The tools that are searched include *Lycos*, *AltaVista* and *Yahoo!*. Once you have input your search terms, you can select the tools that you want to search and the time that you are prepared to spend waiting. The results are then amalgamated on one page.

Major advantages and disadvantages of metasearch engines

There are numerous metasearch engines available, and each works slightly differently, offering different advantages and disadvantages. The *BigHub.com* allows you to conduct a search on multiple databases. As a result, this approach to searching could be invaluable where you want to aim for comprehensive coverage of the web. Other tools connect you automatically to a range of different search tools. The main advantage here would be in prompting you to use tools you may not have otherwise considered. However, there are many problems with using metasearch facilities. In particular, what you are generally searching is a collection of search engines. Therefore, the disadvantages described in relation to using search engines for locating quality information also apply here, namely:

- the huge number of hits for any one search
- the lack of explanatory information about the material which is retrieved
- the time taken to sift through search results
- a restriction to web-based materials and to the publicly indexable web
- a lack of discrimination between materials in terms of their quality.

Further information on metasearch engines

Phil Bradley has conducted a useful comparison of several metasearch facilities, and includes a more detailed explanation of how they work, the number of search tools each covers, and the different facilities which are available for each.[17] In addition, *Search Engine Watch* provides an extensive list of the various tools that are available with a brief description of each.[18]

Finding information in formats other than HTML

Searching PDF files

As discussed earlier, with the exception of *Google*, search engines index only those materials produced in HTML, thereby excluding PDF files. Documents produced in PDF include articles from electronic journals, government reports, and documentation produced by other official bodies. Therefore most search engines are excluding a category of material which has the potential to be of a high quality, particularly to those working in an academic environment, in the health sector or in any other organization where official documentation is likely to have an impact. Gateways and virtual libraries include PDF files where they fit within their subject scope but their coverage is far from comprehensive. Until recently, therefore, it has been difficult to locate files in this format, and access has required prior knowledge of the availability of materials. For example, it has been necessary to check a government department website where such reports are listed as they are produced.

Adobe, the company that produces the software for accessing and disseminating PDF files, has recently produced a tool for searching such documents. *Search Adobe PDF Online* (**http://searchpdf.adobe.com/**) allows you to search for words appearing in the summaries of over one million PDF documents. As displayed in Figure 2.14, entering the term 'diabetes mellitus' gives 1365 documents. The titles are displayed in the first screen, with a brief description from the first line of the summary about the document. Selecting a title leads you to the full summary, where you can select to view the full document. At present, the tool is limited. For example, the brief summaries are automatically generated and therefore do not necessarily provide a useful indication of the content of each document. In addition, the site address displayed in the first screen refers to the address of the summary within the Adobe site rather than the full address of the document. However, by selecting the title, it is possible to view the full summary, which provides detailed information about the document, and the full address (as displayed in Figure 2.14). Despite its limitations, the importance to some

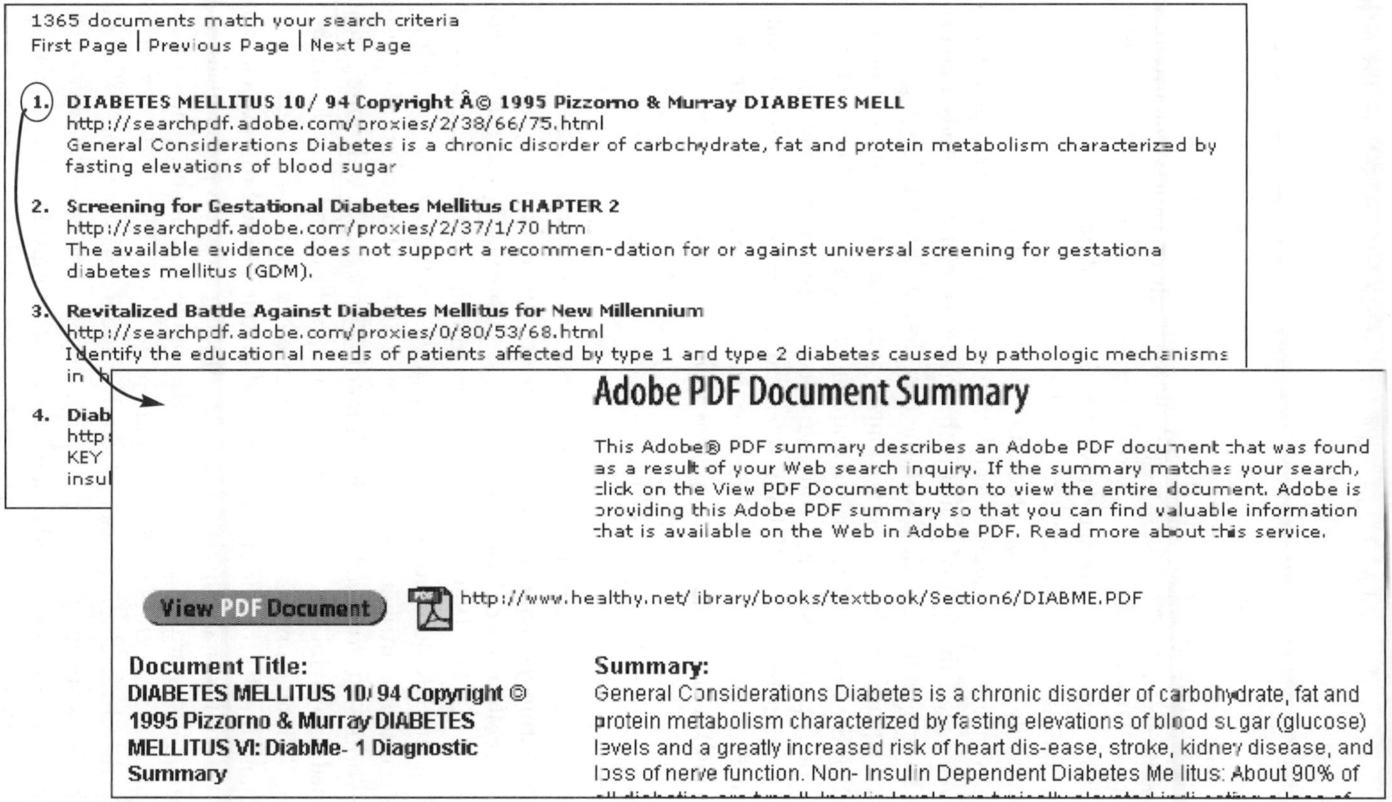

1365 documents match your search criteria
First Page | Previous Page | Next Page

1. **DIABETES MELLITUS 10 / 94 Copyright Â© 1995 Pizzorno & Murray DIABETES MELL**
   http://searchpdf.adobe.com/proxies/2/38/66/75.html
   General Considerations Diabetes is a chronic disorder of carbohydrate, fat and protein metabolism characterized by fasting elevations of blood sugar

2. **Screening for Gestational Diabetes Mellitus CHAPTER 2**
   http://searchpdf.adobe.com/proxies/2/37/1/70.htm
   The available evidence does not support a recommen-dation for or against universal screening for gestationa diabetes mellitus (GDM).

3. **Revitalized Battle Against Diabetes Mellitus for New Millennium**
   http://searchpdf.adobe.com/proxies/0/80/53/68.html
   Identify the educational needs of patients affected by type 1 and type 2 diabetes caused by pathologic mechanism in

4. **Diab**
   http
   KEY
   insul

Adobe PDF Document Summary

View PDF Document   http://www.healthy.net/ibrary/books/textbook/Section6/DIABME.PDF

This Adobe® PDF summary describes an Adobe PDF document that was found as a result of your Web search inquiry. If the summary matches your search, click on the View PDF Document button to view the entire document. Adobe is providing this Adobe PDF summary so that you can find valuable information that is available on the Web in Adobe PDF. Read more about this service.

Document Title:
DIABETES MELLITUS 10 94 Copyright ©
1995 Pizzorno & Murray DIABETES
MELLITUS VI: DiabMe- 1 Diagnostic
Summary

Summary:
General Considerations Diabetes is a chronic disorder of carbohydrate, fat and protein metabolism characterized by fasting elevations of blood sugar (glucose) levels and a greatly increased risk of heart dis-ease, stroke, kidney disease, and loss of nerve function. Non- Insulin Dependent Diabetes Mellitus: About 90% of

Fig. 2.14 *Searching the summaries of PDF files*

internet users of this tool for locating a subset of potentially high-quality information should not be underestimated.

Locating images and other audiovisual materials

Some search engines, such as *AltaVista*, now offer options for locating images. Using *AltaVista*, you can type 'image:' before each of your keywords in the search box. This specifies that any sites retrieved contain your keyword(s) in the text description of an image. However, the lack of quality control and subject description in search engines means that any images that are retrieved are not necessarily going to be of a high quality, nor are they necessarily going to be of relevance to your search. A search for 'image:lung', for example, retrieves 3121 web pages, the first of which is the home page of a Dr Andy Lung containing an image of the author with the text description 'Dr_Lung.jpg'. Other links are equally irrelevant or no longer available. A second option using *AltaVista* is to select the category for searching images (located on the left-hand side of the opening screen). You can select to search for photographs or images, buttons/banners and photos in colour and/or black and white. Images are drawn from two commercial sites in particular, *Corbis* (**http://store. corbis.com/**) and *viewimages* (**http://www.viewimages.com/**), as well as from the internet generally. Unlike the previous option, the results are presented as a page of thumbnail images (small-scale images that you can select to view an image in full).

Specialist sources of image and other audiovisual materials also exist. For example, within medicine, *BioMed* (**http://www.brisbio.ac.uk/**) is currently one of the best collections of biomedical images available via the internet. It started life in the in the late 1980s when veterinary teaching staff at the University of Bristol in the UK donated their teaching slides to form a shared archive of images. Further contributions from colleagues and staff based at other institutions world-wide resulted in the 'Bristol Biomedical Videodisc', which contained approximately 20,000 veterinary, medical and dental images for teaching. These are now accessible via the internet.

The multimedia format of the internet should lend itself to locating images and other audiovisual materials. However, finding an appropriate image is far from straightforward, as there is no single source that enables their effective retrieval. Search engines tend to exclude materials in file formats other than HTML, thereby excluding images and other audiovisual materials. Where it is possible to locate images using a search engine such as *AltaVista*, either a specific instruction is required or a separate option must be selected, and there is no quality control of the images that are retrieved. Many more tools for accessing these types of information exist, such as *BioMed*, and some gateways and virtual libraries. However, their coverage is restricted due to the time constraints involved in locating, evaluating and describing resources. For further details of the range of available options, two useful overviews are *Searching beyond text: multimedia search tools* by Greg Notess,[19] and 'Finding images on the internet' by Phil Bradley.[20] Evaluating the quality of images and other multimedia resources is discussed in Chapter 4.

Searching newsgroups and mailing lists

Newsgroups and mailing lists have been in existence for longer than the web itself. Newsgroups are comparable to a noticeboard – users interested in a specific topic area can post messages on the 'noticeboard' for others to read and respond to. Mailing lists are similar but utilize e-mail for discussing issues of interest between groups of e-mail users. The discussions that take place via both newsgroups and mailing lists can range from the useful to the bizarre – newsgroups in particular are not renowned for being a source of high-quality information. Despite this, both newsgroups and mailing lists are potential sources of useful information for many internet users.

However, their usefulness as a source of information is limited by the lack of comprehensive search tools either to locate lists or newsgroups, or to search the archives of discussions. *Google* currently provides the only facility for searching and browsing newsgroup archives (**http://groups.google.com/**). Previously *Deja.com*, it was only possible at the time of writing to search discussions from August 2000 onwards via *Google* newsgroups, thereby limiting the volume of searchable information. However, in March 2001 the site was 'in the process of adding *Deja.com's* Usenet archive of more than 500 million messages – a terabyte of human conversation dating back to 1995'. More tools are available for finding mailing lists and for searching their archives. For example, *JISCmail* (**http://www.jiscmail.ac.uk/**) is a UK-based higher education discussion list service. It is possible to browse the archives of thousands of mailing lists via the home page. *Mailbase* (**http://www.mailbase.ac.uk/**) predated *JISCmail*, although several mailing lists and their archives are still available via the site. *Liszt* (**http://www.liszt.com/**) is a US-based directory of mailing lists – it is not possible to search the archives of mailing lists via this site but it is possible to browse the directory of brief descriptions about each list. Two further directories that include information about mailing lists are *list UNIVERSE.COM* (**http://list-universe.com/**) and *topica* (**http://www.topica.com/**). Again, further information about searching for this type of information is available from Phil Bradley's website.[21]

Searching the 'invisible web'

As discussed earlier, search engines are restricted to the 'publicly indexable web'. The 'invisible web', sometimes also referred to as the 'deep web', is the information that search engines cannot index because it is hidden behind a search interface, such as in a database, or behind a login screen, such as papers in electronic journals. Restriction to using search engines therefore means exclusion of a whole category of potentially high-quality information.

Some tools are now being developed which provide access to the invisible web. To date, efforts have focused on identifying where invisible web content exists and directing users to the relevant locations. This is the approach adopted by gateways and virtual libraries, which include the descriptions of 'invisible' databases and journals, but you need to connect to each site individually to search the contents. Likewise, this method is also used by *InvisibleWeb.com* (**http://www.invisibleweb.com/**), a catalogue of invisible resources, and *CompletePlanet* (**http://www.completeplanet.com/**), a directory of almost 40,000 invisible web databases. You can browse both directories and connect to each individual resource in order to search the information. In addition, *CompletePlanet* is currently developing *LexiBot*. Using this tool, it is possible to input your search terms; the tool then selects the most relevant options from 600 different invisible web resources and forwards your query to them. It is anticipated that ultimately the service will run each query against the 100,000 'significant' invisible websites that *CompletePlanet* estimates currently exist.

Searching the invisible or 'deep' web is a relatively new concept and the available search tools are currently limited in terms of their capabilities. However, this area is receiving an increasing amount of attention as the potential volume (and quality) of the information missing from search engines is becoming better understood. Again, guides are available to searching this type of information.[9, 22]

Searching for regional or subject-specific information

Many readers will no doubt be aware of the plethora of search tools that advertise coverage of regional or subject-specific information. While space does not allow a detailed examination of these, it is worth mentioning here that many of these tools are developed using the same techniques adopted by search engines. As mentioned earlier, *SOSIG* (a gateway to high-quality resources within the social sciences), connects users to a social sciences search engine to expand their search results. Automated methods are used to identify and index only those materials containing keywords that denote coverage of the social sciences. Therefore, although such tools might be useful in restricting searches to a specific subject area, there is generally no quality control of the information.

Additional problems relate to how the information is identified for inclusion in such services. A UK-focused service, for example, might select only those sites where the internet address ends in .uk. If this is the case, the *BMJ* (http://www.bmj.com/), a journal which is freely available via the internet, would not be identified because the address ends in .com, despite its obvious interest to a UK audience.

Therefore, if you are interested in locating high-quality materials, it is worth noting that such tools should be used with caution – restriction by subject or region does not necessarily equate with restriction by quality, especially if the restriction is undertaken automatically.

Where should you start?

This chapter has examined a range of facilities for searching the internet, from the most heavily used search engines which aim for comprehensive coverage of the web, through to selective services for accessing high-quality materials. In addition, some speciality search tools have been highlighted. So, where should you start?

The first task when looking for high-quality information is to attempt to locate a service which provides access to quality materials within the subject area that you are interested in. A limited number of such services have been discussed under 'gateways and virtual libraries', where an invaluable guide, and probably the best starting place for the vast number of guides which are available, is the *Argus Clearinghouse*. However, this is an evaluative guide to evaluative guides, and therefore its coverage cannot be comprehensive – you may find that there is no guide listed for the subject area that you are interested in. If this is the case, firstly consider the search terms that you are using. When you are searching the *Clearinghouse*, you are not searching every word of every resource but rather the brief descriptions about each site. If you are looking for information on Saigon during the Vietnam War, it is unlikely that a specific guide will exist on 'Saigon' within the *Clearinghouse*. However, using the broader terms 'Vietnam' or 'history' might lead you to guides that contain appropriate information.

Likewise, when you are searching an individual gateway or virtual library, you are not searching every word of every page, but rather the brief descriptions about each resource. If you do not find what you are looking for initially, also consider broadening your search terms. Using broader search terms might lead you to sites that contain appropriate information but where the descriptions do not contain the specific terms that you are interested in. It is also worth browsing the suggested subject headings (where available) and exploring the help information to establish whether you can input the stem of a word to include all possible variations of it.

As discussed under 'subject catalogues and directory services', some of the generic services claim to provide indications of the quality of the sites they describe. However, the quality ratings are not always useful or informative. Located at the end of this chapter is a checklist of what to look for in a search tool if you are attempting to locate high-quality information. Use this to help in assessing whether a service is truly providing indications of resource quality.

Beyond gateways and virtual libraries – where next?

The types of services included in the *Clearinghouse*, and discussed under 'gateways and virtual libraries', aim for coverage of high-quality materials only. There has been little co-ordination to date of coverage across disciplines and user groups. In addition, due to the high level of manual input required in identifying, evaluating and describing materials for such services, they often cover a small number of resources and are often of interest to only a limited number of users. If you have tried the above options and there is no relevant-sounding guide, or you have found a guide but cannot find any information of interest, then you should consider trying the other types of search facilities which have been described in this section, in the following order:

1   subject catalogues and directory services
2   search engines
3   metasearch engines.

If a highly selective guide is not available or contains no relevant materials, general subject directories or catalogues should be the next option. These tend to be larger but less selective in terms of site quality. However, the descriptions generally offer a meaningful indication of the content of resources. If still nothing useful is found, now might be the time to try a search engine. This option offers more comprehensive coverage of the web, but is the least discriminatory and the least descriptive about the sites it covers. Therefore you will need to expend more time and effort in filtering through the search results. Finally, if you still find nothing, a metasearch engine should be the final option, as tools such as the *BigHub.com* claim to cover several databases.

As mentioned earlier, some tools offer the option to broaden searches automatically – *SOSIG*, the Social Sciences Information Gateway, connects users to an automatically generated database of social science resources. Likewise, *Yahoo!* displays both results from its directory (websites), as well as results from the *Google* search engine (web pages).

Figure 2.15 summarizes the main advantages and disadvantages of different types of search facilities in terms of finding quality information. As a general rule, the greater the number of resources covered by a search tool, the less selective the guide is in terms of the quality of the materials included in it. In addition, there tends to be less descriptive information about the sites that are included. This means that you may find a greater volume of information but you will need to do more work to filter the useful from the not-so-useful results.

Although search engines claim comprehensive coverage of the web, in reality the percentage of the material covered is very small. It has been estimated that only 1/500 of the web is visible to search engines. Therefore, if you are using a search engine, try using different engines, as the databases are constantly changing and each covers a slightly different part of the web. In addition, explore the help information and any additional search options to assist you in focusing your searches on material that is likely to be of more relevance to you. Lastly, consider the other types of search facilities that are available – the information that you are seeking may be locked in a PDF file, a database or an electronic journal. Exploring sites such as *InvisibleWeb.com*, *CompletePlanet* and *Search Adobe PDF Online* may lead you to high-quality resources that you might not otherwise have found.

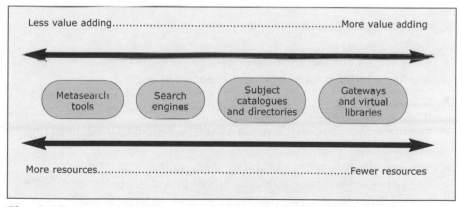

Fig. 2.15 *Main advantages and disadvantages of different search facilities*

CHECKLIST WHAT TO LOOK FOR IN A SEARCH TOOL

This section has provided various suggestions on which search tools to use and when to use them, as well as outlining the advantages and disadvantages of different types of search facilities. If you are interested in identifying a search tool to find high-quality information, the main questions to consider are:

✔ what subject areas does the search tool cover?
✔ who are the intended users of the tool?
✔ are resources selected and evaluated prior to their inclusion in the database?
✔ are resources awarded a rating according to their perceived quality?
✔ are explicit evaluation criteria available which explain how resources are evaluated and on what basis?
✔ are descriptions provided about each resource, and do the resource descriptions provide sufficient information to enable you to assess their relevance?
✔ are the resource descriptions evaluative? i.e. do they indicate the likely value and usefulness of materials?
✔ how frequently are materials revisited to ensure their continuing value and usefulness?
✔ what is the knowledge and expertise of those involved in selecting, evaluating and describing materials?
✔ what types of materials does the search tool cover? does it only include information available via the web, or are other materials also covered?

It is also worth considering:

✔ what search options are available?
✔ are there facilities to narrow and broaden searches?
✔ is it possible to browse by subject categories, and are the subject headings or categories meaningful?
✔ are there any additional options available for using the tool to find information?
✔ are the different options effective, easy to use and useful?
✔ is any help information available which provides guidelines on using the tool? is the help information clear and understandable? is it useful?

References

1 *Resources for searching* [online], available at
http://www.netskills.ac.uk/support/searching/
[2001, March 8].

2 Sullivan, D., *Search Engine Watch* [online], available at
http://www.searchenginewatch.com/
[2001, March 8].

3 Bradley, P., *Welcome to Phil's home page* [online], available at
http://www.philb.com/
[2001, March 8].

4 *Similar Pages* (*GoogleScout*) [online], available at
http://www.google.com/help/features.html
[2001, March 29].

5 Bradley, P., The relevance of underpants to searching the web, *Ariadne*
[online] **24**, 2000, available at
http://www.ariadne.ac.uk/issue24/search-engines/
[2001, March 8].

6 *Our Search: why use Google – Google searches more sites more quickly,
to bring you the most relevant results* [online], available at
http://www.google.com/technology/index.html
[2001, March 29].

7 Sullivan, D., *Media Metrix search engine ratings*, 2001 [online], available at
http://www.searchenginewatch.com/reports/mediametrix.html
[2001, March 8].

8 Sullivan, D., *Search engine sizes*, 2000 [online], available at
http://www.searchenginewatch.com/reports/sizes.html
[2001, March 8].

9 *CompletePlanet: the deep web – surfacing hidden value*, 2001 [online],
available at
http://www.completeplanet.com/Tutorials/DeepWeb/
[2001, March 8].

10 *Argus Clearinghouse: how the guides are rated* [online], available at
http://www.clearinghouse.net/ratings.html
[2001, March 8].

11 Venditto, G., Sites that rate the web: critic's choice, *Internet World*, 8
(1), 1997, 84.

12 Rettig, J., Beyond 'cool': analog models for reviewing digital resources,
Online [online], September, 1996, available at
http://www.onlineinc.com/onlinemag/SeptOL/rettig9.html
[2001, March 8].

13 Tillman, H. N., *Evaluating quality on the net* [online], available at
    http://www.hopetillman.com/findqual.html
    [2000, December 28].

14 Cooke, A., McNab, A. and Anagnostelis, B., The good, the bad and the
    ugly: internet review sites. In Raitt, D. I. and Jeapes, B. (eds.), *Proceed-
    ings of the 20th International Online Information Meeting*, Oxford,
    Learned Information, **20**, 1996, 33–40.

15 Collins, B. R., Beyond cruising: reviewing, *Library Journal*, **121** (3),
    1996, 124.

16 Anagnostelis, B., Cooke, A. and McNab, A.,Thinking critically about
    information on the web, *Vine* (104), 1997, 21–8.

17 Bradley, P., *Multi-search engines: a comparison*, 2000, [online], available at
    http://www.philb.com/msengine.htm
    [2001, March 8].

18 Sullivan, D., *Metacrawlers and metasearch engines*, [online], available at
    http://searchenginewatch.com/facts/metacrawlers.html
    [2001, March 8].

19 Notess, G., *Searching beyond text: multimedia search tools*, 2000
    [online], available at
    http://www.onlineinc.com/onlinemag/OL2000/net11.html
    [2001, March 8].

20 Bradley, P., *Finding images on the internet*, 1999 [online], available at
    http://www.philb.com/findimages.htm
    [2001, March 8].

21 Bradley, P., *Discussion lists, Usenet and archives*, 1999 [online], available at
    http://www.philb.com/mail.htm
    [2001, March 8].

22 Sherman, C. and Price, G., *Worth a look: searching the invisible web –
    resources and concepts for web research*, 2000 [online], available at
    **http://websearch.about.com/internet/websearch/library/searchwiz/
    bl_invisibleweb_apra.htm**
    [2001, March 8].

3

Assessing the quality of an information source

The previous chapter examined the ever-increasing range of tools and facilities that are available for searching the internet, focusing on finding high-quality material. This chapter is designed to help you assess the quality of an information source once it has been located. It provides a detailed guide to those factors or characteristics that affect the quality, value or usefulness of any information source which can be accessed via the internet. However, as mentioned in Chapter 1, any assessment of quality is dependent upon the needs of the individual seeking information, as well as on the nature of the source being evaluated. Therefore the guidelines provided here are not prescriptive, and you should select the appropriate criteria depending on the nature of the source you are evaluating and your own particular needs.

The chapter is divided into ten areas of evaluation:

- identifying the purpose of a source
- assessing coverage
- assessing authority and reputation
- assessing accuracy
- assessing the currency and maintenance of a source
- considering the accessibility of a source
- evaluating the presentation and arrangement of information
- assessing how easy a source is to use
- making a comparison with other sources
- assessing the overall quality of a source.

Each section contains extensive notes on how to approach the particular aspect of evaluation and examples are provided throughout. At the end of each section, a checklist is provided for easy reference.

Identifying the purpose of a source

The purpose of a source refers to its aims and objectives. These include the intended coverage, any stated limitations in terms of coverage (the scope), and the intended audience. Identifying the intended audience is of particular importance as you may need to determine whether information is likely to be presented at a level that is suitable for your needs.

Evaluation will involve determining whether any aims, objectives or limitations are stated within a source or service, and examining any such statements.

Medical Matrix (**http://www.medmatrix.org/index.asp**) is a gateway to health and medical information available via the internet. There is a link from the opening screen to 'About Medical Matrix' (displayed in Figure 3.1). Where a link such as this, or links entitled 'help', 'README' or 'FAQ' (frequently asked questions), are available, it is worth following them, as they often lead to details of the purpose of materials. As displayed in Figure 3.1, the 'about' link in *Medical Matrix* leads to an explicit statement of its purpose and intended coverage – 'posting, annotating, and continuously updating "full content, unrestricted access, Internet clinical medicine resources".' There is also a statement of the intended audience: 'primarily United States physicians and healthworkers who are on the front line in prescribing treatment for disease conditions.' Further details relate to the evaluation of resources for inclusion in the gateway, providing additional insight into the intended coverage of the service.

Any assessment of purpose is inextricably linked to the other areas of evaluation, which are discussed elsewhere in this chapter – in particular an assessment of coverage (see next section). By considering the other areas of assessment, it will be possible to determine whether the intended purpose has been achieved, whether the intended subject areas or materials are covered, and whether the information is appropriate for the intended audience.

CHECKLIST   IDENTIFYING THE PURPOSE OF A SOURCE

✔ is there a statement of the intended purpose of the source?
✔ is there a statement of the aims, objectives and intended coverage?
✔ what are the aims and objectives of the source?
✔ what is the intended coverage, and are there any limitations to it?
✔ who are the intended audience?

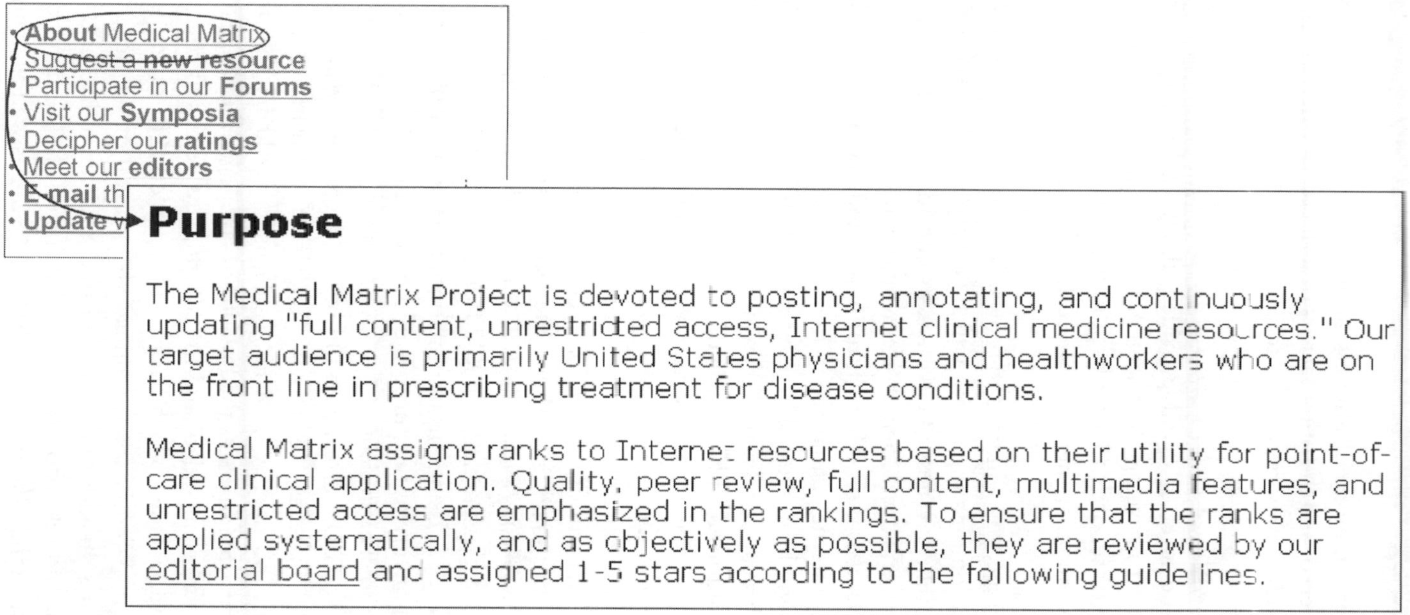

About Medical Matrix
Suggest a new resource
Participate in our **Forums**
Visit our **Symposia**
Decipher our ratings
Meet our editors
E-mail th
Update v

Purpose

The Medical Matrix Project is devoted to posting, annotating, and continuously updating "full content, unrestricted access, Internet clinical medicine resources." Our target audience is primarily United States physicians and healthworkers who are on the front line in prescribing treatment for disease conditions.

Medical Matrix assigns ranks to Internet resources based on their utility for point-of-care clinical application. Quality, peer review, full content, multimedia features, and unrestricted access are emphasized in the rankings. To ensure that the ranks are applied systematically, and as objectively as possible, they are reviewed by our editorial board and assigned 1-5 stars according to the following guidelines.

Fig. 3.1 *Statement of purpose in the 'Medical Matrix' information gateway*

Assessing coverage

The principal factor determining the usefulness of any information source is often the subject area covered, and the other factors described elsewhere in this section are often of secondary importance. Factors affecting the coverage of a source are: the subject areas and the types of materials covered; the comprehensiveness of coverage within a given area; the range of different subjects covered (the breadth); the level of detail provided about each subject (the depth); and any limitations to coverage (the scope). In addition, the retrospective coverage of a source or service (how far back in time material is covered) affects comprehensiveness and may therefore affect the value and usefulness of a source.

In order to assess coverage, you will need to browse the source itself, or conduct a search for information on a topic with which you are familiar. You can then determine the comprehensiveness of coverage by considering whether all aspects of a subject have been covered which you would expect to be covered.

The *Internet Movie Database*, or *IMDb* (**http://www.imdb.com/**) is a well known and widely used internet database of film information. A film and theatre studies teacher might be interested in pointing her students towards this site for details of films, directors and actors. Having heard about the site from another teacher, she would need to know whether it is suitable for her class. Two links are provided from the opening screen of the *IMDb* which are likely to provide useful information about its intended purpose – a link for first-time users and a link to 'help' information. However, in this instance the links are not particularly helpful. The aim of the site 'is to be the most fun and useful resource on the internet for movie fans around the world', and the scope 'all sorts of information on over 200,000 movie & TV titles, plus even more on over 400,000 actors and actresses, nearly 40,000 directors and hundreds of thousands of other people . . .'. Using this information, the teacher would only be able to build a limited picture of the purpose of the site and make an assessment about its suitability for her students.

In order to evaluate the *IMDb*, a search could be conducted. For example, 'war' retrieves 744 'title' matches, i.e. movies, television programmes and videos with this word in the title. A knowledgeable user would be able to examine the films that are listed to assess the breadth of coverage (the range of different types of films that are included) and the comprehensiveness of coverage (whether all films are included which they would expect). For example, films range from *When the Wind Blows*, an animated portrayal of the impact of nuclear war, to *Star Wars*. In addition, films are listed in different languages, from different countries, and television series are also included. The dates of the films are recorded, including *Abraham Lincoln* from 1924, as well as many other films from the 1920s and 1930s, indicating that retrospective coverage by this site is good. Moreover, several titles from 2000 and 2001 are retrieved, indicating the currency of the database.

Level of detail for the intended audience

The level of detail or depth of coverage relates to the intended audience of a source. You will need to evaluate whether sources provide sufficient information and whether the information is pitched at an appropriate level for your needs.

Figure 3.2 displays information in the *IMDb* for the film *Gladiator*. As displayed in Figure 3.2, the *IMBd* provides extensive information beyond a listing of the actors involved in the film. It is possible to read a detailed plot outline, view a list of the full cast and crew, read external reviews of the film and view the trailer online. If you were assessing this site, you would need to decide whether enough information is provided for your needs – in the example mentioned above, the teacher would need to assess whether the level of detail is sufficient for a class of film and theatre studies students.

Assessing whether information is pitched at an appropriate level involves reading through the text and attempting to determine whether it is either too simplistic or too complex for the audience involved. The text in Figure 3.2 from the *IMDb* might be considered suitable for a wide range of students because it is aimed at a general audience. As mentioned under 'Assessing coverage' (page 64) *Medical Matrix* states that it is aimed 'primarily' at 'United States physicians and healthworkers who are on the front line in prescribing treatment for disease conditions.' However, from an examination of the information within the site, it is apparent that it is likely to appeal to a much wider audience. For example, browsing the gateway for materials relating to 'pregnancy' retrieves not only materials aimed at healthcare professionals, but also material defined as 'patient education' – fact sheets and other resources relating to conception, fertility and other pregnancy-related issues. The descriptions are written in a non-technical language that would appeal to both patients and professionals.

Pointers to further information

Figure 3.3 displays some of the links that are available from the British Library website (http://www.bl.uk/). Pointers to further information, such as hypertext links to other sites or references to printed materials, can enhance the coverage of a source or service. In this example, the links provide access to a more

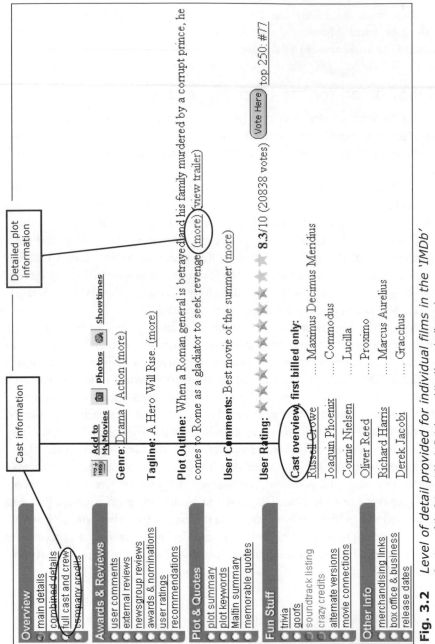

Fig. 3.2 *Level of detail provided for individual films in the 'IMDb'*
Courtesy of the Internet Movie Database – http://www.imdb.com/

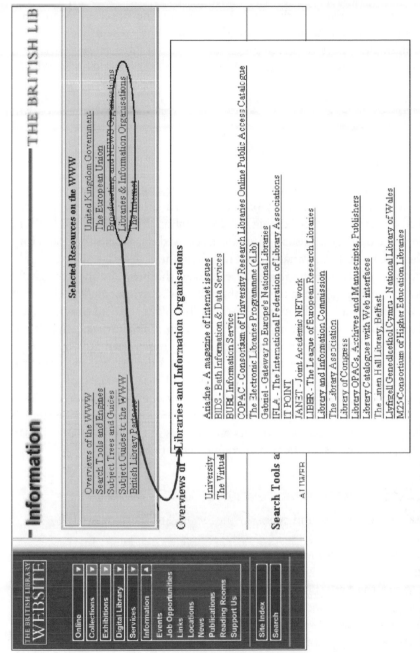

Fig. 3.3 Links to further information from the British Library website
Source and page owner: the British Library

extensive range of materials than is possible within the site itself. Many sites include some descriptive information about each link, which adds value to them and enables users to select potentially relevant sites more easily. One further consideration is whether the links have been selected and on what basis. It is evident that these links have been selected on the basis of their relevance but there is no information on whether they have been selected according to their quality.

Mirror sites

Some sites are 'mirror sites' which, as their name suggests, are copies of an original site. Mirror sites are generally provided to enable faster access to materials (discussed further under 'considering the accessibility of a source'), and both the mirror and the original site usually provide access to the same information. However, there may be local variations in terms of their coverage. For example, *AltaVista*, one of the search engines discussed in the previous chapter, can be accessed via the original site in the USA (**http://www.altavista.com/**) as well as via numerous other locations, including Australia (**http://au.altavista.com/**), Canada (**http://www.altavistacanada.com/**) and the UK (**http://uk.altavista.com/**). If you were evaluating *AltaVista*, you would need to determine whether you are using an original or a mirror site, whether the mirror and the original site cover the same materials, and the respective advantages and disadvantages of accessing each. For example, the UK mirror site for *AltaVista* contains additional content of regional interest and is likely to offer faster access for users outside the US. *AltaVista* provides information about its mirror sites in the details about the service (**http://www.altavista.com/av/content/av_network.html**).

CHECKLIST ASSESSING COVERAGE

✔ what subject areas and types of materials are covered by the source?
✔ what range of different subjects is covered?
✔ are the subject areas covered comprehensively?
✔ what are the limitations in terms of coverage?
✔ what is the retrospective coverage of the source?
✔ what level of detail is provided, and is the level of detail sufficient for the audience? is the information pitched at an appropriate level?
✔ are there any links to further sources of information? is any descriptive information available for any links? are the links selected, and if so on what basis? are the links valuable and useful?

✔ is the site an original or a mirror site? does the mirror site cover the same materials as the original? what are the advantages and disadvantages of accessing the mirror versus the original site?

Assessing authority and reputation

An assessment of the authority of an information source is based upon a range of factors, but primarily the knowledge and expertise of those responsible for producing it. A source is generally considered authoritative if it has been written by a subject expert, or produced by an institution with recognized knowledge and expertise in the field. Authority is inextricably linked to reputation, including the reputation of the source itself, as well as the reputation of those responsible for producing it. A good reputation is created because a source has been successful, useful or valuable on previous occasions, or because its author or institution are well known for their knowledge and expertise in an area. The authority and reputation of a source is likely to affect the extent to which you will rely on the information it contains, and therefore influences perceptions of its relative quality. For example, you are less likely to rely upon a page entitled 'Smoking does not cause lung cancer' in the *Journal of Theoretics* (**http://www.journaloftheoretics.com/Editorials/Editorial%201-4.html**) than information from the World Health Organization (**http://www.who.int/**), the UK government Department of Health (**http://www.doh.gov.uk/**) or the US government National Institutes for Health (**http://www.nih.gov/**). Aside from the claims made by the first site, the information is from a little-known journal compared to three well known and highly reputable organizations.

Several techniques can be used to ascertain authority and reputation. For academic works, a literature search could be conducted to determine whether the author has published in the field before, and whether he or she has published in refereed journals. The expertise of an author may also be evaluated by determining whether he or she is a professional working in the field or a lay person with a passing interest in a subject. Some sites include a statement of the expertise and credentials of the authors, and this can be useful when attempting to make an assessment.

Alternatives to individual or institutional authority

It may be difficult to identify an individual or an institution responsible for a site. However, there are many other indicators that can be used to assess authority and reputation. One consideration is the address of a source. For example, **.gov.uk** and **.gov** in an address indicate governmental sites in the UK and the USA respectively, and .ac.uk and .edu indicate academic institutions. Further details about analysing web page addresses are provided in Chapter 4 under 'Organizational sites, personal home pages and other websites' (page 97).

You might also consider the reputation and experience of any other organizations involved in the production of resources, such as publishers, sponsors or funding agencies. Commercial and academic publishers in the print world have formed their own quality-control processes out of a necessity to produce a profit and/or maintain standards. The internet, in comparison, has afforded anyone with the opportunity to become his or her own publisher. However, commercial and academic publishers remain driven by the same incentives, whether they are producing material in print or over the internet, and it is therefore worth considering their involvement in the production of any material. Any reviews of a site or service can also provide an indication of reputation and authority, particularly if a review has been published in a well respected journal within the field. As discussed on pages 23–4, web citation searching techniques can also be used to indicate authority. One further consideration is the use of counters – these often appear at the end of the first page of a site, and indicate how many people have visited the site during a specified time period. Thus they can be used to assess a site's popularity. However, the use of counters has obvious limitations. A site's popularity does not necessarily equate with its quality, and counters include visitors to the first page of a site who may venture no further.

Many readers might consider authority and reputation too subjective to merit consideration. The assumption that the work of a reputable author or institution is likely to be of higher quality than those that are less well known is not always true. Reputations and expertise change, and a newcomer to a field can obviously produce high-quality work. Factors affecting source quality are not mutually exclusive, and it is essential that you consider the authority and reputation of a source in relation to, for example, its coverage, and the currency and accuracy of the information it contains.

CHECKLIST ASSESSING AUTHORITY AND REPUTATION

✔ what is the reputation and experience of the author or institution responsible for the information? is the source written by a subject expert or produced by an institution with recognized knowledge and expertise in the field? are details available of the author's credentials?

✔ what is the reputation and experience of any other organizations involved in the production of the information, such as publishers, sponsors or funding agencies?

✔ what is the reputation of the source? is the source well known?

✔ what is the address of the site? does the address indicate an authoritative institution?

✔ are there any reviews available discussing the source? do they indicate that the site is reputable and authoritative? are the reviews themselves authoritative?

✔ is there a counter on the site? does the number of visits to the site suggest that it is popular?

Assessing accuracy

Accuracy generally refers to the factual accuracy – the correctness – of a source of information. In many respects, the need to determine accuracy underpins the whole process of evaluation – it is often the reason for looking critically at any information. Despite this, many authors on the subject have avoided the question of *how* to assess accuracy, simply asking, 'Is the information accurate?'. This is not surprising. The ease of assessing accuracy is affected by both the nature of the information and the expertise of the evaluator. For example, mathematical information can be either correct or incorrect, whereas theories can be subjective and there may be no right or wrong answer. Some evaluators will be able to search a source for information about which they have some knowledge and expertise in order to make an assessment of accuracy, while others may have little or no expertise about the subject. Despite these problems, addressing the question 'Is the information accurate?' is an essential step to evaluation, and considering how to answer it cannot be avoided. Some guidance can be found in the field of healthcare, where methods and techniques are being developed to do just this – some of these are considered below. In addition, it is possible to look beyond complete accuracy to indicators of the *likely* accuracy of information – some considerations are also discussed here.

Appraising information critically

Healthcare practice in the UK and elsewhere in the world has been the subject of substantial change during the 1990s. There has been a shift in emphasis from doctors basing their practice on personal intuition or their own experience towards *evidence-based* healthcare. Simply, this means basing healthcare decisions on *evidence* – on the research findings relating to a particular illness and how it should be treated. However, the findings of research can vary – one study might offer a physician one set of advice, while another may be contradictory. This has been evident in recent months in the UK with the controversy over the

71

measles, mumps and rubella (MMR) vaccination. While one study questions the safety of the combined vaccination,[1] others advocate its safety.[2, 3] What should physicians believe?

The quality of research can vary from study to study, and therefore the accuracy of the information also varies. As part of the shift towards evidence-based healthcare, standards have been defined for the quality of research and there is now a widely recognized hierarchy of evidence.[4] This hierarchy lists types of study according to the extent to which the information can be used to inform healthcare decision-making. At the top of the hierarchy are systematic reviews of randomized controlled trials. A randomized controlled trial is a study where a population is randomly divided into two groups – the first group receives the treatment under investigation, and the second receives the standard or no treatment. The results are compared. A systematic review of randomized controlled trials involves the systematic identification and comparison of all such trials for one treatment. This means drawing on the results of lots of smaller studies to provide a much stronger indication of the likely outcome of using a particular treatment. Further down the hierarchy of evidence are listed individual randomized controlled trials, as well as other types of research, leading to the opinions of experts based on their day-to-day practice at the bottom of the hierarchy.

Randomized controlled trials and systematic reviews are types of research that are generally peculiar to medicine. Therefore it may not be possible to define a hierarchy of information according to its likely accuracy for other fields. However, an additional part of the process of developing evidence-based practice is the need for practitioners to evaluate or critically appraise the quality of any research, wherever it sits within the hierarchy. Critical appraisal within this context refers to evaluating the quality of a piece of research and therefore judging its likely accuracy. There are several papers and tools designed to assist with this process. For example, *Surgical-tutor.org.uk* includes the following questions for the critical appraisal of a paper:[5]

- who wrote the paper?
- do they or the institution have a proven academic record?
- is the paper interesting and relevant?
- did the study introduction address the relevant points?
- were the aims clearly stated?
- was an appropriate group of subjects studied?
- was the sample size justified?
- was the study design appropriate?
- were the aims of the study fulfilled?

- were the sources of error discussed?
- are the relevant findings justified?
- are the conclusions of the paper justified?

It may be possible to draw on the questions listed for the critical appraisal of healthcare information to evaluate the accuracy of other types of research, irrespective of the subject matter. Potentially relevant issues include: who wrote the paper; whether they have a proven academic record; the relevance of the paper; whether there is a clear statement of the aims; use of appropriate research methods; fulfilment of the study aims; and justification of the findings and the conclusions. Therefore, although this approach is dependent upon the availability of 'research' information, it does offer some useful considerations for assessing accuracy.

Beyond factual accuracy

Obviously much of the information that is available via the internet could not be defined as research, and even if it were, you may not have the necessary expertise to appraise the information critically using the questions listed. However, there are numerous other factors that may affect the accuracy, or user perceptions of the accuracy, of a source of information. These include: whether information is based upon any research; the availability of references to published information; whether information has been through a refereeing, editing or any other quality-control process; the potential for bias introduced by authors, publishers or sponsors; and the professionalism or overall quality of a source as indicated by spelling, grammatical or typographical errors. Some sources provide a facility for sending corrections to any inaccurate information – which is not only useful but also suggests a concern for accuracy. Other related factors discussed elsewhere include the authority and reputation of the source, the knowledge and expertise of any authors or organizations involved in producing the information, and the currency of the information.

The potential for bias is an area of particular concern. No source is ever completely free from bias, but identifying the motivation of those involved in producing the information will enable you to judge the extent to which you can rely upon it. For example, a search for 'nutrition', 'sports' and 'athletes' in *AltaVista* retrieves over two million hits. As displayed in Figure 3.4, the first is *Nutrition advice for athletes* (**http://www.hhdev.psu.edu/research/athletes.htm**); the second *Nutrition for athletes* (**http://www.ausport.gov.au/nut.html**); and the third *GU sports nutrition for athletes and athletic training, competition, endurance* (**http://www.gusports.com/**). All three sites sound potentially rele-

73

1. *Nutrition* Advice for *Athletes*
   Athletes Should be Careful About the **Nutrition** Messages They Hear. Many of the nutritional messages aimed at the general public may be inappropriate...
   URL: www.hhdev.psu.edu/research/athletes.htm
   Translate ▤ Related pages Facts about: Pennsylvania Stat...

2. *NUTRITION FOR ATHLETES*
   Nutrition for **Athletes**. Dr Louise Burke - Consultant Dietitian at the Australian Institute of Sport. All **athletes** are encouraged to follow the rules...
   URL: www.ausport.gov.au/nut.html
   Translate More pages from this site ▤ Related pages

3. gu *sports nutrition* for *athletes* and athletic training, competition, endurance
   GU, the country's original energy gel, is the perfect **sports nutrition** product for the weekend warrior, team sport enthusiast or professional athlete...
   URL: www.gusports.com/
   Translate More pages from this site ▤ Related pages

Fig. 3.4   *Search results in 'AltaVista' for 'nutrition', 'sports' and 'athletes'*

vant. However, reading the descriptions for each site displayed in Figure 3.4 provides some insight into the likely accuracy of the information. For example, the description for the second site reads, 'Nutrition for Athletes. Dr Louise Burke – Consultant Dietician at the Australian Institute of Sport'. An academic working at a reputable and authoritative-sounding institution has produced this site and it is therefore likely that the information provided here will be accurate. Furthermore, selecting the link to this site leads to detailed guidelines on nutrition for athletes with references to published information. Alternatively, the third description begins: 'GU, the country's original energy gel, is the perfect sports nutrition product' – the site is designed to advertise a product and so any information is likely to be biased by a commercial imperative.

Further detail can be gleaned from the site addresses. The address for the third site contains **.com**, indicating a commercial organization. In comparison, the second site contains **.gov.au**, indicating information from the Australian government, and the first **.edu**, indicating information from an American academic institution. Website addresses, and how to use them in an evaluation, are considered further in Chapter 4 under 'Organizational sites, personal home pages and other websites' (page 97).

CHECKLIST   ASSESSING ACCURACY

✔ is the information contained in the source factually accurate?
✔ does the information have a research basis? what is the quality of the research?
✔ are there any references to published sources of information?

- ✔ has the information been through any quality-control processes, such as refereeing or editing?
- ✔ is the information likely to be biased by any individuals or organizations involved in its production? what is the motivation of those involved in the production of the source?
- ✔ is the information professionally produced? are there any typographical, spelling or grammatical errors? is there a facility to send corrections to inaccurate information?

Assessing the currency and maintenance of a source

The currency of a source relates to how up-to-date it is, and maintenance refers to whether a source is likely to be kept up-to-date. Currency and maintenance are often central factors affecting our use of the internet to look for information, as there is a general perception that the internet provides access to the most current information possible. Moreover, currency is an important consideration because outdated information can become useless as well as inaccurate or misleading. However, currency will be of increased importance in relation to some material and within some subject areas, while for other material it may not require evaluation. For example, a ten-year-old tutorial on basic human anatomy will still be valuable because our knowledge of this topic has not changed during this time, but a site providing access to news information will need to be updated frequently in order to ensure its accuracy. For example, Figure 3.5 displays an introduction to a frequently asked questions (FAQ) file for information about *Star Trek* (**http://www.ee.surrey.ac.uk/Contrib/SciFi/StarTrek/FAQ.html**) which was accessed in January 2001 but was last updated in January 1994. The significance of this date will depend upon the need for current information and the potential impact of a seven-year time-span on the accuracy of information about *Star Trek*.

Currency and maintenance are assessed by examining the date when any information was produced (either on the internet or initially as a printed source), when the source was last updated, when it will next be updated, and the frequency of updating. Such details may be available from the source itself, such as an explicit date of when the information was produced (as with the *Star Trek* FAQ). In addition, there may be a statement or policy regarding the frequency of updating and the updating process. For example, the online version of *The Telegraph* (**http://www.telegraph.co.uk/**), a newspaper in the UK, states that it is 'updated daily at 1.00 a.m. UK time'. In addition, 'updates for UK news, international news, sports news and city news are posted throughout the

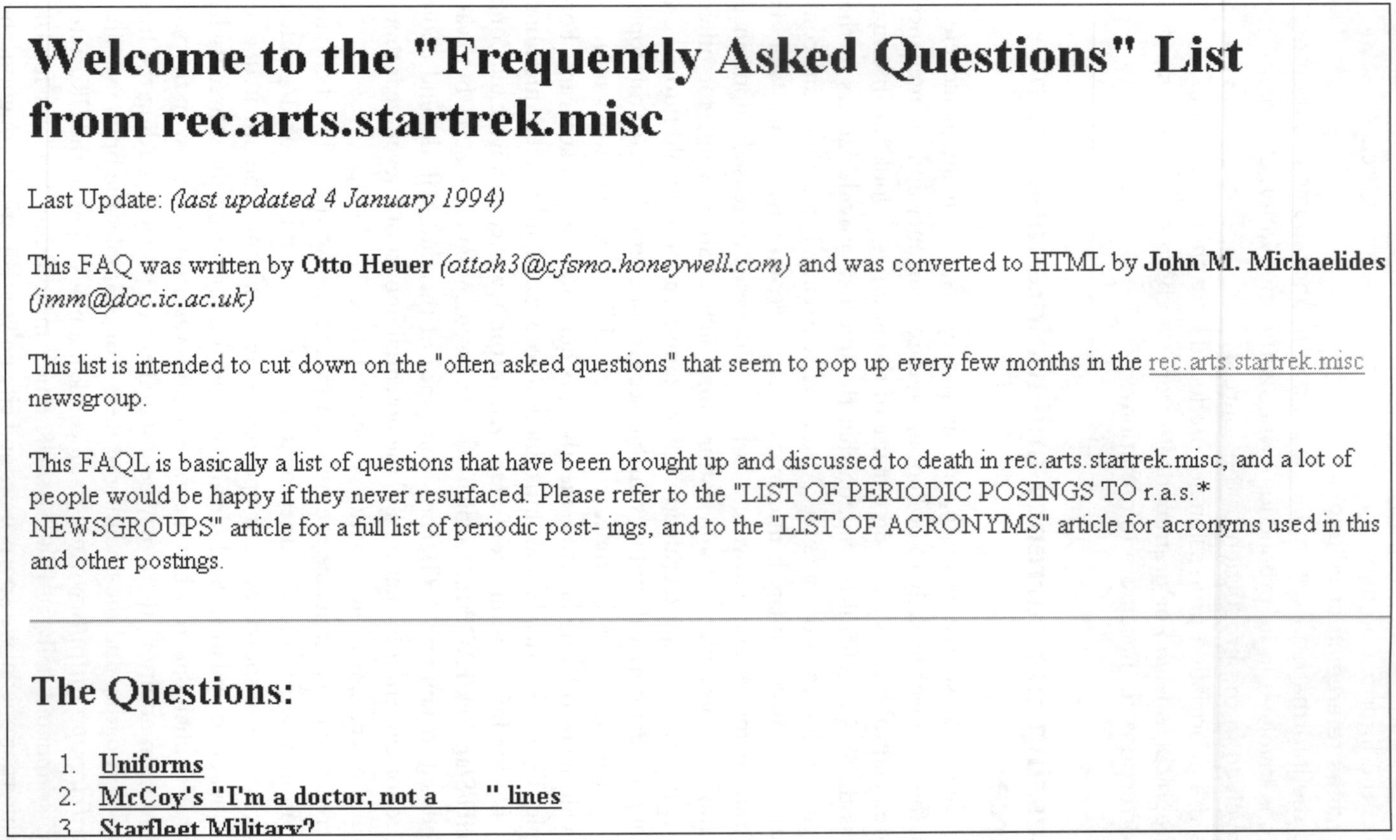

Welcome to the "Frequently Asked Questions" List from rec.arts.startrek.misc

Last Update: *(last updated 4 January 1994)*

This FAQ was written by Otto Heuer *(ottoh3@cfsmo.honeywell.com)* and was converted to HTML by **John M. Michaelides** *(jmm@doc.ic.ac.uk)*

This list is intended to cut down on the "often asked questions" that seem to pop up every few months in the rec.arts.startrek.misc newsgroup.

This FAQL is basically a list of questions that have been brought up and discussed to death in rec.arts.startrek.misc, and a lot of people would be happy if they never resurfaced. Please refer to the "LIST OF PERIODIC POSINGS TO r.a.s." NEWSGROUPS" article for a full list of periodic post- ings, and to the "LIST OF ACRONYMS" article for acronyms used in this and other postings.

The Questions:

1. Uniforms
2. McCoy's "I'm a doctor, not a ___ " lines
3. Starfleet Military?

Fig. 3.5 *'Star Trek' FAQ*

course of the day.' However, many sites do not state how frequently they are updated. Furthermore, sites may not be updated as frequently as promised, and a 'last update date' might only refer to parts of a site. Consequently you may need to search for current information. For example, the *IMDb* (Figure 3.1) is not explicit about the frequency of updating of its database. You could search the database for any recently released films, or for films which are still being produced – as mentioned, several 2000 and 2001 releases were included in the database at the time of writing, suggesting the currency of the database. You might also need to monitor a source over time to ensure that it maintains the same level of currency.

Maintenance

You could browse through a source in order to create an impression of whether it is generally well-maintained. One factor to consider is the currency of any hypertext links. As mentioned, some sites include a policy regarding the updating process. Such a policy may include details of whether an individual or group is responsible for maintenance, their knowledge and expertise, and their motivation for doing so. If individuals or groups maintain a site voluntarily, they may be more likely to lose interest and therefore not maintain the site effectively in the long term. Contact information for site maintainers is also a useful feature and suggests a concern for site maintenance. Indicators that sites are 'under construction' may suggest the maintenance of a source and you might consider returning to a site at a later date for reassessment.

CHECKLIST   ASSESSING THE CURRENCY AND MAINTENANCE OF A SOURCE

✔ is there an explicit date for the information? when was the source originally produced, either in printed form or on the internet?

✔ is the information up-to-date? when was the information last updated? when will the information next be updated? how frequently is the information updated?

✔ is there a statement of policy regarding the frequency of updating and the updating process?

✔ is the site generally well maintained? are any links to external sources live?

✔ is there a maintenance policy?

✔ is there an individual or group responsible for maintenance? do they maintain the site voluntarily? what is their knowledge and expertise?

✔ are contact details available for a site maintainer?
✔ does the source need to be monitored or reassessed at a later date to ensure continued currency and maintenance?

Considering the accessibility of a source

Generally, the main factor determining whether we use a source of information is the subject area that it covers. However, accessibility might affect your choice of sources to be used – this might include whether you decide to pay for access, to wait for a page to download, or to use material on a regular basis. Many of us choose to use the internet because it is convenient, networked computers are easily accessible, and it is faster and easier than going to a library. In addition, the internet is often used because it is free – we are reluctant to pay high prices for information from elsewhere.

Speed of access

Speed of access is of particular concern, and factors affecting speed include the location of sources, the number and size of any images, and whether thumbnail images have been used to improve access speeds. Thumbnail images are small images that can be selected to display a much larger graphic – Figure 3.6 displays a selection of thumbnail images from the *Southern Trekking and*

Fig. 3.6 *Use of thumbnail images to improve access speeds*

Mountaineering Club home page (**http://www.st-mc.org.uk/**) – clicking on each image will result in the full graphic being displayed. This enables the page to download more quickly than if the full-sized images had been used, and users can decide whether they want to wait to view particular pictures in more detail.

The availability of a mirror site can also enable faster access. As already mentioned, *AltaVista* can be accessed via the original site in the USA, as well as via other locations, including the UK, Canada and Australia. Individuals in these locations are likely to access *AltaVista* much faster using one of the local mirror sites than if they use the original site in the USA.

In addition, sites are faster to access if it is possible to view a text-only version of the information. Again, using the example of *AltaVista*, the default graphical page includes a link to a 'text-only version' (**http://www.altavista.com/cgi-bin/query?text**) which downloads more quickly. As displayed in Figure 3.7, the same details are displayed to the user in the search results, meaning that the content is not sacrificed for faster access speeds. Where a site contains images, it is often helpful if the author has provided a meaningful description of each image in the alternative text tag within the HTML of the page. This ensures that pages are meaningful to any user, irrespective of whether images are viewed.

Fig. 3.7   *Text-only search results in AltaVista*

Software restrictions

A further consideration is the mode or modes of access available – whether sites are only available using the latest version of multimedia web browsers, or whether they can also be accessed using older versions of the software, using a text browser, or via FTP or telnet. A site that is limited to the latest version of multimedia browsers will exclude users with restricted facilities for accessing the internet. For example, frames are widely used on the internet to break a screen up into two or more sub-pages. It is worth considering whether it is possible to view a non-frames version of the information as later versions of web browsers are required to enable their use.

Specific software or hardware may also be required to access the full 'bells and whistles' version of some material. For example, as mentioned in the previous chapter, many journals and magazines use PDF. PDF is a file format developed by Adobe for use with its Acrobat Reader,[6] which enables users to print articles in a high-quality presentation format. PDF documents can be displayed and printed in a form which is identical to the original paper-based publication, enabling the use of more sophisticated text and graphics formats than is possible using HTML. Figure 3.8 is an example of an article from the *BMJ* (http://www.bmj.com/) displayed in PDF using Acrobat Reader. Similarly, as mentioned earlier, it is possible to view a trailer of *Gladiator* online from the *IMDb*. However, users must first download additional software in order to use this facility. Where additional software is required, it should be easily accessible (there should be a link to a relevant site for downloading the software), and instructions should be available for downloading and using the software.

Other access restrictions

Access to sources via the internet may be restricted by the language used, the need for registration, or the need to prove eligibility or membership of a particular organization.

The Lancet (http://www.thelancet.com/) is a high-quality medical journal that has been available for many years as a paper-based publication. The opening page, displayed in Figure 3.9, provides two access routes – either to register or to log in. Clicking on the option to register leads to an electronic registration form that requests some personal information and includes an easily completed questionnaire. Users select a username and password, and are able to access the whole site (if they have subscribed to the paper-based journal) or parts of the site (if they have not subscribed). The log-in option leads to a prompt for a username and password. Thus registration for *The Lancet* is a fairly straightforward process.

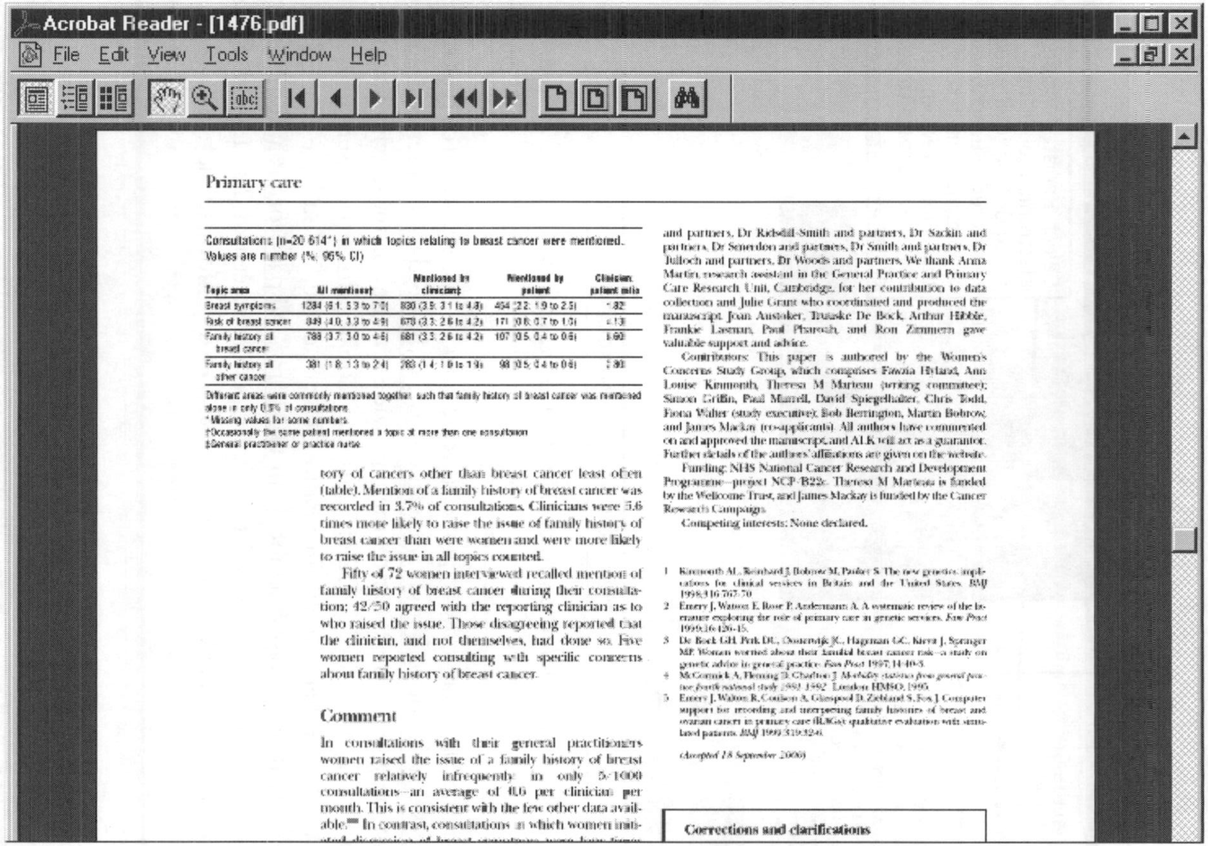

Acrobat Reader - [1476.pdf]

File Edit View Tools Window Help

Primary care

Fig. 3.8 Journal article from the 'BMJ' displayed in PDF using Acrobat Reader

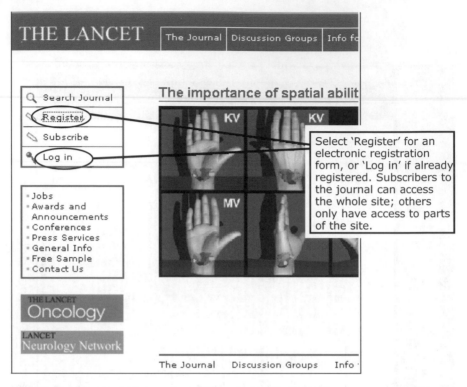

Fig. 3.9 *The opening page of 'The Lancet' displaying access routes*

Internet users are now required to remember so many passwords that some sources enable you to bookmark pages to avoid the need to re-enter a password each time you use a site, and others provide a route for those who have forgotten their passwords. Other sites use cookies to store usernames and passwords or other similar information. For example, if you have enabled the cookies facility on your machine, your username and password is automatically input when you select 'log in' from the opening screen of *The Lancet*. Such options therefore facilitate the process of accessing information.

Cost

Cost is an obvious consideration in the use of information. Under certain circumstances, you may need to identify whether there is a charge for accessing information, and what charging schemes are available, as well as whether it is possible to view some information for free. As mentioned, *The Lancet* provides two options for users: full-text access to subscribers of the printed edition and limited access to registered users of the website. As an evaluator, you would need to determine the cost of the journal, how much information is freely available, and the value and usefulness of any free information in comparison with the original publication. In addition, some services charge extra for accessing an electronic version of paper-based materials, and you might need to consider the relative value of paying to access the electronic version. Under certain circumstances, a user might also wish to consider the cost of one source in comparison with another that provides access to similar information (this is discussed below under 'Making a comparison with other sources' (page 91).

Copyright

Copyright in relation to electronic information is a complex area and its general consideration is beyond the scope of this book. However, one consideration in terms of evaluation is the availability of copyright information. You may want to re-use textual or graphical materials, such as in a publication or presentation. Copyright law relating to the use of electronic information, and information available via the internet in particular, varies from country to country. However, as a basic rule, any information which is encountered via the internet will be covered by copyright, including images, the text of web pages, and the contents of e-mail and Usenet messages. It is therefore useful if the authors or producers provide a statement of the copyright ownership of materials, details of how materials should be cited in a publication or attributed to an author, as well as the individual who should be contacted where copyright permission is required.

Reliability of access and ease of finding sources

One final issue is the reliability of access. Some sites are unavailable at particular times of the day, often for the purposes of site maintenance or updating. Where applicable, the times should be specified in the details about the site, and the amount of 'down-time' should be kept to a minimum. In addition, where sites move location, it is useful if they provide a forwarding link to their new location!

CHECKLIST CONSIDERING THE ACCESSIBILITY OF A SOURCE

✔ is the source fast to access? does the location affect the speed of access? have thumbnail images been used to improve access speeds? is there a local mirror site?

✔ is it possible to view a text-only version of the information? is the meaning of the information lost by not viewing graphics? is there a meaningful description of any images in the ALT-TEXT tag of the HTML source code?

✔ what software is required to view the information? do you need the latest version of Netscape Navigator or Internet Explorer?

✔ is it possible to view a non-frames version of the information?

✔ is any additional software or hardware required? is any additional software easily accessible? are instructions available from the original source for downloading and use of the software?

✔ are there any restrictions to access, such as the need to prove eligibility or membership of an organization?

✔ do you need to register to use the site, and is registration straightforward?

✔ is it possible to bookmark an internal page, or have cookies been used, to avoid the need to re-enter passwords? is there a route for users who have forgotten their passwords?

✔ what language is the information in?

✔ does it cost anything to access the source? what charging schemes are available? is some information available for free? how useful and valuable is the free information in comparison with what is charged for?

✔ is there a statement of copyright ownership? are there details of how materials should be cited in a publication or attributed to an author? is contact information available?

✔ is the source reliably accessible, or is it frequently unavailable? are the times specified when the site is unavailable?

✔ is the site stable, or does it frequently move location? if the site moves, is forwarding information provided?

Evaluating the presentation and arrangement of information

As with accessibility, the presentation and arrangement of information is generally secondary to its content – most of us are concerned primarily with the information contained in a source, and we will use relevant information regardless of how it has been presented. Nielson, for example, argues that 'users comment on the content [of a web page] first', and 'if the content is not relevant, then they don't care about any other aspect of the design.'[7] In addition, 'good presentation' is often a matter of personal taste: some of us will feel a particular feature is essential while others may feel the same feature is redundant.

However, design issues all too frequently enhance or compromise the usability of a resource. In a recent article in *Information World Review*, Infield asks:

> What about those sites built like mazes with the information you are seeking hidden behind long and tortuous passages of mouse clicks? After the umpteenth wrong turn you give up in frustration. I don't know about you but I don't tend to rush back to those kinds of sites.[8]

Indeed, Potts laments that 'not since the arrival of desktop publishing has information design suffered such an onslaught of amateur, incompetent and bad practitioners.'[9] Therefore resources need to be judged accordingly.

Aids to finding information within a source

The presentation and arrangement of information on the screen can influence the ease of assimilating it. This includes whether screens are clearly laid out and aesthetically pleasing, whether there is too much information on each screen, whether the text is easy to read and whether headings stand out. Figure 3.10 is a screenshot from the *BUBL Information Service* (http://bubl.ac.uk/) – one of the virtual libraries described in the previous section. The page is clearly laid out and all the links are easily displayed on one screen. It is possible to navigate from here to any of the major sections of the service, and the resources that are linked to from each hypertext link are self-evident. It is also worth considering whether a source is consistently and logically presented and arranged. Figure 3.11 is a second screen from within the *BUBL Information Service* – comparison of the two screens highlights the consistency in presentation and arrangement throughout the source, which would help users in finding their way around the material.

Features such as a site map, contents list, index, menu system or search facility will be beneficial in helping users to find the information they are looking for, as well as in familiarizing themselves with the materials that are available in a source. Figure 3.11 displays the options for accessing information within *BUBL Link*. Several access points are available, providing a range of options to facilitate retrieval. You could attempt to locate information using these tools in order to determine their effectiveness. Where categories have been used to organize

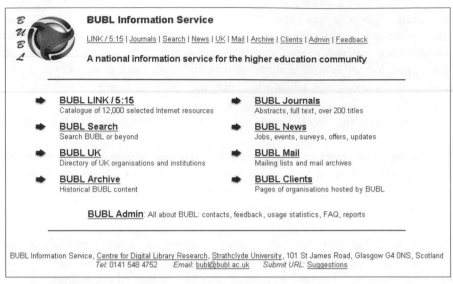

Fig. 3.10 *The opening page of the 'BUBL Information Service'*

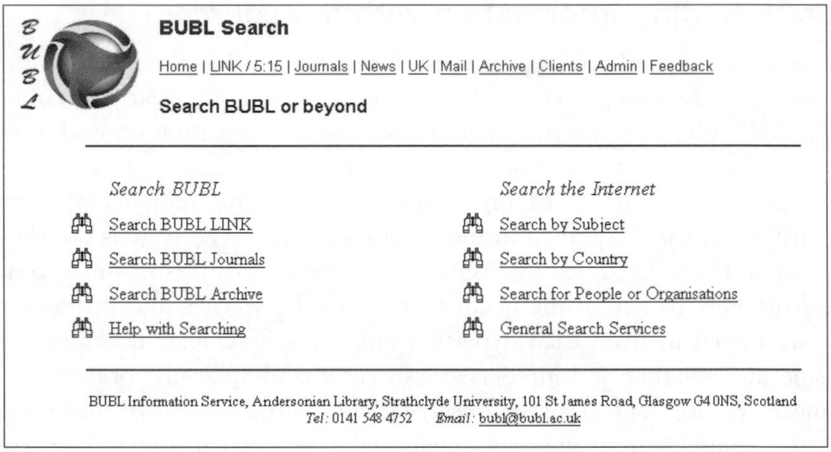

Fig. 3.11 *Accessing information in the 'BUBL Information Service'*

information, you might assess whether the information has been appropriately and usefully organized.

Further considerations are the number of clicks required to locate relevant information, whether steps are unnecessarily repeated, and whether useful shortcuts are available, such as a 'home' icon to take you directly to the start of a document or resource. In addition, some web pages are extremely long and users must scroll painstakingly through them to find what they want. One alternative is providing links between different sections of the same page, or splitting a document into parts and providing links between the different sections. However, the opposite extreme might be too many separate pages for small sections of the same document, continually forcing users to download different parts but without offering the option to scroll through larger sections. Obviously, the length of a page is a highly subjective issue but you might consider whether a useful balance has been achieved and whether the organization is appropriate to the content.

The presentation of hypertext links, and how a link is defined and included in the text, can also help or hinder access to the information. Different authors present hypertext links in different ways. One option is to be explicit and include text such as 'Click here for . . .' or 'This is a link to . . .'. Other options are simply to use an appropriate word without interrupting the flow of the text (this assumes that, because hypertext links are usually in a different colour and underlined, it is self-evident what they are) or to use the URL (the address of the site that is linked to). Most authors use either the second or third option (see, for example, Figure 1.2 and Figure 2.9) because it is obvious from the link what is being pointed to, and the presentation of the links does not interrupt the reading of the text.

Images, frames, Java . . .

Some individuals prefer simplicity in presentation, while others favour the use of frames, graphics and moving images or text. Moving images or text can be created using Java (a programming language) or Javascript and Dynamic HTML. Frames are used to break a screen up into two or more sub-pages, allowing a site producer to display more than one page at the same time. A popular use of frames is to display the contents listing for a site in one frame, while the user simultaneously views individual pages within the site in a second frame. The user can browse information in one frame without this affecting the contents listing in the other.

Under certain circumstances, the use of frames, graphics and moving images can add value to a site. Figure 3.12 is the opening screen to *Yahooligans!* (http://www.yahooligans.com/), a search tool designed specifically for children. The opening screen includes far more graphics than the opening screen of *BUBL* (Figure 3.10) because the service is designed to attract a younger audience. However, as mentioned in the previous section, the use of such features can reduce access speeds, and may also be off-putting to some people. Therefore such technologies should be appraised in terms of whether they have been used appropriately, whether they are necessary and add value to a source, or whether they do little more than slow down access. It could be argued that

Fig. 3.12 *Opening screen for the 'Yahooligans!' search tool.*

graphics are necessary here because of the intended audience, while in a service such as *BUBL* they would be superfluous. Another issue is the location of graphics or images in relation to the text. Obviously graphics should be placed near to the text to which they relate, or else appropriate referencing should be used to signpost the reader.

A further issue is advertising. Initially, many internet users were strongly opposed to the use of advertising, but its use on the internet is now obviously much more widespread. However, advertising still needs to be used appropriately and it should not detract from the information itself. For example, the advert displayed on the opening screen of *Yahooligans!* does not dominate the screen, nor does it draw the user away from the basic function of the page, i.e. to search or browse *Yahooligans!*. If a user is interested in more detail about the product being advertised, they can opt to click on the advert concerned. Evaluation of commercial information and advertising is discussed further in Chapter 4.

CHECKLIST EVALUATING THE PRESENTATION AND ARRANGEMENT OF INFORMATION

✔ is the source clearly presented and arranged? is each screen clearly laid out and aesthetically pleasing? is the text easy to read and do the headings stand out?

✔ is the presentation and arrangement of each page consistent throughout the source?

✔ is there a site map, contents list, index, menu system or search facility? are any such facilities effective?

✔ is the source logically presented and arranged? is the information categorized, and has it been appropriately organized?

✔ are individual pages within a site appropriately divided up? are there too few long pages or too many short pages?

✔ how many 'clicks' does it take to find what you want? are steps unnecessarily repeated? are shortcuts available to access information in as few clicks as possible?

✔ how are hypertext links defined? are they meaningful? do they interrupt the flow of the text?

✔ are there any graphics or moving images? are they necessary? have they been used appropriately? do they add value to the text? are they logically presented in relation to the text?

✔ have frames been used? are they necessary? have they been used appropriately? do they add value to the text?

✔ are there any advertisements? have they been used appropriately, or do they distract the user from the information or the main purpose of the page?

Assessing how easy a source is to use

Generally, you will have built an overall impression of whether you feel a source is easy to use while actually using it in order to investigate the other criteria which have already been discussed. Moreover, the factors affecting ease of use are inextricably linked to the accessibility of sources, as well as the presentation and arrangement of information. Sources should be easy to access, it should be easy to move around a source and locate information, and any searching or browsing facilities should be straightforward and easy to use. A specific consideration is whether sites are intuitive and user-friendly, or whether training or familiarity is required before material can be used effectively.

User support services

User support services can make it easier to use a site. Examples include help information, training courses, a telephone helpline and contact information. You might consider appraising the value and usefulness of any user support services, including the level of detail of help information, whether it is clear, and whether it is context-sensitive (i.e. different help is available according to the point you are at in using the source). Other considerations are the meaningfulness of system messages, the response times for telephone helplines, and whether there is any response to e-mails or telephone messages.

Databases are one type of resource where user support can be of particular importance. For example, the *Web of Science* service (**http://wos.mimas.ac.uk/**) provides access to a range of databases, including the *Citation Indexes*. The original internet version of the *Citation Indexes* was only accessible via a telnet service, which was confusing to new users and required some degree of familiarity before it could be used effectively. The service is now available via a web interface which requires little training before it can be used. Prior to logging on to the service, help information is available in the form of a FAQ file (**http://wos.mimas.ac.uk/wos_faq.html**), user guides and other training documentation (**http://wos.mimas.ac.uk/documentation.html**), as well as an e-mail address for the *Web of Science* helpline (**wos@mimas.ac.uk**). Once you have connected to the service, there is a link to context-sensitive help information. This help information is detailed and clear, and provides examples of how to conduct searches and use the service.

CHECKLIST ASSESSING HOW EASY A SOURCE IS TO USE

✔ is the source generally easy to use?

✔ is the source easy to access?

✔ is the source user-friendly and intuitive, or is training and/or experience required in order to use the source effectively?

✔ is it easy to move around the source and locate information?

✔ are any searching or browsing facilities straightforward and easy to use?

✔ is any help information available? is the help information clear? is the help information context-sensitive? is the help information useful?

✔ are any system messages meaningful and useful?

✔ are any training courses or training documentation available?

✔ is there a telephone helpline, e-mail address or any other user support service available? do you receive a response to e-mails or telephone messages, and is the response time acceptable?

Making a comparison with other sources

In any assessment of the quality of a source, it is essential to determine its value in relation to others that are available. All of the criteria and evaluation details which have been discussed already could be used as points of comparison: you could compare sites in terms of their purpose, coverage, authority and reputation, accuracy, currency and maintenance, accessibility, presentation and ease of use. Indeed, you will probably find that you automatically draw comparisons between different sources in order to decide which is the best to use under certain circumstances. This is likely to occur, not only when you are evaluating materials, but also while you are looking at search results and when you are using different sites and services. Some comparisons have already been drawn here. For example, during the examination of the results of a search on sports, athletes and nutrition (see Figure 3.4), comparisons were drawn between the likely accuracy of different sites.

In order to illustrate this area of assessment further, Figures 3.13 and 3.14 display the opening screens from two job vacancy services, *jobs.ac.uk* (**http://www.jobs.ac.uk/**) and the *NISS Vacancies* service (**http://www.vacancies.ac.uk/**). These services are broadly similar in terms of the subject areas covered – they both provide details of jobs within the UK higher education sector. In addition, they both provide keyword searching and browsing facilities, the categories of job advertisements are broadly similar, and the advertised jobs are submitted by users (which determines the amount of information provided about each job). Both are produced by authoritative organizations, the services appear to be maintained daily (each job advertisement includes a date when it was added), and contact information is included in both. Furthermore, both sites are clearly laid out and easy to use, and the job advertisements themselves are reached in the same number of clicks.

However, there are some differences between the two services. For example, it is possible to restrict your browsing in *jobs.ac.uk* by job type, the type of contract offered and the type of institution, as displayed in Figure 3.13. In addition, *jobs.ac.uk* provides links to other sources of job information, therefore enhancing the coverage of the site. The *NISS Vacancies* service includes a link at the top of the opening screen (shown in Figure 3.14) to browse the week's new additions. Although this particular option is not available via *jobs.ac.uk*, it is possible to have new advertisements e-mailed every Saturday morning – an option which some might feel is preferable as they would not need to remember to access the site each week.

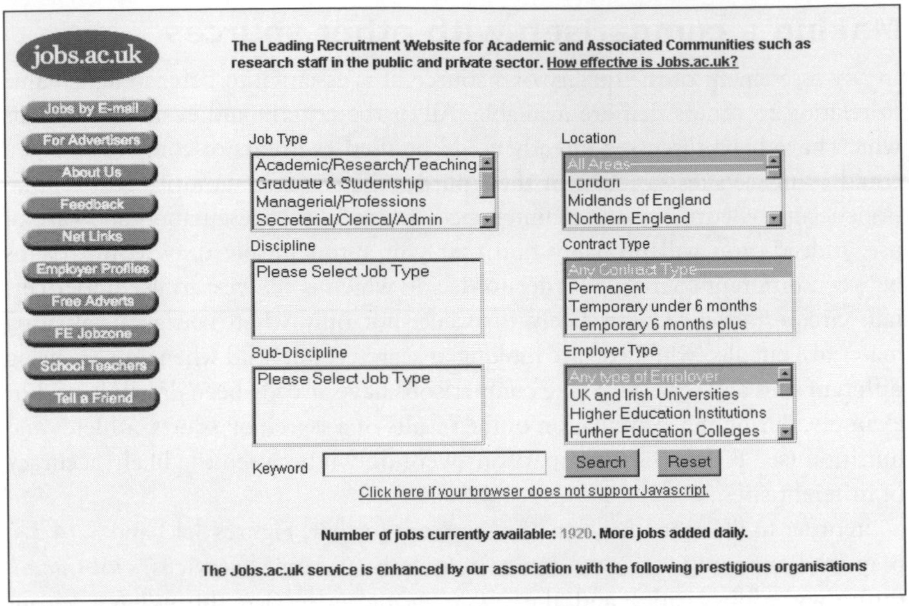

Fig. 3.13 *Opening screen of the vacancies service, 'jobs.ac.uk'*

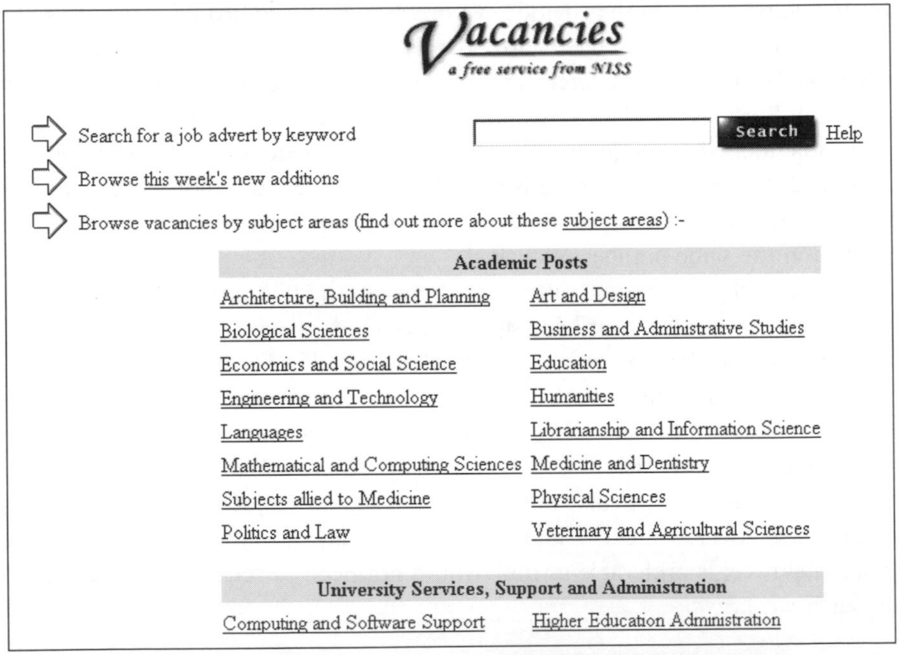

Fig. 3.14 *Opening screen of the 'NISS Vacancies service'*

Comparative costs and value for money

Under certain circumstances, you may need to assess the comparative cost of sources and their relative value for money. In addition, the potential extra benefits obtained by accessing information via the internet should be considered where information is also available in other formats. For example, the electronic version of *The Lancet* might be compared with the paper-based version. Value-added features of the electronic version include the option to e-mail comments on articles, and a search facility, but a paper-based copy of the journal is obviously more portable and might be considered easier to flick through at random.

Uniqueness

One aspect of comparing different sources is uniqueness – whether a site provides coverage of a subject which no other sources offer, whether a source has any unique features or facilities, or whether a source provides access to information in a unique format. For example, several collections of DNA data are available to researchers via the internet. Although the different sites often offer similar features and facilities for accessing the data, the data itself is often uniquely available from one site – the *Genome Database* (**http://www.gdb.org/**) is unique in offering the complete genome sequences of some organisms in a single file. Sources which are unique in some way are likely to be used regardless of their other attributes and characteristics, especially if it is the unique feature which you are particularly interested in.

CHECKLIST MAKING A COMPARISON WITH OTHER SOURCES

✔ is the source unique in terms of its content or format, or does the source offer any unique features or facilities?
✔ what is the purpose of the source compared with others?
✔ what is the coverage of the source compared with others?
✔ how authoritative and reputable is the source compared with others?
✔ how accurate is the source compared with others?
✔ how current and well maintained is the source compared with others?
✔ how accessible is the source compared with others?
✔ is the information contained in the source well presented and arranged compared with others?
✔ how easy is the source to use compared with others?

✔ what are the benefits of accessing this information via the internet compared with other formats?

✔ what is the cost of the source and its value for money in comparison with others?

Assessing the overall quality of a source

A final stage in evaluating any source of information must be to take a step back and consider the overall impression that the source has given. An overall impression is generally based upon perceptions or experiences of the value and usefulness of a source, or of the information it contains, and such an impression is developed through familiarity or extensive and frequent use. You may begin to form an overall opinion as you are evaluating a site, and you are likely to start to draw conclusions about materials after considering the various criteria described here.

Reviews and recommendations

Those involved in selection and evaluation will rarely have the time or resources to use a site extensively or to consider every issue mentioned in this section. Therefore two useful sources of further advice are published reviews and recommendations from other users. A wide range of different journals and magazines provide reviews of websites and other internet materials. In addition, the previous chapter discussed a range of virtual libraries and subject-based gateway services. These could be consulted, firstly to determine whether a site is included in any appropriate databases of quality materials, and secondly to consult any available reviews. You might also be able to elicit the comments of friends or colleagues who have already used a site, or have been using a site extensively over a period of time. By examining reviews or eliciting recommendations, you will be provided with an indication of someone else's overall impression of the quality, value and usefulness of a source. Caution is needed, however, because sites can change and resources might require reassessment. Furthermore, different materials are used for different reasons and one person's assessment of quality might not be the same as another's.

CHECKLIST ASSESSING THE OVERALL QUALITY OF A SOURCE

✔ what is your overall assessment of the source? what conclusions can you draw after having considered the evaluation issues discussed in this chapter? is the source valuable and useful, and is the information contained in it valuable and useful?

✔ are any reviews available or is the site included in any databases of high-quality materials?

✔ is it possible to elicit comments from someone who has used the source or who uses it regularly? what is their overall impression of the source?

References

1 Wakefield, A. J. and Montgomery, S. M., Mumps measles rubella vaccine: through a glass darkly, *Adverse Drug Reactions and Toxicological Reviews*, **19** (4), 2000, 265–83.

2 Peltola, H., et al., No evidence for measles, mumps and rubella vaccine associated inflammatory bowel disease or autism in a 14-year prospective study, *Lancet*, **351** (9112), 1998, 1327–8.

3 Taylor, B. M. E., et al., Autism and measles, mumps and rubella vaccine: no epidemiological evidence for a causal association, *Lancet*, **353** (9169), 1999, 2026–9.

4 *Levels of evidence and grades of recommendations*, 1999 [online], available at
   http://cebm.jr2.ox/docs/levels.html
   [2001, March 8].

5 *Critical appraisal: guidelines for the critical appraisal of a paper*, 2001 [online], available at
   http://www.surgical-tutor.org.uk/papers/appraisal.htm
   [2001, March 8].

6 *Adobe* [online], available at
   http://www.adobe.com/
   [2001, March 8].

7 Nielsen, J., Is navigation useful?, *useit.com*, (January), 2000 [online], available at
   http://www.uscit.com/alertbox/20000109.html
   [2001, March 8].

8 Infield, N., Content may be king . . . but design still rules, *Information World Review*, (December), 2000, 57.

9 Potts, D., Content may be king . . . but design still rules, *Information World Review*, (December), 2000, 56.

4

Evaluating particular types of sources

Chapter 3 examined ten areas of assessment relating to the evaluation of any source of information that is available via the internet. However, a wide range of types of sources is available and different people access and use these for different reasons. Consequently, users are often interested in specific quality issues. For example, someone using a personal home page might be more concerned with the authority of the information, while a user of an FTP archive might wish to assess access speeds. This chapter examines the factors to consider when evaluating specific types of internet sites.

The source types have been categorized as follows:

- organizational sites, personal home pages and other websites
- mailing lists, newsgroups and other forms of communication via the internet
- full-text documents
- databases
- electronic journals and magazines
- sources of news information
- advertising, sponsorship and other commercial information
- image-based and multimedia sources
- current awareness and alerting services
- FTP archives.

Each source type is defined, the various factors that might be considered during an assessment of each source type are explained, and a worked example is provided. In addition, each section includes a checklist of the assessment factors relevant to each source type.

Chapter 3 provides a detailed guide to those factors that affect the quality of any information source available via the internet. Many of the same issues are relevant to the sources discussed here, and in order to prevent repetition, readers are referred to the appropriate point in Chapter 3 where applicable. If readers are evaluating a source that does not fit into any of the categories discussed here, they should use the generic criteria in Chapter 3. The criteria relating to each source type are not prescriptive – as with the generic criteria, you will need to select the appropriate criteria depending upon the nature of the source you are evaluating and your own needs.

Organizational sites, personal home pages and other websites

Organizational sites are collections of web pages that are created and maintained by a particular organization. These include company home pages, university home pages, the site of a professional group, and of any other society or organization. Often organizational sites include personal home pages. A personal home page is a web page, or a collection of web pages, which is maintained by an individual and relates to that person's own interests. A vast range of other types of web pages is also available and, in addition to organizational sites and personal home pages, this section includes the evaluation of websites with a subject focus. There are obvious overlaps between these three types of web pages – personal home pages and organizational sites often include materials relating to a specific subject area, and personal home pages and subject-based pages are often part of a wider organizational website. Many of the same criteria are therefore applicable to these resource types.

Assessing organizational sites, personal home pages and other websites

Almost all of the generic criteria discussed in Chapter 3 are applicable to the evaluation of organizational sites, personal home pages and other websites. However, there are issues that are of particular concern.

Possibly the most common reason for accessing the home page of a particular organization is to find out facts about it, such as its address or a phone number. Therefore it is essential that basic factual information pertaining to an organization (e.g. phone number, address, e-mail address, opening times, etc.) should be available. It is also essential that this basic information should be easy to locate within the site and that materials should be maintained, because outdated information will become inaccurate. While it is not usually necessary to maintain information about an organization on a very frequent basis, it is essential to be able to determine when the materials were last updated in order to estimate their likely accuracy. Therefore each page should include a date indicating when it was last updated. Likewise, users often access personal home pages because they want the e-mail address or other contact information for an individual. Therefore this information should also be readily available and easy to locate on personal home pages, and there should be an indication of when the information was last updated.

The knowledge and expertise of those involved in creating and maintaining a site can affect its overall value and usefulness, as well as the authority and likely accuracy of any information. Therefore you might consider the issues highlighted in Chapter 3 relating to authority, reputation and expertise. As mentioned in Chapter 3, site reviews, including those from a gateway or virtual library, and counters, can indicate the reputation and popularity of a site. The presentation and arrangement of the source is also of concern, as this can make it easier or harder to find information. You might want to consider whether a source is clearly, consistently and logically presented, and the availability and effectiveness of any features such as a site map, index or search facility.

Coverage of organizational sites, personal home pages and other websites

Some sites provide little more than basic contact information for an organization or an individual, while others provide detailed information, as well as links to related sites of interest. As mentioned in Chapter 1, personal home pages can be problematic because they may contain little more than images of 'These are my friends', 'This is my cat' or 'This is where I live'. However, the importance of the coverage of a resource and the level of detail provided will depend upon your own needs for accessing the information. You might want to ascertain whether a page provides access to any 'real' information, and if you are interested in the subject content, areas of particular concern are:

- the subject areas and types of materials covered
- the comprehensiveness of coverage of a site within a specific area
- whether there are any pointers to further information which might enhance the coverage.

Some sites are designed as 'link sites' (they simply provide hypertext links to relevant materials without contributing any original content), while others offer detailed information on a particular topic. Where sites only link to other resources, the value and usefulness of the links should be considered, including.

*   the range of materials covered
*   whether they have been selected and on what basis
*   whether descriptive information is provided about the various links to provide users with a means of assessing their potential usefulness.

You should refer to the appropriate details in Chapter 3 on assessing coverage for further information.

Example   *The Vincent Van Gogh Gallery*
             http://www.vangoghgallery.com/

Step 1: Look for clues in the search results and the URL

Artists and their paintings are areas of interest for many authors of websites and pages – there are 112,000 hits for a *Google* search on 'Vincent Van Gogh' alone. However, it is possible to make some basic judgements about the likely quality of the sites listed from what you are told in the search results and by examining each site's address.

As was discussed in Chapter 2, search engines rank results according to their relevance. Usually this is based on an analysis of the number and location of the chosen search terms within each site. In contrast, *Google* (**http://www.google. com/**) bases its rankings on the number of times a site has been linked to from elsewhere, the assumption being that the greater the number of links to a site, the higher its quality. Therefore, where *Google* is concerned the most relevant (and potentially the highest-quality) sites should be listed first, and browsing more than the first couple of pages of results is often unproductive.

The first site listed in *Google* is the *Vincent Van Gogh Gallery*, described as 'a comprehensive resource for information about Van Gogh and images of his works'. The ranking and the description would probably prompt you to select this site as a first port of call. Other sites include the *Van Gogh Museum* (**http://www.vangoghmuseum.nl/**). From personal knowledge, you would probably be aware that Van Gogh was Dutch, and possibly also that there is a Van Gogh museum in Amsterdam. The **.nl** in the website address indicates that this is a Dutch site, and the lack of an organizational domain indicates a

national resource. Different countries and organizational domains are repre-
sented differently in URLs. A site with .**edu** in the address is from an
educational establishment in the USA, .**com** a commercial organization in the
USA, and .**gov**, a government body in the USA. Sites from countries outside the
USA contain an additional country code (e.g. .**uk**). However, if a page has no
country code, it does not necessarily mean the information is from the USA. In
addition, the domain names vary according to the country – e.g. governmental
bodies in the UK are .**gov.uk**, but educational establishments are .**ac.uk**). For
more information about country codes and domain names, see *alldomains.com*
(**http://www.alldomains.com/**), which includes data about country codes and
the sub-domains within each country.

Another site listed much further into the thousands of search results is *Sonia
Baur's home page* (**http://www.unc.edu/~bauer/**), which includes in the
description 'one of my favorite artists is Vincent Van Gogh'. The title and
description would probably be sufficient to indicate that this will not provide
valuable information on Van Gogh. It is also worth noting the tilde (~) character in the website address. This is often used within the address to denote a
personal home page within a larger organizational site. However, you should
not automatically assume that a site containing a tilde in the address is a personal home page, or that sites not containing a tilde in the address are not
personal home pages.

Step 2: Find out what the site tells you about itself

The first page of the *Vincent Van Gogh Gallery* provides a statement indicating
the provenance, purpose and coverage of the site – the site has been available
for five years and describes itself as 'the most thorough and comprehensive Van
Gogh resource' on the web, including '100% of Vincent Van Gogh's works and
letters'. There is a site inventory claiming almost 4,000 images and an equal
number of pages of information.

At the end of the first page are several links to additional information about
the site and its author, David Brooks. A good starting place for evaluation is
always to follow links such as these as they will usually provide useful background information, and you can also often find out where information has
come from and who has produced it. The author claims that he 'has been
studying Van Gogh's life and works for nearly ten years', but also states elsewhere that he 'was never a great scholar of the fine arts' and has 'no formal
education in them'. This would possibly lead you to question the authority and
therefore the likely accuracy of the information. However, there are other indicators of authority, including extensive facts relating to the origins of the

author's interest in the artist. The site also receives sponsorship from a commercial company that produces posters and prints. There is also a counter at the end of the first page – there have been 2,675,669 hits since December 1996, indicating the site's popularity and its length of establishment. There is also a link to 'accolades' – a collection of badges that the site has been awarded from several rating and reviewing services. However, as was discussed in Chapter 2, such ratings can be of questionable value and usefulness, and you would need to connect to each in turn to assess whether the service still exists, and on what basis the site has been evaluated.

Step 3: Browse the site to assess its coverage

Figure 4.1 shows part of the opening screen to the *Vincent Van Gogh Gallery*. As mentioned earlier, the site claims that it is a comprehensive resource for Van Gogh and you would need to browse some of these links in order to assess whether or not it achieves this goal. As displayed in Figure 4.1, there are links to several collections of material, and browsing these indicates that indeed this is a comprehensive resource. Each category contains a list of paintings, its origin and the location of the original. Selecting the name of a painting results in an image of the painting being displayed with further information about it. There is also an overview of the artist and his paintings, a FAQ file for the most frequently asked questions about the site and the artist, and a listing of current exhibitions. Other useful features include a clickable world map – selecting any of the highlighted sections of the map leads to locations across the world which hold Van Gogh's paintings. The hyperlink 'links' leads to descriptions of selected resources about Van Gogh that are available via the internet.

As displayed in Figure 4.1, the page is clearly presented and materials have been usefully organized. The hypertext links are meaningful, which further facilitates the process of finding resources, and the different pages throughout the site are presented in a familiar format. Furthermore, the author includes updating information and an e-mail address. However, the site could benefit from a map or an overall index, as browsing the available materials can become confusing.

Step 4: Look for additional information

A general impression of this site is that it is an invaluable resource for Van Gogh materials. It is comprehensive in its coverage, and it is well organized and clearly presented. However, the fact that it is produced by an individual claiming no expertise in the area could be disconcerting. If you are faced with a

Categories

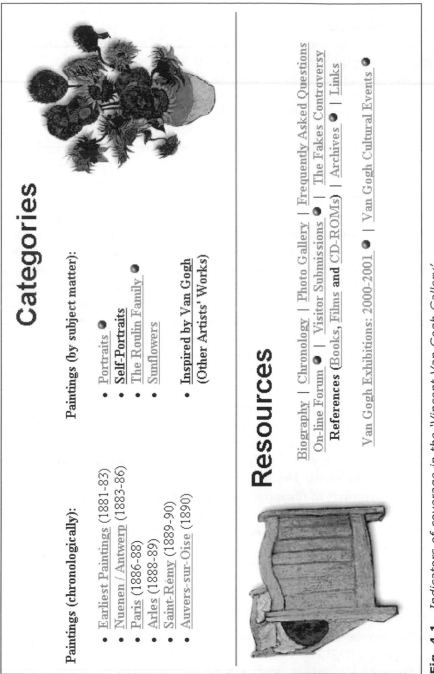

Paintings (chronologically):

- Earliest Paintings (1881-83)
- Nuenen / Antwerp (1883-86)
- Paris (1886-88)
- Arles (1888-89)
- Saint-Rémy (1889-90)
- Auvers-sur-Oise (1890)

Paintings (by subject matter):

- Portraits ●
- **Self-Portraits**
- The Roulin Family ●
- Sunflowers
- **Inspired by Van Gogh**
  (Other Artists' Works)

Resources

Biography | Chronology | Photo Gallery | Frequently Asked Questions
On-line Forum ● | Visitor Submissions ● | The Fakes Controversy
References (Books, Films and CD-ROMs) | Archives ● | Links

Van Gogh Exhibitions: 2000-2001 ● | Van Gogh Cultural Events ●

Fig. 4.1 *Indicators of coverage in the 'Vincent Van Gogh Gallery'*

contradictory situation such as this it can be beneficial to seek further guidance. A search in the *Librarians' Index to the Internet* (**http://lii.org/**), one of the virtual libraries described in Chapter 2, provides the following information about the site:

> The Vincent Van Gogh Information Gallery is a most comprehensive site on the artist, with around 3,500 pages and a similar number of graphics. There's a section on his earliest works; a map locating those paintings housed in museums and public institutions worldwide; biographical information includes photographs, a chronology, and excerpts from letters between Vincent and his brother, Theo. A growing section is InSites on Van Gogh's major paintings, with provenance, exhibition history, and the site author's commentary. There are also annotated lists of books, films, CD-ROMs, and Web sites. One of the very best 'fan' sites I've seen.

Although this description is slightly out-of-date (the site was originally named the *Vincent Van Gogh Information Gallery* and there are now almost 4000 images), the description indicates that other information professionals in the field consider this to be a worthwhile resource. In addition, inclusion of the site in the *Librarians' Index to the Internet* alone indicates its perceived quality. Another option is to find out whether any authoritative and reputable sites link to the resource. Again using *Google*, type **link:www.vangoghgallery.com** in the space provided – this will search for any sites that link to the *Vincent Van Gogh Gallery*. Almost 3,500 sites are retrieved, including several university art departments and libraries, once again indicating that this is a resource which others have identified as useful.

CHECKLIST   EVALUATING ORGANIZATIONAL SITES, PERSONAL HOME PAGES AND OTHER WEBSITES

✔ what is the purpose of the site?
✔ are contact details for the person or the organization concerned readily available? is it easy to locate contact information within the site?
✔ what is the coverage of the site? does the site provide basic information about an individual or an organization, or are additional materials provided? does the site cover a particular area comprehensively? what subject areas and materials are covered? are there any pointers to further information and do they enhance the coverage of the site? if the site links to other materials, are the links

valuable and useful? what materials are covered by the links? is descriptive information provided about the links? is the descriptive information useful?

✔ what is the reputation and expertise of the individual or the institution responsible for the information? is there any sponsorship for the site, and does the sponsorship suggest a good reputation? is there a counter for the site, and does it indicate that the site is popular? are there any reviews for the site, or has the site been included in any gateways or virtual libraries?

✔ what is the likely accuracy of the information?

✔ is the information current and is the site well maintained? is there an update date for each page of information, or is it otherwise possible to ascertain its currency?

✔ is the site easily accessible?

✔ is the information well presented and arranged? is the information clearly, consistently and logically presented and arranged? are there any features such as a site map, an index or a search facility? how effective are they in assisting users to find information?

✔ is the site easy to use, and are there any user support facilities?

✔ how does the site compare with other similar sites? is the site unique?

✔ what is your overall impression of the quality of the site?

Mailing lists, newsgroups and other forms of communication via the internet

Mailing lists, also sometimes called discussion lists or listservs, are e-mail-based lists available to a group of users who are interested in a particular topic area. Software is used to enable users to subscribe to a list, and they can then post messages to the whole group, participate in discussions and receive all of the messages which are posted to the group. Newsgroups, also known as Usenet or Usenet newsgroups, are similar as different users can discuss a particular area of interest. However, users need not subscribe to participate as anyone can view the messages provided they have access to the required software. In addition, newsgroups are hierarchically arranged into topic areas. Previously a newsgroup reader was required in order to view or post a message to a newsgroup, but newsgroups may now be accessed using a web browser.

There are three ways in which newsgroups and mailing lists are commonly used: users either post queries and actively participate in the discussion, or they 'lurk' (i.e. read the messages and follow the discussion without participating), or they browse the earlier discussions looking for information. Depending upon your needs and the circumstances of evaluation, you may be concerned with assessing an individual message, or with evaluating the whole newsgroup or mailing list; the appropriate criteria should be selected from those described below.

Newsgroups and mailing lists are differentiated by the means of access. However, there are similarities in the nature of the information disseminated via the two routes, and consequently there are many similarities in the techniques which might be used to assess the quality of that information. Furthermore, many mailing lists are also accessible as newsgroups and vice versa. Both types of sources are therefore discussed together here, although the criteria are differentiated where applicable. In addition, the criteria can also be used to evaluate other forms of communication via the internet, such as individual e-mail messages, chat rooms and other communication forums.

Assessing newsgroups and mailing lists

The generic criteria discussed in Chapter 3 relating to identifying the purpose of a source and assessing its coverage are applicable to either individual messages or whole newsgroups and mailing lists. In order to make an assessment, you will need to determine whether or not there is a home page or FAQ for the list or group, which is likely to provide useful information about the intended coverage and audience. In addition, the availability of an archive will affect the usefulness of a newsgroup or mailing list as an information source, and another consideration is the retrospective coverage of the archive (some archives are maintained for as little as a month). Several directories were highlighted in Chapter 2 for locating newsgroups and mailing lists, and for searching their archives – searching these will often provide useful information about a list or group, and/or point you towards a home page and the archive if these exist.

A particular issue is the type of material covered by mailing lists and newsgroups – some lists might be used to post job advertisements or advertisements for new websites, while others will be intended for the discussion of a specific issue. Where an archive is available, you could browse recent messages in order to determine whether discussion focuses upon the intended area. Alternatively, you may need to subscribe to a group for a short period of time to make an assessment. Other considerations are whether real exchange and discussion takes place via a group, as indicated by the proportion of questions answered and whether discussion threads develop, or whether the group largely consists of one-off messages. If an individual, usually described as the moderator, is responsible for monitoring or moderating the content of a group, the discussion might be more focused on the intended subject area. It is often possible to determine whether a group is moderated by examining the discussion itself or by consulting any introductory information.

Participants in newsgroups and mailing lists

The participants in a group can influence its overall value and usefulness, as well as the topics that are discussed. Newsgroups and mailing lists are useful for contacting a large number of people, for contacting people all over the world or in a particular locality, or for contacting a subset of a population. Therefore, potential factors requiring examination are:

- the number of people involved
- whether the list is local, national or international
- the actual composition of the group.

These criteria are more relevant to mailing lists where participants subscribe to the list, and there may be a publicly viewable membership list on a home page. However, where a list of members is unavailable, or in the case of newsgroups, you could examine recent messages as an indication of the participants.

Accuracy and authority of newsgroups and mailing lists

The questionable accuracy and authority of information received in e-mails generally, and retrieved via newsgroups and discussions lists in particular, is often considered their main drawback. However, users do not necessarily expect to rely upon the information, and newsgroups and mailing lists are often used less as a source of high-quality information than as a useful way of contacting people and seeking their advice or opinions. Therefore some criteria relating to accuracy are relevant, such as whether the author of a message is a well known expert, or whether a refereed journal article is cited in a message. However, you should bear in mind the informal nature of the information and the purpose for which it will be used. In addition, a mailing list or newsgroup may have a reputation as a useful source of ideas and opinions, and a review in a gateway or virtual library would indicate this.

Hernández-Borges, et al. have developed a methodology for analysing the likely authority of various paediatrics mailing lists.[1] *MEDLINE* was searched for the names of list subscribers, and an impact factor was calculated for each of the subscribers using the *Science Citation Index* to determine how many times each author had been cited. An average impact factor was calculated for each list, as well as an average impact factor per participant and per message to the group. An average number of postings per author was also calculated. The authors claim that their methodology offers a technique for assessing the quality of mailing lists because it is 'based on the accumulation of defined impact factors generated by published articles of the various members of the discussion groups, a way for any scientific group to gain prestige in a given field of science'. Although this technique sounds useful, the process is probably too complex for many evaluators to consider seriously.

Accessibility and volume of traffic in newsgroups and mailing lists

The accessibility issues discussed in Chapter 3 are not generally applicable here. Those issues which do require consideration are whether there are any restrictions to access (some mailing lists have a closed membership), and the mode of access (whether a mailing list or a newsgroup). This information will be available either from a directory or from the home page of the list or newsgroup concerned. A further issue is the likely volume of traffic to a group, which can become unmanageable. In order to monitor the volume, you could browse the newsgroup, examine the mailing list archive where available, or subscribe to a mailing list for a limited time period. As shown in Figure 4.2, *Google* (http://groups.google.com/) includes details about the levels of activity of each of the newsgroups in its archive using a simple bar chart. Other directories provide similar information. For example, *topica* (**http://www.topica.com/**) lists the number of subscribers and the average number of postings for each group in its directory.

The availability of facilities for searching the archive will affect its accessibility, and it is useful if the archive is browsable by date, author and subject thread. A searchable archive may be available from a home page, or files of discussion might be transferable from an FTP site. Another useful facility is the ability to receive messages in a digest of the day's or week's postings as one message. The frequency of the digest would perhaps need to be considered.

Pedersen proposes a method for categorizing the volume and type of information from mailing lists.[2] This would involve calculating the average number of messages per day to a list, and categorizing the messages according to whether they are administrative, announcements, discussion, pointers to further information, etc. He suggests the group characteristics could then be summarized as, for example, 'very light traffic consisting entirely of announcements' or an 'active forum . . . dominated by relevant discussion'. Again, although this is a useful consideration, the process is probably too complex for many evaluators to undertake.

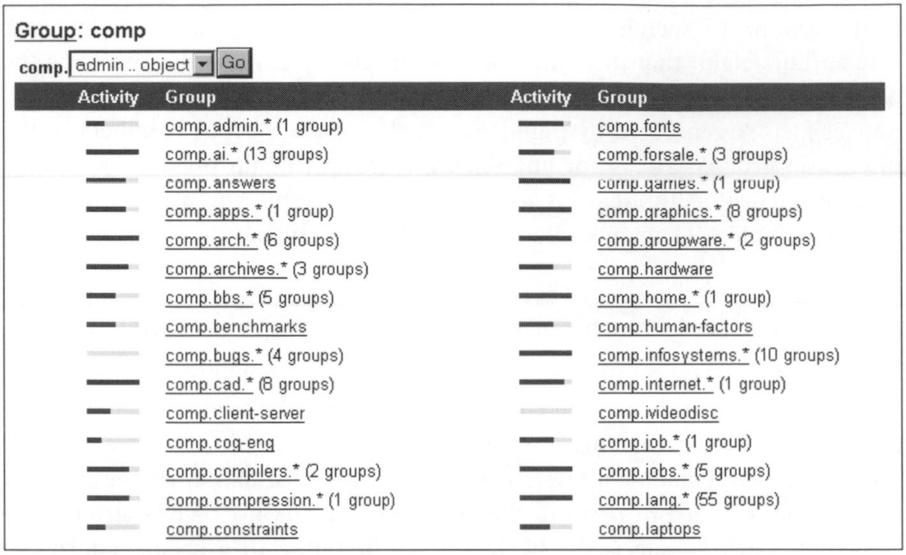

Fig. 4.2 *Levels of activity in comp. newsgroups from 'Google'*

Presentation and ease of use for newsgroups and mailing lists

The generic issues relating to presentation and arrangement, ease of use and user support are mainly irrelevant here. Alternative considerations are whether the group has adopted conventions for labelling messages according to whether they provide information about jobs, conferences, etc., as this can facilitate the process of sifting through the volume of postings. Other issues relate to administration. If there is an individual responsible for list administration, any problems which arise, such as mail loops (an individual's e-mail system automatically replies to a group, they receive that reply, the system automatically replies back again, etc.), may be dealt with more quickly. Likewise, administrative and help information may be available via a home page or might be posted regularly to the group. Such information should cover, not only the intended coverage and audience as mentioned, but also how to subscribe, unsubscribe and post messages to the group. The usefulness of any such information will obviously need to be assessed.

Example   *pchelp* mailing list
http://groups.yahoo.com/group/pchelp/

Step 1: Search available directories for information

Suppose that you have bought a new computer and you are interested in finding a mailing list where you can post messages with any queries. Browsing *Liszt* (http://www.liszt.com/) for 'computers', followed by 'hardware' leads to a range of different lists, including *pchelp*. According to *Liszt*, this mailing list is for 'any PC software, hardware, internet related topics'. *Liszt* provides details about how to subscribe and unsubscribe, and there is a link to the list's home page.

Step 2: Examine the home page for background information

Figure 4.3 shows the information available from the *pchelp* mailing list home page (http://groups.yahoo.com/group/pchelp/). Although the description in the top-left-hand corner offers no additional detail to that provided by *Liszt*, there is a wealth of valuable facts here that would help in assessing whether or not this is a useful place for posting queries about a new computer. We are told that the list has an open membership, that it is unmoderated, that anyone may post to the list, and that the archives are publicly accessible and searchable. Posting and sub-scription information is available, as well as contact details for the list owner. We are also told that there are 264 members of the list, and that the list started in December 1998 (although the browsable archive suggests that discussion actually commenced in January 1999). This indicates a well established group with a large membership. The figures indicate that the volume of traffic is somewhat erratic, but that generally there is a fairly high level of postings to the list.

Step 3: Browse the archive and/or subscribe for a short time period

The only effective method of assessing the likely value of a newsgroup or mailing list will be either to browse the archive, or if this is not possible, to subscribe for a short time and follow the discussion. This site allows you to both search the archives and browse messages by date. Selecting '49' leads to a list of messages for March 2001, including the message displayed in Figure 4.4. Links to all of the messages in the same thread are also listed, as shown. Several people have posted responses to the question asked here, indicating that the list does not con-sist of one-off messages but involves discussion. Examining any of the individual messages indicates that this is an open environment where questions are asked and others respond with comments and suggestions. This therefore suggests a potentially useful mailing list for our scenario.

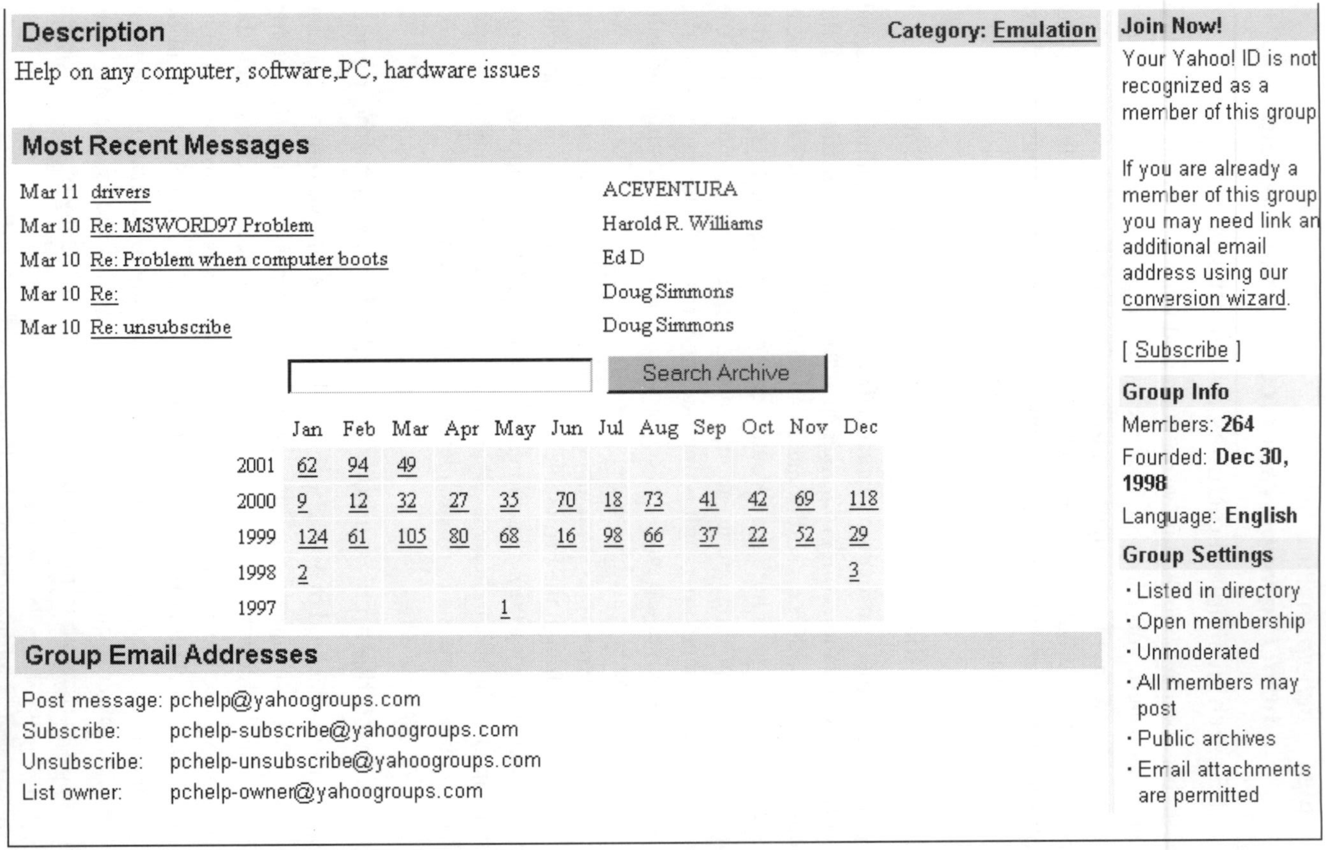

Description

Help on any computer, software, PC, hardware issues

Category: Emulation

Join Now!

Your Yahoo! ID is not recognized as a member of this group

If you are already a member of this group you may need link an additional email address using our conversion wizard.

[Subscribe]

Most Recent Messages

Date	Subject	Author
Mar 11	drivers	ACEVENTURA
Mar 10	Re: MSWORD97 Problem	Harold R. Williams
Mar 10	Re: Problem when computer boots	Ed D
Mar 10	Re:	Doug Simmons
Mar 10	Re: unsubscribe	Doug Simmons

Search Archive

	Jan	Feb	Mar	Apr	May	Jun	Jul	Aug	Sep	Oct	Nov	Dec
2001	62	94	49									
2000	9	12	32	27	35	70	18	73	41	42	69	118
1999	124	61	105	80	68	16	98	66	37	22	52	29
1998	2											3
1997					1							

Group Info

Members: **264**

Founded: **Dec 30, 1998**

Language: **English**

Group Settings

- Listed in directory
- Open membership
- Unmoderated
- All members may post
- Public archives
- Email attachments are permitted

Group Email Addresses

Post message: pchelp@yahoogroups.com
Subscribe: pchelp-subscribe@yahoogroups.com
Unsubscribe: pchelp-unsubscribe@yahoogroups.com
List owner: pchelp-owner@yahoogroups.com

Fig. 4.3 Information from the 'pchelp' mailing list home page

Reply | Forward | View Source | Unwrap Lines

Message 1473 of 1515 | **Previous** | **Next** [Up Thread] Message Index

From: "Harold R. Williams" <willhn@f...>
Date: Mon Mar 5, 2001 4:08pm
Subject: Re: MSWORD97 Problem

I have a problem that needs resolution, if possible. In trying to
organize my genealogy files I used the Label making tool on MSWORD 97 to
run some 3180 Avery file folder labels. The program works just fine
except that I can not change the font to a larger or different font. It
stays wi...
but for ...
really n...
suggesti...
Harold W...
willhn@f...

Replies	Author	Date
1474 Re: MSWORD97 Problem	Robert McMahon	Mon 3/5/2001
1475 Re: MSWORD97 Problem	DENNIS NILSSON	Tue 3/6/2001
1477 Re: MSWORD97 Problem	Harold R. Williams	Tue 3/6/2001
1479 Re: MSWORD97 Problem	Robert Graf	Tue 3/6/2001
1481 Re: MSWORD97 Problem	Doug Simmons	Tue 3/6/2001
1482 Re: MSWORD97 Problem	Robert Graf	Tue 3/6/2001
1484 Re: MSWORD97 Problem	Harold R. Williams	Wed 3/7/2001
1514 Re: MSWORD97 Problem	Harold R. Williams	Sat 3/10/2001

Fig. 4.4   *Postings to 'pchelp'*

CHECKLIST   EVALUATING MAILING LISTS, NEWSGROUPS AND
OTHER FORMS OF COMMUNICATION VIA THE
INTERNET

✔ what is the purpose of the mailing list or newsgroup?
✔ what is the coverage of the mailing list or newsgroup?
✔ does real exchange and discussion take place via the mailing list or
newsgroup, or does it largely consist of one-off messages?
✔ is the mailing list or newsgroup moderated?
✔ what is the reputation of the mailing list or newsgroup?
✔ is there a list of group members or participants? who are the participants in the group? how many participants are there? is the group
local, national or international? what is the likely knowledge and
expertise of the participants? are there any restrictions to accessing
or subscribing to the group? does the group have a closed
membership?
✔ for individual messages: what is the likely accuracy of the information? what is the reputation and expertise of the author? what is
the date of the message? is an original source of information cited
in the message?
✔ what is the average volume of traffic? is the volume manageable?
✔ is it possible to receive messages in a digest? how frequently is the
digest distributed?

✔ has the group adopted conventions for labelling messages?

✔ is an archive available? are files of discussion downloadable from an FTP site? what is the retrospective coverage of the archive? is there a facility for searching the archive? is the archive browsable by date, author and subject thread? is help information available for searching the archive?

✔ is an individual responsible for the group administration? is any administrative or help information available? is the information periodically posted to the group? how useful is the information? are details of subscription, withdrawal of subscription and posting messages included?

✔ how does the mailing list or newsgroup compare with others?

✔ what is your overall impression of the quality of the mailing list or newsgroup?

Full-text documents

This section relates to the evaluation of individual documents that are available via the internet. This might include government reports, journal articles or other research papers, and help files or FAQs. Many of the generic criteria from Chapter 3 are applicable to the evaluation of full-text documents, but there are some considerations discussed below that are peculiar to their evaluation. In addition, full-text documents are often the electronic equivalent of a paper-based publication, such as a government report, and consequently the criteria may not be peculiar to the availability of information via the internet.

Assessing full-text documents

As mentioned, many of the generic criteria discussed in Chapter 3 are applicable here. Particular considerations are the purpose of the document, the subject area covered, whether the subject has been covered comprehensively, and whether there are pointers to further information. The currency of the information should also be determined, although the importance of this will depend upon the nature of the information and whether there is a need for it to be up-to-date. Factors associated with accessibility, presentation and arrangement, ease of use and user support may be applicable, although this will depend upon the format of the information. You may also want to compare an individual document to others, and to consider the uniqueness of the information.

Assessing authority and accuracy

The general factors discussed in Chapter 3 relating to assessing authority and accuracy are applicable here. Particular considerations are:

- the reputation and expertise of any individuals or organizations involved in the production of the document
- the likely accuracy of the information, including whether the information has a research basis, whether there are any references to published sources of information, and whether the information has been through any quality-control processes, such as editing or refereeing
- the motivation of those involved in the production of the information, and whether the information likely to be biased by their involvement.

As discussed in Chapter 3, different techniques are available for determining the accuracy of information. You may be faced with the need to assess the accuracy of an academic article or research paper, but unless you have the necessary expertise, this may be problematic because the quality of the research is a central consideration. You could therefore consider the wider range of issues discussed in Chapter 3 relating to assessing accuracy and perceptions of accuracy.

You may be presented with a document that provides no indication of where it has come from and there may be no links to a home page or parent document. As discussed earlier, the URL of a web page can provide useful information about a resource. In addition, a useful technique for finding out where a particular page originates from is to delete the last part, or parts, of the URL (after the last '/') to see where the new, shorter URL takes you. For example, 'Abortion: some medical facts' (**http://www.nrlc.org/abortion/ASMF/asmf.html**) appears initially to be a useful and informative document about abortion, covering different techniques, possible complications and the potential psychological consequences. There is no indication of where the information has come from in the opening screen, who has produced it, or why. Reducing the URL to **http://www.nrlc.org/abortion/ASMF/** leads you to nowhere of interest. However, **http://www.nrlc.org/** is the home page of the National Right to Life Committee. This is an anti-abortion lobbying organization, and if you were interested in accurate and reliable information about this topic, you would probably conclude that this document is likely to be biased by its producers.

Example   Evaluating a foot and mouth FAQ
**http://www.maff.gov.uk/animalh/diseases/
fmd/qa1.htm**

Step 1: Find out as much as possible about where the information has come from

Figure 4.5 displays part of a FAQ about foot and mouth disease. A major concern with FAQs is often the authority and the likely accuracy of the information, so if you encountered this page you would want to find out as much as possible about it in order to determine its likely quality. The screen shot in Figure 4.5 displays some of the useful details provided in the FAQ that indicate the quality of this item. In particular, the MAFF logo is displayed and MAFF owns the copyright to the information – MAFF is the Ministry for Agriculture, Fisheries and Food, a UK government department. In addition, if this information were not available, you could examine the URL (**.gov.uk** indicates a UK government body), and you could delete parts of the URL to establish where the FAQ originates from (ultimately this will lead you to the MAFF home page at **http://www.maff.gov.uk/**). We are therefore immediately presented with an indication of the likely authority of this information.

Step 2: Assess the currency, coverage and level of detail of the information

Having made a rudimentary assessment of authority, you would need to

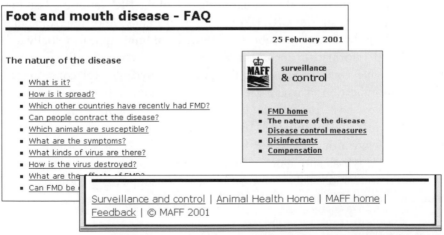

Fig. 4.5   *Useful details for evaluation in a foot and mouth disease FAQ*
© Crown Copyright. Reproduced from MAFF website 2001, by permission of the Controller of HMSO

further evaluate the usefulness of the FAQ by reading the information itself. Suppose that you are a lay person with an interest in the implications of foot and mouth disease. Examining the questions displayed in Figure 4.5 indicates the coverage of the FAQ, and reading some of the information suggests that it is indeed aimed at the lay person – there are no technical terms, for example. There is a date indicating the currency of the information – this page was accessed during a foot and mouth outbreak in the UK, and the information was only two weeks old. In addition, there is an e-mail address for a webmaster. However, this is a brief document and browsing both the questions and answers indicates it is not a comprehensive source on the topic. In addition, aside from the links to other MAFF pages, there are no pointers to further relevant information, there are no references to support the statements made here, and there is no indication of the intended purpose of the FAQ.

Step 3: An overall impression of the FAQ

The overall conclusion for this FAQ must be that it is an authoritative and up-to-date source on the foot and mouth outbreak in the UK, which would be useful to a lay person. However, its coverage is limited, there are no pointers to further information, and there is no indication of the basis for the information.

CHECKLIST   **EVALUATING FULL-TEXT DOCUMENTS**

✔ what is the purpose of the document?
✔ what is the coverage of the document? is the subject covered comprehensively? are there any pointers to further information?
✔ who has produced the document? what is the reputation and expertise of any individuals or organizations involved in the production of the document? is this an authoritative source of information? what is the address of the site, and does it indicate an authoritative institution?
✔ what is the likely accuracy of the information?
✔ does the information have a research basis? what is the quality of the research?
✔ are there any references to published sources of information?
✔ has the information been through any quality-control processes, such as editing or refereeing?

✔ what is the motivation of those involved in the production of the information? is the information likely to be biased by any individuals or organizations involved in its production?

✔ is there a last update date for the document and is the information current?

✔ is the information well presented and arranged?

✔ how does the document compare with others that cover a similar subject?

✔ what is your overall impression of the quality of the document?

Databases

Databases are a collection of records, each of which contains details of a different data item, whether numeric, textual or image-based, and which is usually available in a searchable format. A wide range of different types of databases is available via the internet, including library catalogues, commercial catalogues and bibliographical databases. Some databases were previously available electronically or as a printed index, while others have been developed specifically for use via the web or telnet. Many of the criteria therefore refer to databases generally, while others are peculiar to the use of databases via the internet.

Assessing databases

A good starting point when evaluating a database is any introductory information or help files, as these are often a useful source of facts about who has produced the database, its intended purpose, its coverage and the intended audience. In addition, it is often helpful to consult any resource guides for the relevant discipline. For example, inclusion of a database in a guide to reference works, such as *Walford's*, will provide an indication of its reputation, as well as a synopsis of its purpose and coverage. Likewise, inclusion of a database in an appropriate gateway or virtual library will also indicate that it is considered a quality resource within its field.

Coverage and level of detail in database records

The subject areas and types of materials covered by a database, including the comprehensiveness and the retrospective coverage of a database, are obviously central considerations. Details should be available from the information about the database. In addition, you will need to conduct a search on a subject with which you are familiar in order to verify any claims made by the producers. When reviewing bibliographical databases, you could assess comprehensiveness by determining the number of journals or other materials indexed within a particular discipline. In addition, the coverage of a database will be enhanced by links to any other electronic sources, such as to the full text of articles in a bibliographical database – details are usually available in the help information, although again you may need to conduct some of your own searches.

An important factor to consider is the level of detail provided in each record of the database, and the value and usefulness of that information. For example, bibliographical databases are used via the internet to search for references to published information. If users can make an informed assessment about the relevance of a publication from the information provided by a database, then that database will be of more value – therefore you will need to identify whether abstracts are available, and if so, for what percentage of the records in the database. Database providers may stipulate this or you could examine a sample of records in order to make an assessment. A further issue is whether abstracts have been truncated by word length, as this can prove frustrating where valuable information has been omitted. Furthermore, you may wish to consider the expertise of the authors involved in producing the data as an indication of its likely usefulness.

Accuracy In databases

Many of the general accuracy issues discussed in Chapter 3 are not applicable here. However, citation accuracy is essential in bibliographical databases as the wrong page numbers or journal volume will result in wasted time. Likewise, any typographical or spelling errors can render any database less useful. You could examine a selection of references to estimate their accuracy, or where possible, examine the index for commonly misspelled terms. Using the index, records can be displayed as an alphabetical list of, for example, author names or journal titles, making it much easier to spot spelling mistakes or inconsistencies. It is also worth considering whether any quality-control procedures are in place to help ensure the accuracy of any data. Moreover, an e-mail address for users to notify the service of any inaccuracies suggests a general concern for accuracy.

Currency and maintenance of databases

Because databases are commonly used to access the latest information about a topic or issue, currency and maintenance are central considerations in their assessment. In order to judge currency, it may be possible to ascertain how frequently the database is updated, whether from any introductory information or by searching the database for recent additions. Another factor is the time delay between the publication of materials and their appearance in a bibliographical database. Again, it may be possible to determine this from any introductory information or by searching for recent publications. You may also want to revisit a database to ensure that it is regularly updated, or that it is updated as frequently as the database producers claim.

Presentation, arrangement and search facilities in databases

The presentation and arrangement of a website providing access to a database will affect the ease of access and retrieval of the information it contains. In addition, you will need to consider the searching and browsing facilities that are available. The particular facilities will depend upon the individual source and its purpose, but they should enable you to retrieve information quickly and easily. In addition, different modes of access should be available for accessing the same data. In relation to bibliographical databases, certain basic features should be available, such as the option to search by author, title or subject keyword, as well as the option to limit by publication type and date range. Some databases offer more sophisticated searching facilities, such as automatic keyword mapping and the option to amend and re-run search statements. Any available search or browse facilities should be assessed in terms of their effectiveness, their ease of use and their value. They should also be evaluated according to whether they meet the needs of the intended user group.

Further issues relate to the ease with which data can be output and downloaded from the database, including the option to export data into another package. For example, academic users might maintain a personal database of bibliographical references, and it is therefore useful if references can be transferred to a reference management package without the need for data conversion. In addition, some databases offer facilities to output results via e-mail, and the available output options should be examined. If material is available for loan or purchase from a database, it should be possible to order material directly via the source and contact information should be readily available.

Further issues relating to databases

The generic issues discussed in Chapter 3 relating to accessibility are of relevance here, particularly the speed and reliability of access, or whether there are any restrictions, such as a charge to access a database or to download records. The issues relating to ease of use, user support and the availability of help information are of particular concern. You may need to use a database to determine whether it is intuitive and user-friendly, and examine any help information to assess its usefulness.

Many databases are unique in terms of their coverage and this should be a consideration during assessment. In addition, during recent years, various versions of *MEDLINE* have been made available for free via the internet. Anagnostelis and Cooke have produced guidelines for comparing different versions of the same database – considerations include the difference in currency between any free versions, and comparisons of coverage between different databases.[3] This issue is no longer peculiar to *MEDLINE*, and you will need to consider whether different versions of the same database are available, whether it is via the internet or another access route. All of the generic criteria mentioned in Chapter 3 can be used to compare different sources, but particular areas of concern should be the comparative cost and value for money of different versions, their currency, coverage and ease of use.

....

Example   Evaluating *PubMed*
http://www.ncbi.nlm.nlh.gov/PubMed/

Step 1: Evaluative indicators on the opening screen

As mentioned above, a number of different versions of *MEDLINE* are now available via the internet, and one of these is *PubMed*. The authority of *MEDLINE* as a database for healthcare and medical resources is unquestionable – it is produced by the US National Library of Medicine and it is the most widely used bibliographical database in the field. The National Library of Medicine produces this version of *MEDLINE*, thereby indicating its likely usefulness.

The opening screen to *PubMed* is displayed in Figure 4.6. As shown, there is a statement of the coverage of *PubMed* on the opening screen – access to over 11 million citations from the *MEDLINE* database, as well as citations from additional life science journals. It also states that *PubMed* includes links to the full text of journal articles, and there are links to several molecular biology resources (located beneath the *PubMed* logo). Links from the left-hand menu of the opening screen lead to additional information about the service. In particular, there is an overview of the service that contains details about *MEDLINE* generally and the journals covered by the database. There is also a vast help file and several FAQs relating to different aspects of the service, such as ordering articles, exporting references to reference management software

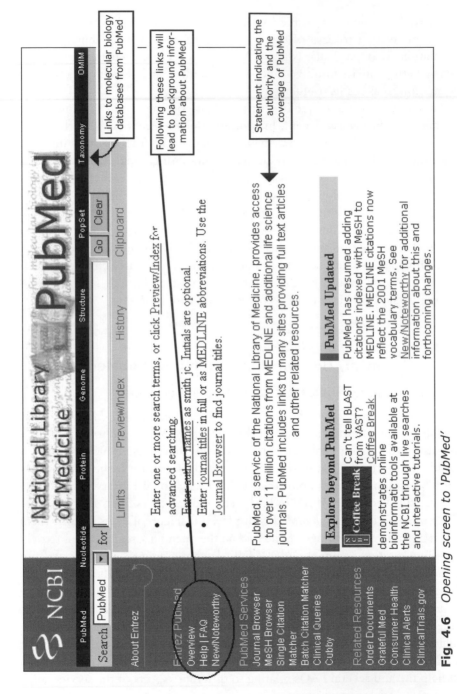

Fig. 4.6 *Opening screen to 'PubMed'*

PubMed is produced by the National Library of Medicine

and saving search strategies. As mentioned earlier, these are useful starting points in database evaluation because they provide background details, as well as information on the available features and facilities.

Step 2: Search PubMed to assess the available options

As displayed on the opening screen, there is a blank space where you can input your search terms, and brief help information about how to search is provided directly underneath. However, there are many more options for searching *MEDLINE* via the *PubMed* site. For example, you can browse the controlled Medical Subject Headings (MeSH), which are used to index materials in the database, and add these to a search. Several options are available for limiting searches, such as by age group, date range and publication type. You can also modify and re-run search strategies using the 'history' option, and browse the journal index or the author index. Another feature is the 'clinical queries' option – this enables you to filter your search results to retrieve only those articles with a research basis, a potentially useful feature for clinicians and other healthcare professionals seeking a limited number of highly relevant papers.

Simply entering a few terms in the space provided from the opening screen of *PubMed* will usually retrieve some references. For example, entering 'nose-bleeds' and 'hypertension' retrieves details of four papers. However, this approach to searching *MEDLINE* is by no means effective. All records in *MEDLINE* have been indexed using controlled subject headings (MeSH), and an effective subject search should search for the appropriate MeSH, as well as any terms appearing in article titles and abstracts (textwords). Conducting a search for either 'nosebleeds' as a textword or 'epistaxis' (the correct MeSH), as well as 'hypertension' (as either a MeSH or a textword), results in almost 100 papers. Therefore a vast quantity of potentially relevant material was omitted from the first search, and where medical information is concerned, any one of those papers might have contained information that was essential to the care of a patient. Therefore, a major drawback of *PubMed* is that it encourages users to conduct a 'quick and dirty' search. In addition, opting to search for the correct MeSH is both time-consuming and complex – training and familiarity are required in order to utilize these options.

Step 3: View some of the papers in the database

Once you have conducted a search in *PubMed*, the results are displayed in a brief format. Several options are available – you can specify how many documents you want to view and how much information you want to display about each paper, or you can modify a search by specifying a date limit, adding new terms or restricting a search to certain fields within the database. In addition, there are options to save or print results. Clicking on the author names for a paper leads to all of the information in the database about the reference, including a detailed and informative abstract for about 80% of the papers. In addition, where the full text of a journal article is available via the internet, *PubMed* provides a link to the relevant website. However, following such links invariably leads to a prompt for a username and password – *PubMed* does not discriminate between journals that are available via the internet for free and journals that require a subscription. There is also an option to order documents online (there is a charge for using this service).

Step 4: Compare *PubMed* with other versions of *MEDLINE*

Several different versions of *MEDLINE* are now available via the internet. In addition, many medical libraries continue to provide access to *MEDLINE* via CD-ROM. Medical libraries are now faced with the decision of whether or not to continue paying for access to *MEDLINE* when it is now available for free via the internet. In this situation, obviously the individuals concerned would need to compare the different versions in order to decide which to use.

The above description of searching *PubMed* might seem somewhat harsh, and you would need to compare the available search options with other databases in order to put this view into perspective. For example, some versions of *MEDLINE* automatically prompt users to look for the correct MeSH (thereby encouraging more effective searching than *PubMed*), while others provide fewer options than *PubMed*. Additional issues for comparison include the currency and coverage of different versions of *MEDLINE*. *PubMed* provides access to the full *MEDLINE* database, as well as additional life sciences journals. There are links to the full text of articles (although not all journals are available to all users), as well as links to several sources of molecular biology data. These options are generally not available in other internet versions of *MEDLINE*, and certainly are not available in CD-ROM-based versions of *MEDLINE*. In addition, *PubMed* contains the *PreMEDLINE* data – basic reference information that is added on a daily basis before the articles have been fully indexed. To give a comparison, many CD-ROM versions of *MEDLINE* are updated on a monthly basis, and many internet versions are updated on a weekly basis. A further consideration is that there are no restrictions to accessing *PubMed* – the database is freely available to anyone with an internet connection. Therefore, although *PubMed* can be difficult to search effectively, there are many additional advantages to its use, particularly the cost and its currency.

....

CHECKLIST   EVALUATING DATABASES

✔ what is the intended purpose, coverage and audience of the data-base? is this information available from any introductory information or help files?

✔ what is the coverage of the database? what subject areas and mater-ials are covered? is the database comprehensive within a particular area? what is the retrospective coverage of the database? is inform-ation available about the material which is included in the database?

✔ does the database contain links to further sources of information?

✔ are different versions of the same database available? are there any differences in coverage?

✔ how much information is provided in each record of the database? is the amount of information useful, and sufficient for the needs of the user?

✔ in the case of bibliographical databases: do they consist of references only or are abstracts available? for what percentage of the records are abstracts provided? have the abstracts been truncated by word length?

✔ is it possible to identify the authors responsible for the information in the database? what are their knowledge and expertise?

✔ what is the reputation of the database? is the database included in any guides to reference works, such as Walford's, or in a gateway or virtual library?

✔ are there any typographical or spelling errors? are there any errors in bibliographical citations? are there any quality-control procedures in place?

✔ is the database current and well maintained? how frequently is the database updated? is there a time delay between the publication of materials and their appearance in the database?

✔ what searching and browsing facilities are available? are any search-ing and browsing facilities useful, effective and easy to use? what outputting and downloading options are available? is it easy to output and download data from the database? can data be exported to other packages? is this easy to do?

4 in relation to bibliographical databases: is it possible to search by author, title or subject keyword? can searches be limited by pub-

lication type and date range? are there any additional searching or browsing features? are the search and browse facilities effective, easy to use and useful?
✔ is it possible to order material directly from the database?
✔ is contact information available?
✔ is the database easily accessible? are there any restrictions to access? is there a charge for accessing the database or downloading records?
✔ is the database easy to use and are there any user support facilities?
✔ how does the database compare with other similar databases?
✔ what is your overall impression of the quality of the database?

Electronic journals and magazines

Electronic journals and magazines are often an electronic version of a paper-based publication, although an increasing number are now produced only in an electronic format. Electronic journals and magazines are often accessed via the internet because they are not otherwise available, or because it is more convenient or cheaper than going to a library to find the paper-based copy. They are therefore evaluated in much the same way as any printed versions, and many of the criteria are not specific to publications available via the internet. In addition, the criteria relating to the evaluation of electronic journals and magazines are equally applicable to any other publications which are produced periodically, such as annual reviews or newspapers (although additional criteria for evaluating sources of news information are provided later in the chapter). You may be interested in evaluating a whole journal or magazine, or an individual article – the level of evaluation will depend upon your own needs. If you are interested in evaluating an individual article, then you should consult the section on full-text documents.

Assessing electronic journals and magazines

The subject area covered is often the chief reason for using electronic journals and magazines, and many of the criteria already described in Chapter 3 for identifying the purpose of a source and assessing its coverage are applicable. Further issues include whether the whole publication is available via the internet, and if only parts are available, how those parts have been selected. For example, some sites are simply used to advertise a journal or magazine and therefore offer limited coverage (e.g. the current issue, the contents pages or selected abstracts). A further factor is whether an archive is available that enables users to access back copies of a publication, and the retrospective coverage of the archive.

Authority and reputation of academic journals

The general factors affecting the authority and reputation of any source are applicable to journals and magazines. However, there are complex issues associated with assessing the reputation and authority of academic journals that require further attention. Within a given discipline there is a hierarchy of academic journals which is based upon a combination of factors, including the reputation of the journal, its length of establishment and its impact factor (a measure of the number of times a journal has been cited over a given period of time divided by the number of articles published in it). The position of a journal within the hierarchy influences perceptions of the quality of the articles published in it, and the result is cyclical: the higher the position of a journal within the hierarchy, the greater the number of articles submitted to the journal, the more stringent the refereeing process, and thus the higher the quality of the published material. Some of these issues would obviously be applicable to non-academic publications too.

Issues for evaluation include whether the journal is refereed, the stringency of the refereeing process (this might be determined by examining rejection rates for the journal if this information is available), its reputation, and its genealogy (the length of establishment and whether there is a printed equivalent of the publication). In order to identify the impact factor of a journal, you will need access to the *Journal Citation Reports* (**http://jcrweb.com/**) – this service is available only to subscribers (your local library service may be a subscriber). Methods of assessing the reputation of a journal include determining whether it is covered by important bibliographical databases within the discipline, such as *MEDLINE* and *EMBASE* for medical journals, *ERIC* for education journals, or *LISA* for journals in librarianship. Further aspects are the reputation and experience of the editorial board (their details are usually available on the website), and the reputation and experience of any sponsors or other organizations involved in the production of the publication. For example, sponsorship by a learned society indicates an academic need for a journal rather than a commercial opportunity.

However, the reputation of a journal is not always a useful indicator of quality. For example, a highly reputable medical journal such as *The Lancet* is not of interest to every healthcare professional because of its broad subject coverage – the subject area covered by a publication and your own needs will remain central to the evaluation process. Moreover, a newly established electronic journal with no paper-based equivalent may have a reputable editorial board and the support of a reputable learned society, and there may be demand for the journal in its particular subject domain. The various criteria cannot be used in isolation, and while authority and reputation are important, they should be considered in relation to factors such as coverage, currency and accuracy.

Further issues relating to electronic journals and magazines

The factors discussed in Chapter 3 relating to currency and maintenance are applicable to electronic journals and magazines. Additional issues are the length of time between acceptance of an article by a journal and its subsequent publication, as well as whether there is any time difference between publication of printed and electronic versions of the same issue. You may need to browse previous issues to generate an average of these figures. In addition, due to the nature of electronic information, it may be possible to revise and update articles – if an article has been revised, the details should be clearly visible from the website.

The general factors relating to the accessibility of journals, and their presentation and arrangement, are also applicable, although there are some additional considerations. Cost is a central concern and you may need to consider the charging options available, as well as the availability of any free information. Where an archive is available, there should be options to search by subject, author, volume and issue number, and it should be possible to limit searches by date range. An index for the site as a whole will be useful, and it should be easy to locate the latest copy of a journal or magazine, as well as any back issues. A contents list should be available for each issue, and there should be links between the citations at the end of articles and the main body of the text. Additional features that take advantage of the electronic format include the option to update articles, to e-mail comments about articles, and to link directly into other electronic resources. In addition, many journals offer the option to receive the contents pages of each issue of a journal as it is published via e-mail. Where such facilities are available, you will need to appraise them according to whether they add value to the publication.

As discussed in Chapter 3, some sites use PDF to display or print journal or magazine articles as they would appear in a paper-based publication. You may need to determine whether this option or other options are available, as well as whether it is easy to download the necessary software and access the article concerned.

The comparison issues are also applicable. In particular, you might consider the advantages of the electronic format over its paper-based equivalent where applicable, the relative currency of an electronic version compared to the printed version, including the frequency of updating, and the coverage of the paper-based journal or magazine by the electronic version.

Example   Evaluating *Ariadne*
http://www.ariadne.ac.uk/

Step 1: Examine the opening screen

Ariadne is an electronic journal that was first produced as part of the *Electronic Libraries* (*eLib*) programme in the UK. The opening screen (displayed in Figure 4.7) provides useful information about the intended audience of the journal:

> Ariadne magazine is aimed at both librarians and information science professionals in academic libraries, and also to interested lay people in the UK Higher Education community. Its principal geographic focus is the UK, but it is widely read in the US and worldwide.

There are also details about the aims of the journal – it 'describes and evaluates sources and services available on the internet, and of potential use, to librarians and information professionals' – and its intended coverage:

> It reports to the library community at large on progress and developments within the UK *Electronic Libraries Programme*, and on other JISC-funded services (the DNER and RDN services for example). It also reports on information services worldwide, keeping the busy practitioner abreast of current digital library initiatives.

There are also details about the frequency of updating (every three months), the funding arrangements and levels of use. However, not all electronic journals will be as helpful as *Ariadne* in providing this information on the opening screen, and often you will need to follow links such as 'about this journal' and 'about this journal's website'. You may even need to refer to the publisher's home page. Wherever you locate this information, you will need to examine the site to ascertain more about the publication and whether it meets its stated aims and objectives.

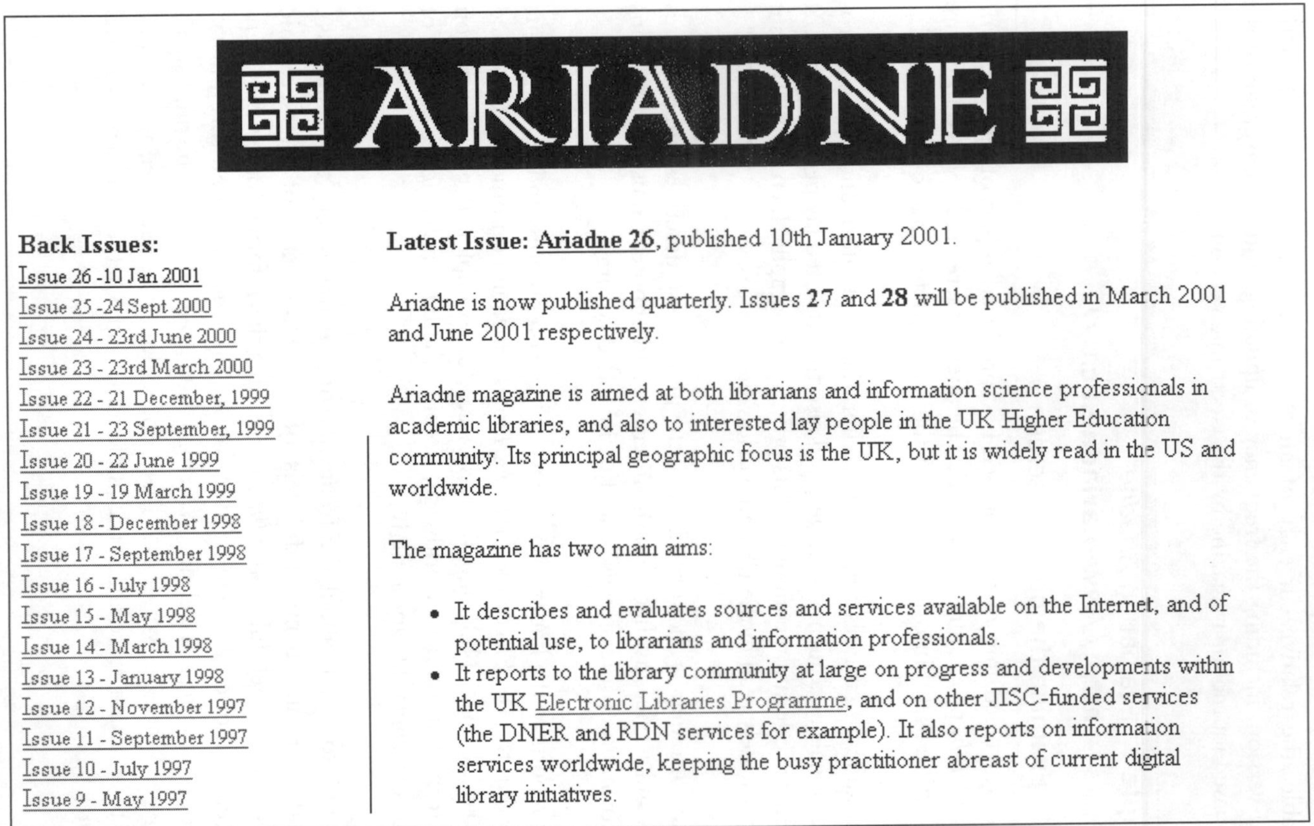

ARIADNE

Back Issues:

Issue 26 -10 Jan 2001
Issue 25 - 24 Sept 2000
Issue 24 - 23rd June 2000
Issue 23 - 23rd March 2000
Issue 22 - 21 December, 1999
Issue 21 - 23 September, 1999
Issue 20 - 22 June 1999
Issue 19 - 19 March 1999
Issue 18 - December 1998
Issue 17 - September 1998
Issue 16 - July 1998
Issue 15 - May 1998
Issue 14 - March 1998
Issue 13 - January 1998
Issue 12 - November 1997
Issue 11 - September 1997
Issue 10 - July 1997
Issue 9 - May 1997

Latest Issue: Ariadne **26**, published 10th January 2001.

Ariadne is now published quarterly. Issues **27** and **28** will be published in March 2001 and June 2001 respectively.

Ariadne magazine is aimed at both librarians and information science professionals in academic libraries, and also to interested lay people in the UK Higher Education community. Its principal geographic focus is the UK, but it is widely read in the US and worldwide.

The magazine has two main aims:

- It describes and evaluates sources and services available on the Internet, and of potential use, to librarians and information professionals.
- It reports to the library community at large on progress and developments within the UK Electronic Libraries Programme, and on other JISC-funded services (the DNER and RDN services for example). It also reports on information services worldwide, keeping the busy practitioner abreast of current digital library initiatives.

Fig. 4.7 *Details about 'Ariadne' from the opening screen*
Ariadne is produced by UKOLN, the UK Office for Library Networking

Step 2: Browse the site

As displayed in Figure 4.7, there is a link from the opening screen to the current issue of the journal, and browsing this issue gives a clearer picture of its contents and arrangement. Each issue contains a contents page, which is divided into editorials, main articles, regular columns and reports on events, as well as other 'odds and ends'. There is a link to each article, details of the author(s) and a sentence describing each article. Browsing the contents page of the current issue indicates that the journal is indeed of interest to librarians and information professionals interested in the internet and networked information sources, and selecting any of the links leads directly to the full text of each article. You do not need access to additional software to view the full text – material is only available in HTML format. In addition, although *Ariadne* provides an e-mail address for the journal as a whole, there is no indication that users are encouraged to respond to individual articles, and e-mails are not displayed on the website.

Browsing the current issue indicates that the site is clearly and logically arranged. The presentation format is consistent throughout – the journal title is displayed at the top of each screen with a statement of where you are within the site, and the same options or short-cuts are displayed on each page ('main contents', 'section menu', 'e-mail *Ariadne*' and 'search *Ariadne*'). A link to the current issue of the journal is clearly displayed on the opening screen and there are also links to the back issues – these are displayed as a list in reverse chronological order (shown in Figure 4.7). The whole of the journal is available for free online as the archive begins with Issue 1 – this also indicates the genealogy of the journal, as Issue 1 dates from 1996. It is also possible to search the whole site, including the back issues, and the search facility is easy to use with help information provided.

Step 3: Find out more about *Ariadne*

There is no indication from the website that *Ariadne* is a refereed journal, and there are no details about an editorial board. However, as already mentioned, there is a description of the funding arrangements for the journal on the first page. *Ariadne* is published by the UK Office for Library Networking (UKOLN), which, as stated on the site, is funded by the UK Council for Museums, Archives & Libraries and the UK Higher Education Funding Councils. The journal also receives funding from the European Union. These are all reputable organizations, indicating the authority and reputation of *Ariadne*. A search on *LISA*, the principal bibliographical database for journal articles in librarianship and information science, reveals that articles from *Ariadne* are indexed. If you wanted further information, it would also be possible to contact the web editor as an e-mail address is provided.

Step 4: An overall impression of *Ariadne*

Ariadne is provided for free via the internet; it is a relatively new journal, having only been established in 1996; the website does not indicate that there is a paper-based equivalent, there is no indication that it is refereed, and there are no details about the editorial board. This might lead to the conclusion that it is not a high-quality or worthwhile publication. However, it explicitly states on the opening screen that it is designed to keep information professionals up-to-date on projects and services relating to the internet and networked resources. Examination of a recent issue indicates that indeed the journal does this, with editorials, full articles, regular columns and much more. In addition, the funding bodies, and the fact that the journal is indexed in *LISA*, add weight to its authority and reputation. Although the website for *Ariadne* does not exploit to the full the capabilities of electronic access, it is easy to use, and the information is clearly, consistently and logically arranged. Therefore, within the context that this is a fairly informal publication for the discipline, it could be described as a high-quality publication.

CHECKLIST EVALUATING ELECTRONIC JOURNALS AND MAGAZINES

✔ what is the coverage of the site? what are the aims and objectives of the site providing access to the journal or magazine? is the whole journal or magazine available? if only parts are available, how are those parts selected? is the site intended simply for advertising purposes?

✔ what is the purpose of the journal or magazine?

✔ what is the coverage of the journal or magazine?

✔ is there an archive for accessing back issues of the journal or magazine? what is the retrospective coverage of the archive? is the archive searchable by subject, author, volume and/or issue number? is it possible to limit searches by date range? how useful and effective is the search facility?

✔ what is the reputation of the journal or magazine? is it an authoritative journal or magazine? what are the reputation and experience of the editorial board? what are the reputation and experience of any other organizations involved in the production of the journal or magazine?

✔ in relation to academic journals: what is the impact factor of the journal? what is the genealogy of the journal? how long has it been available? is there a paper-based equivalent? is the journal refereed, and how stringent is the refereeing process? is the journal indexed in any appropriate bibliographical databases?

✔ is the site well maintained? is there a time delay between article acceptance and publication in the journal? what is the time delay? is there a time difference between production of the printed and electronic publications? is there a facility for updating articles? are details provided of any updating procedures?

✔ is the site easily accessible?

✔ is the information well presented and arranged? is there a site index? how easy is it to locate individual issues within the site? is there a contents list for each issue? is it easy to locate individual articles? are there links between citations and the main body of the text in each article?

✔ are there any additional features, such as an option to e-mail comments on articles or to link directly into other electronic sources? can you receive the contents pages of each issue of a journal as it is published? do these facilities add value to the journal or magazine?

✔ can articles be displayed in PDF? is it easy to download the necessary software and access the article concerned?

✔ is the site easy to use, and are there any user support facilities?

✔ how does the site, journal or magazine compare with other similar sites, journals or magazines?

✔ what is your overall impression of the quality of the site, journal or magazine?

Sources of news information

This section relates to materials where the purpose of the information is to describe current events, whether local, national or international. Obvious examples are newspapers, such as *The Guardian* (**http://www.guardian.co.uk/**) and *The Times* (**http://www.thetimes.co.uk/**), or the website for a television station, such as the *BBC News* (**http://news.bbc.co.uk/**) and *CNN* (**http://www.cnn.com/**). However, many other sites contain a news component – for example, the MAFF site discussed earlier provides current information about foot and mouth disease. In addition, a site may provide up-to-date information on a particular topic – *Ariadne* has been considered as a journal providing current awareness information about electronic sources and services for librarians and other information professionals. Essentially the criteria that you use will depend upon your reason for using the information – the criteria discussed below relate specifically to evaluating the news component of any site.

Assessing sources of news information

Most of the generic criteria discussed in Chapter 3 apply to the evaluation of sources of news information. However, particular areas of concern are coverage, currency, authority and accuracy. In addition to the general coverage criteria, a site may be the electronic version of a paper-based publication or television/radio broadcast, and therefore you will need to consider whether all of the content is available online, and if not, how the material has been selected. There may be additional content, or additional features available in the electronic version – in which case you may need to compare the two versions in order to assess their relative usefulness.

Currency is obviously an important consideration, including whether each page of information contains an explicit date, whether the information is up-to-date, and how frequently or regularly the information is updated. Details may be explicit from the site itself, and there may be a policy regarding maintenance, but you may need to monitor some resources to ensure continued currency and maintenance.

Authority and accuracy, as mentioned, are also areas of concern. Issues include where the information has come from – in particular the organization producing the news – and their authority and expertise in the area. If possible, consider whether any information is likely to be biased by any organizations or individuals concerned with the production of the source. Where newspapers are concerned, printed publications usually segregate editorial content or opinion pieces so that it is possible to acknowledge their bias – this should apply also to electronic versions of the same information. Further considerations are whether the information has been edited, or whether there are any other quality-control procedures in place.

The presentation and arrangement of the information, the accessibility of the site, and the ease of using a resource, are all areas for consideration – you should consult the general criteria discussed in Chapter 3 for these aspects of evaluation.

Example   Evaluating the *Barnsley Chronicle Online*
http://www.barnsley-chronicle.co.uk/

Step 1: Find out about the site

The internet is an ideal mechanism for disseminating news information. Not only is it possible to update the news as it happens, but also the information can be accessed from almost anywhere in the world. For this reason, access to local newspapers is especially appealing – previously papers such as the *Barnsley Chronicle* were generally available only from within the local area, but access to the internet has changed this situation.

There is a link to information about the paper from the opening screen of the *Barnsley Chronicle*. However, this is somewhat disappointing for anyone evaluating the site because there is only a brief statement from the editor, a 'who's who' guide to people working for the paper, and a brief history. We are told that the paper is 150 years old, that its purpose is 'chronicling the lives and activities of the people of its town', and that the website has been available since 1995. There is no information about how often the paper is produced, how regularly the website is updated, and the content that is available online (whether the whole of the paper is available, and if not which parts have been selected and on what basis). As displayed in Figure 4.8, there is a date in the centre of the opening screen, but you would need to monitor the paper over time to assess the currency of the information and the regularity of updating. Alternatively, contact details are available from the website, and you could e-mail a webmaster to obtain this information.

Step 2: Browse the content to assess the coverage of the site

As mentioned, there is no indication of how much content is available online compared to the printed version of the paper. There is an archive, but browsing this indicates that only selected content is available via the internet. Browsing the site generally suggests that there is additional content which is probably not available from the paper-based publication. For example, it is possible to access information about schools in the local area, including their inspection reports. This might be extremely useful, particularly if you were considering moving to the area. Again, you might need to contact someone working at the paper to find out further details. Alternatively, you could purchase a copy of the paper and make a direct comparison.

As shown in Figure 4.8, there are opportunities for advertising via the website. In March 2001, there were adverts from a property company and a retail development in Barnsley. Such advertisements have obvious implications in

Fig. 4.8 *The opening screen of the 'Barnsley Chronicle Online'*

terms of the potential bias of any information relating to these topics. However, no information is without bias, and most local newspapers include advertising as a means of generating income and ensuring the future of the publication. It is unfortunate that there is no statement about any advertising policy and its implications for the information from the website, but this should perhaps be considered in relation to the fact we are looking at a local newspaper site.

Step 3: An overall impression of the site

Many limitations of the *Barnsley Chronicle* website have been highlighted. Additional issues include the fact that the opening screen is somewhat cluttered (see Figure 4.8), that it is not easy to navigate the site and find what you are looking for, and that it is not possible to search the paper for information of interest. Ultimately, however, the site is a unique source of information on Barnsley and its people, and for this reason it is a potentially useful resource.

CHECKLIST EVALUATING SOURCES OF NEWS INFORMATION

✔ what is the purpose of the site?
✔ what is the coverage of the site? what topics are covered, and are they covered comprehensively?
✔ is the site an electronic version of a printed publication, or is it the site for a television or radio station? does the site provide access to the whole content, and if not how has the information been selected?
✔ what is the reputation and expertise of any individuals or organizations involved in the production of the site? is this an authoritative source of information?
✔ what is the likely accuracy of the information? has the information been through any quality-control processes, such as refereeing?
✔ is the information likely to be biased by any individuals involved in its production?
✔ is there an explicit date for the information? is the information up-to-date? when was the information last updated? when will the information next be updated? how frequently is the information updated? is there a statement of policy regarding the frequency of updating and the updating process? does the source need to be monitored or reassessed at a later date to ensure continued currency and maintenance?
✔ is the site easily accessible?

✔ is the information well presented and arranged?
✔ is the site easy to use and are there any user support facilities?
✔ how does the site compare with other similar sites?
✔ what is your overall impression of the quality of the site?

Advertising, sponsorship and other commercial information

As Alexander and Tate comment, 'advertising and sponsorship are hardly new phenomena . . . they have long been the mainstays of newspapers and television shows, as well as art, music, sporting and countless other activities.'[4] However, as the authors also point out, the internet poses new problems because of the amalgamation of advertising, sponsorship and other types of commercial information with information generally. As an evaluator, it is likely that you will be faced with the difficulties of untangling useful information from information that is likely to be heavily biased by sponsorship, advertising or any other type of commercial involvement.

Assessing advertising, sponsorship and other commercial information

Alexander and Tate define advertising as 'the conveyance of persuasive information, frequently by paid announcements and other notices, about products, services or ideas', and sponsorship as 'financial or other support given by an individual, business or organization for something, usually in return for some form of public recognition.' The issue that is of particular concern here is the influence that an advertiser or sponsor may exert over the accuracy and objectivity of information. As mentioned already, a learned society may sponsor an electronic journal, thereby indicating an academic need for the information. Alternatively, a cancer journal sponsored by the tobacco industry is obviously less likely to contain accurate and reliable information because of the motivation of the funders. You will need to consider who is responsible for producing the information, what the motivation is of any individuals or organizations in making the information available, and whether the information is likely to be biased by their involvement.

A further concern is whether or not it is easy to distinguish between information and advertisements. For example, in paper-based magazines, there is generally a clear distinction between advertisements and other material, as they are distinguished by a title such as 'advertising feature'. On many websites this is also the case. Figure 3.12 shows the opening screen to the *Yahooligans!* site.

It is easy to distinguish between the information provided by *Yahooligans!* and the advertisement, particularly as the advertisement is labelled with 'ad'. However, this is not always the case, and you may need to link to logos to find out whether they lead you to external sites which are advertising products.

Alexander and Tate refer to 'a continuum of objectivity on the web' – from sites that accept absolutely no advertising to those that are entirely composed of advertising. You will need to ascertain the purpose of any information, and decide whether this has any implications for its accuracy. However, the role and importance of advertising and sponsorship can really only be considered in relation to what the information will be used for. Ultimately the importance of any commercial involvement in a site will depend on the source that you are evaluating and how you intend to use it.

Example   Evaluating *LifePlus Health Benefits*
http://www.staywellvitamins.com/lifep.htm

Step 1: Identify who is responsible for the information

LifePlus Health Benefits is a document about the health benefits of several complementary and alternative medical interventions. There is a vast amount of detailed information about a range of interventions, and reading the text suggests an authoritative document with detailed and accurate information. However, scrolling almost to the end of the document leads to the information shown in Figure 4.9. As displayed, there are some indicators that this information is from a commercial site, notably the link 'To Order' and the statement, 'Anytime – Any product – Buy 6 get 1 free'.

Step 2: Identify the purpose of the information

There is a link from the document to the 'Life Plus Home Page', and following this link leads you to the home page of a commercial organization. It is therefore clear that any information available from this site is likely to be heavily biased by a commercial imperative. Another indicator is the lack of available evidence for the claims made in the document. From the home page, there is a link to personal 'testimonials' displayed in Figure 4.9 given by individuals who have used the company's products and have been cured of all ills, but there is no other indication of the basis for the information.

Ultimately, you would need to decide whether you want accurate and reliable information about complementary and alternative medicine. If this is the case, then obviously it is very unlikely that you would use this information.

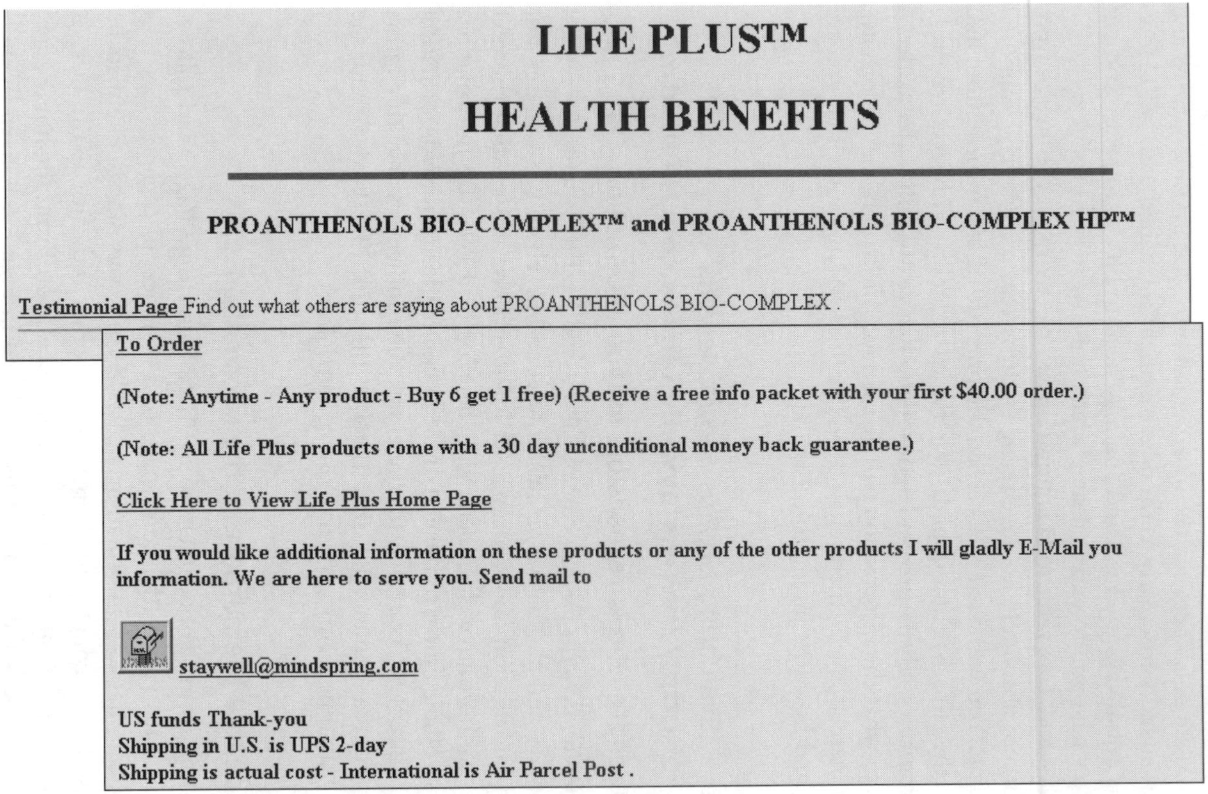

LIFE PLUS™

HEALTH BENEFITS

PROANTHENOLS BIO-COMPLEX™ and PROANTHENOLS BIO-COMPLEX HP™

Testimonial Page Find out what others are saying about PROANTHENOLS BIO-COMPLEX.

To Order

(Note: Anytime - Any product - Buy 6 get 1 free) (Receive a free info packet with your first $40.00 order.)

(Note: All Life Plus products come with a 30 day unconditional money back guarantee.)

Click Here to View Life Plus Home Page

If you would like additional information on these products or any of the other products I will gladly E-Mail you information. We are here to serve you. Send mail to

staywell@mindspring.com

US funds Thank-you
Shipping in U.S. is UPS 2-day
Shipping is actual cost - International is Air Parcel Post.

Fig. 4.9   Indications of a commercial site selling products

However, if you were interested in buying a product, then the site provides the necessary contact details and information to make a purchase.

CHECKLIST   EVALUATING ADVERTISING, SPONSORSHIP AND OTHER COMMERCIAL INFORMATION

✔ what is the purpose of the site? is the site designed purely to advertise a product, or to advertise the products and services of a particular company? is it easy to distinguish between advertise-ments and other information?

✔ who is responsible for producing the information? what is the moti-vation of any individuals or organizations in making this information available? is the information likely to be biased by any individuals or organizations involved in its production?

✔ what is the coverage of the site?

✔ s the information current, and is the site well maintained?

✔ is the site easily accessible?

✔ is the information well presented and arranged?

✔ is the site easy to use and are there any user support facilities?

✔ how does the site compare with other similar sites?

✔ what is your overall impression of the quality of the site?

Image-based and multimedia sources

The internet is increasingly being used as a source of graphical and multimedia information. Reasons for use include to illustrate work, for presentations, to supplement other textual materials, or for computer assisted learning (CAL) materials (multimedia teaching packs designed to enhance the learning experi-ence through the use of computing technology). Image-based and multimedia sources may include a large textual component, but the purpose of the criteria in this section is to enable appraisal of sites in terms of their image or other non-textual content. Evaluation may be required for a whole site which pro-vides access to images or other media, or for an individual image which forms part of an otherwise text-based source of information. You should select the appropriate criteria from those described below depending upon the circum-stances of evaluation.

Assessing image-based and multimedia sources

In relation to the purpose and coverage of a site or source, evaluation should include the topics covered by individual images, video or sound clips, the range of different subjects covered as a whole, and the comprehensiveness of coverage within an area. For example, a site might contain images of the life cycle of an animal, and considerations would include whether all the major stages have been covered, the number of images for each stage, and whether the depth of coverage is appropriate for the user (e.g. a university student will require more detail than a school pupil). Explanatory text about any images or other media can enhance their value. Factors for assessment include the level of detail, the balance of text and images or other media, and whether the explanatory text is sufficient for your needs. In addition, pointers to further information may enhance the coverage of a site.

The nature of images and other non-textual media as a source of information may mean that their reputation and authority, their accuracy and their currency are less important. However, a site which adopts a particular perspective may result in biased images, and images may become outdated. Factors for consideration therefore include whether there is a date of when each image, video clip or sound was produced, whether these will be updated, and the motivation and expertise of those responsible for producing them. One further concern is the authority of resources that are designed for educational purposes – you will need to consider whether material is provided commercially or by an academic institution, as this can affect perceptions of credibility.

Accessibility of image-based and multimedia sources

The generic criteria discussed in Chapter 3 for assessing accessibility are applicable here. Factors of particular concern are:

- the availability of contact and copyright information – it is frustrating to locate an appropriate image or resource, and then to be unable to identify any copyright information or the contact details for the person responsible for its production
- the computer storage format used – this will need to be compatible with the software and hardware available to the user
- the storage size of materials – this will affect access speeds, and sites might usefully provide a local mirror site or use thumbnail images to improve access speeds.

The accessibility of CAL materials will be of especial concern because students may have limited access to the internet or access via slow computers. It may be possible to download a self-contained package using FTP for local use, or again, there may be a local mirror site. The mode of access should be evaluated in relation to the speed of access, as well as ease of use.

Presentation and arrangement of image-based and multimedia sources

The presentation and arrangement of a site providing access to non-textual resources will affect ease of access and use, and again the generic criteria apply. A particular issue is the availability of navigational features to assist users in moving between different images. In addition, you should assess the availability of any features or facilities that take advantage of the multimedia format. For educational materials, examples include interactive tutorials and self-test materials. Considerations include the availability of such features, whether they add value to the content, and whether they enhance the learning experience. Further factors are the clarity of images or video clips, whether they are in colour or black-and-white, and whether images are two-dimensional or three-dimensional. Information on the size and resolution of the images may be available, which will affect their quality and clarity. However, the quality of materials may be difficult to reconcile with the speed of access, as the higher the quality of the images, or the more sophisticated the video and sound clips, the larger the file size and therefore the longer they will take to download.

Comparison of image-based and multimedia sources

An assessment of the value of image-based and multimedia materials will require comparison with others that are available. You could compare online images to those available in books, and assess whether a site offers access to a unique source of materials, or provides access to information in a unique or innovative format through the use of multimedia.

....

Example   Evaluating the *Bristol BioMed Image Archive*
        http://www.brisbio.ac.uk/

Step 1: Find out about the service

The opening screen to the *Bristol BioMed Image Archive* is displayed in Figure 4.10. A striking aspect of this site is the clarity of the opening screen. You are presented with a brief description of the site – 'A collection of medical, dental and veterinary images for use in teaching'. There is also a space to enter search terms, and links to all of the appropriate sections within the site. As an evaluator, the first port-of-call would be the 'about' section. This provides a brief history of the service – it started life in the late 1980s when veterinary teaching staff at the University of Bristol donated their teaching slides to form a shared archive of images; further contributions from colleagues and staff based at other institutions world-wide resulted in the Bristol Biomedical Videodisc, which contained approximately 20,000 veterinary, medical and dental images for teaching. These are now accessible via the internet site. Details are also available about the copyright of the site and copyright ownership of each individual image (this resides with the image donor), current funding arrangements and access arrangements. As also shown in Figure 4.10, there are links to help information, an e-mail address (for feedback to the site), registration, and privacy and usage rules. Anyone can access the archive, but in order to download

Fig. 4.10 *Opening screen of the 'Bristol BioMed Image Archive'*
© Bristol BioMed

images for teaching purposes, a brief registration form must be completed. There is no charge for using the service, and registration is straightforward.

Step 2: Try looking for images

Options are available from the opening screen to search or browse the archive. You would need to use these to assess their usefulness. If you select 'search options' from the opening screen, followed by 'all options', the search page shown in Figure 4.11 will be displayed. There are several options for searching – entering 'chimp' in the space provided will retrieve any images which contain this word, plus any variations of the word (chimps, chimpanzee, chimpanzees), because there is an automatic stemming feature. It is also possible to search for authors of images, image donors or the Medical Subject Headings (MeSH) which are used to describe the contents of each image. The results are presented as small-scale images (thumbnails), which are quick to download. If you select an image, the detailed information displayed in Figure 4.11 will be

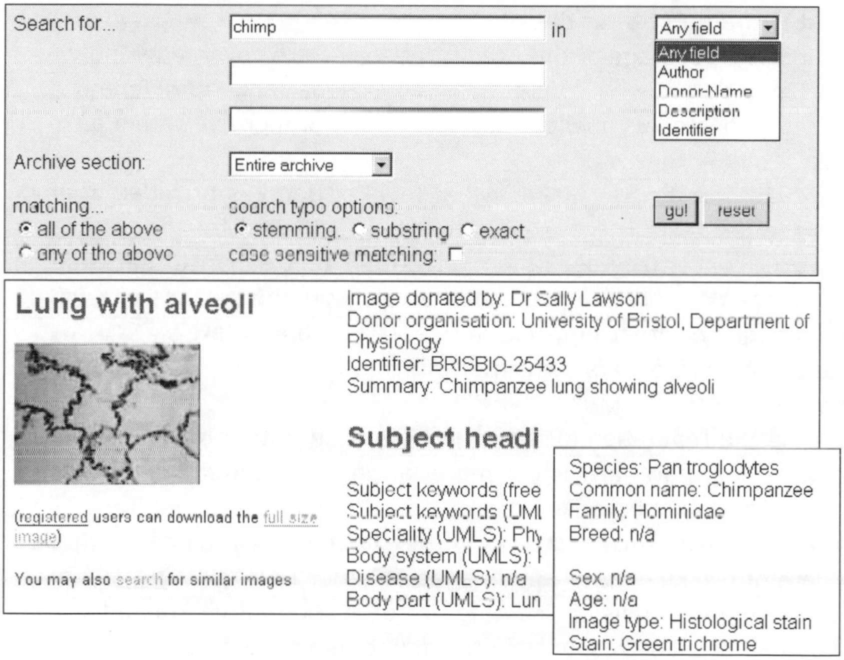

Fig. 4.11 *Search options and textual information about each image in the 'Bristol BioMed Image Archive'*
© Bristol Biomed

retrieved. This includes the name of the image donor, details about the image itself and what it displays, and the MeSH headings used to describe the image.

Step 3: An overall impression of the *Bristol BioMed Image Archive*

An overall impression of the *Bristol BioMed Image Archive* is that it is an extremely high-quality teaching resource. It is clearly presented and arranged, the images are of high quality, and it is very easy to locate images of interest. In addition, the brief textual information about each image is useful. However, the archive will obviously only appeal to a narrowly defined audience – those teaching medicine, dentistry or veterinary medicine. In addition, there is no indication that the archive is being expanded to contain a greater number of images.

CHECKLIST   EVALUATING IMAGE-BASED AND MULTIMEDIA SOURCES

✔ what is the purpose of the site?

✔ what is the coverage of the site? what topics are covered by individual images, video or sound clips? what is the range of different subjects covered as a whole? is the site comprehensive within an area?

✔ is explanatory text available? what level of detail is provided in any explanatory text? is the explanatory text sufficient for the needs of the user concerned? does the explanatory text enhance the value of the images or other non-textual materials? is the balance of text and images or other non-textual materials appropriate?

✔ are there any pointers to further information which enhance the coverage of the site?

✔ what is the reputation of the source? is it an authoritative source? for teaching materials: is the material provided commercially or by an academic institution?

✔ is the information current, and is the site well maintained? is there a date of production for any images or other non-textual materials? are there any details of updating? what is the motivation and expertise of those responsible for maintaining the materials?

✔ is the site easily accessible?

✔ is there a mirror site?

✔ have thumbnail images been used?

✔ is copyright information available?

✔ are contact details available?

✔ for teaching materials: is it possible to download a self-contained package using FTP for local use, or are materials accessed via a website? does the mode of access affect the speed?

✔ what is the file format that is used? what is the size of the files?

✔ is the information well presented and arranged? is it easy to navigate between different images or materials? are images or other non-textual materials clear? what is the image resolution?

✔ are images in colour or black-and-white? are images two-dimensional, three-dimensional or video clips?

✔ are there any features or facilities which take advantage of the multimedia format? do any such features or facilities add value to the content of the site?

✔ is the site easy to use and are there any user support facilities?

✔ how does the site compare with other similar sites?

✔ what is your overall impression of the quality of the site?

Current awareness and alerting services

Current awareness and alerting services are designed to alert users to a particular topic or issue. Various types are available via the internet, including websites for the contents of current journals, or mailing lists on sources of funding for those involved in research. Examples mentioned in Chapter 3 were two job vacancies services available via the web, one of which offered an e-mail-based alerting service. Essentially, the criteria used will depend upon the format of the service (whether it is a website or available via e-mail), as well as your own needs.

Assessing current awareness services

Almost all of the generic criteria discussed in Chapter 3 will be applicable to current awareness and alerting services that are accessible via the web. However, issues relating to accessibility, presentation and arrangement, and ease of use will be less applicable to services that are available via e-mail.

As with almost any source of information, you will need to appraise the coverage of the services. One factor in addition to those already discussed in Chapter 3 is whether it is possible to submit a profile to a service in order to restrict the information received to the subjects of most interest to you. Obviously you would need to assess the effectiveness of any such facilities, possibly through trial use if this is possible, or by consulting existing users of the service. In relation to mailing lists, an additional issue is whether it is easy to identify the subjects covered by individual postings, such as through the use of conventions for the subject headings of postings. Such facilities can enable users to assess quickly and easily whether they wish to read a posting.

Currency is another area of concern – you will need to determine the frequency of updating of a site (or the frequency of distribution of a mailing list) and the currency of the information that is distributed. A further consideration is the timeliness of the information (whether information is received when it is most needed). Considerations include whether journal contents information is received at the same time as publication of the journal itself, or whether job or funding application details are received prior to the closing dates for application. Cost and any restrictions to access should also be determined, as many services charge or require registration.

Again, as with most types of sources, you may also want to compare different services in order to consider whether one of them offers any unique features or covers a unique subject area.

....

Example   Evaluating a tables of contents alerting service from
             Elsevier Science
             http://www.elsevier.nl/

Step 1: Find out about the service

Elsevier Science is a well-known publishing company involved in the production and distribution of several scientific journals. If you select 'Journal Tables of Contents' from the first page of Elsevier's website, followed by 'Contents-Direct', this will lead you to details about its *ContentsDirect* alerting service. This is an e-mail-based service which 'delivers Elsevier Science book and journal tables of contents directly' to the user's computer, providing 'the very latest information on soon-to-be published research'. Elsevier publishes a large number of scientific journals, and therefore this is an ideal-sounding service for researchers, particularly as many are likely to already browse the contents listings for journals to stay abreast in their field. This service means that information about the journal contents is delivered directly to the user before it has been published.

Step 2: Register to use the service

In order to assess the coverage and the ease of use of this service, you would need to register. You must complete a registration form – although it is a fairly

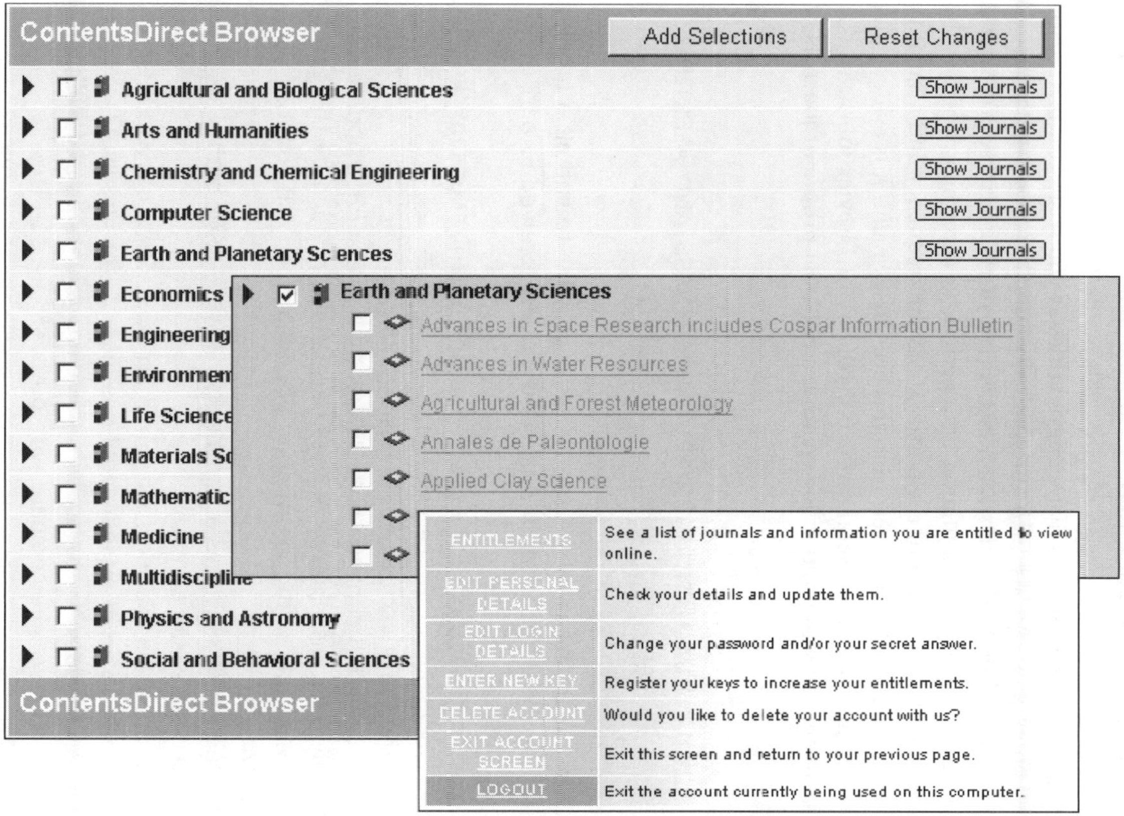

Fig. 4.12 *Creating a personal service in 'Elsevier ContentsDirect'*
Reprinted with permission from Elsevier Science

lengthy form, it is not time-consuming to complete. Once this is done, you can begin to select the journals that you are interested in. As displayed in Figure 4.12, a list of subject areas is displayed; selecting 'Earth and Planetary Sciences', for example, results in a list of the journals published by Elsevier in this field. To select any journals, you simply click in the boxes adjacent to each journal name. You can select as many journal titles as you wish, completely for free. The contents listings are then automatically e-mailed on a regular basis.

If you were undertaking a thorough evaluation of this service, you would need to register, perhaps for a limited time period, to determine whether the claims regarding the currency of the postings and the frequency and regularity of updating are accurate. However, from this brief assessment, it is evident that this would be a potentially useful service to readers of Elsevier journals. The service is enhanced by the option for creating a personal profile of journals of interest.

CHECKLIST EVALUATING CURRENT AWARENESS AND ALERTING SERVICES

✔ what is the purpose of the service?
✔ what is the coverage of the service? is it possible to submit a profile to the service in order to limit the information received to particular subject areas?
✔ what is the reputation and expertise of any organizations involved in the production of the service?
✔ what is the likely accuracy of the information?
✔ is the information current? how frequently is the service updated or the mailing list distributed? is the information provided by the service timely – i.e. is the information provided when it is most needed?
✔ is the service available as a mailing list, a website or both?
✔ is the service easily accessible?
✔ is the information well presented and arranged? is it easy to identify the subjects covered by individual postings for mailing lists?
✔ is the service easy to use and are there any user support facilities?
✔ how does the service compare with other similar services?
✔ what is your overall impression of the quality of the service?

FTP archives

FTP stands for File Transfer Protocol, the protocol that enables the transfer of files from one computer to another across networks or the internet. An FTP archive is a collection of files of software, textual materials or numerical data which can be accessed and retrieved using FTP. FTP archives were previously only accessible using an FTP utility, but it is now possible to access them using standard web browsers such as *Netscape Navigator* or *Internet Explorer*, and many sites are designed specifically for use via the web. The issues discussed here relate to an evaluation of the sites themselves rather than an evaluation of the software or data they contain, as this is outside the scope of the book.

Assessing an FTP archive

The generic criteria relating to purpose and coverage discussed in Chapter 3 are applicable to an assessment of FTP archives. The types of software or data available from a site will obviously be a central consideration, and other issues include the format of any software, and whether software for different platforms or types of computer is available. In addition, sites might provide access to upgrades and older versions of data or software, as well as trial versions of software, and it should be possible to distinguish easily between the different file types. The availability of a mirror site is often useful in improving access speeds, and you may wish to compare the coverage and frequency of updating of the mirror site with that of the original location. You could also compare an archive with others in order to determine whether it provides unique coverage of software or data, or whether there are any particularly useful features or facilities that assist in file transfer.

Some aspects of authority and reputation are applicable. A site may have an excellent reputation as a source of software or data, and might be used on account of its name or reputation. A related issue is the origin of any data or software, and details about this should be available. Many of the accuracy issues are not applicable to FTP archives, but a site may provide some quality-control facilities which could provide a useful filter. Sites may also certify that all files have been checked for viruses.

Many of the currency and maintenance issues are also applicable, particularly if you are interested in downloading software upgrades or updating data files. You may need to know how regularly a site is updated, and whether there is a time delay between software development or data generation and its availability from the site. As with other sources, contact information for a site maintainer is often useful.

149

Accessibility, presentation and ease of use of FTP archives

The internet is used because it is a fast and convenient means of accessing files. Thus, the criteria relating to accessibility are important, including whether there is a mirror site to improve access speeds. An additional issue is whether or not files have been compressed – i.e. they have been saved in a format that requires less storage space. Because the files are smaller, it takes less time for them to download. Where files have been compressed, details of the software necessary to decompress the files should be readily available. Information should also be available on file sizes, software version numbers and the expiry date for any trial versions. Help information, perhaps in the form of a README file (usually a text file discussing the contents of the site) or a site FAQ, might be useful. If relevant, consider the value and usefulness of any information that is provided. There should be an option to browse or search materials by filename, platform or type of application. Where a search facility is available, help information will also be useful.

Example Evaluating the *WinSite* archive
http://www.winsite.com/

Step 1: Find out about the *WinSite* archive

Following the 'About WinSite' link from the opening screen of the *WinSite* archive leads to some useful information about the site. The site describes itself as 'the planet's largest software archive for Windows shareware and trialware on the internet', providing some indication of its intended purpose and coverage. We are also told that the site was first founded in 1995, indicating a well-established source of Windows software. Although the 'About' document refers to mirror sites across the world, it was not possible at the time of writing to locate a list of these or their locations. This is a disadvantage, as mirror sites would ensure faster access from outside the USA.

Step 2: Use the *WinSite* archive to download software

The archive is accessible through a website and options from the opening screen include browsing and searching for software. Browsing the archive is straightforward – selecting the 'browse' option from the opening screen leads to seven options: 'new', 'hot', 'popular', 'handhelds', 'Windows 3x', 'Windows 9x' and 'Windows NT/2000'. This not only makes it easy to select the type of software and platform required, but also provides an indication of coverage.

Selecting 'Windows NT/2000' leads to the list of file areas and descriptions displayed in Figure 4.13 – examples include 'Business Applications' and 'Education Software'. Selecting the latter leads to the list of file details (also displayed in Figure 4.13). As can be seen, useful details are provided including the file name, file size (indicating how long the files are likely to take to download), the date the file was added to the archive and a description of the file. The screen shot was taken in March 2001, and the dates suggest that this site is frequently updated and well maintained, as none of the files are older than 18 months. Selecting 'Kihlman's SQL tutorial' leads to the screen displayed in Figure 4.14, which contains an option to download the file. Additional infor-

WinSite Windows NT/2000 File Categories

File Area	Description
access	Microsoft Access Files
business	Business Applications
demo	Demo Packages and Crippleware
desktop	Desktop Applications, Screen, Image, and BitMap Files
drivers/other	Misc. WinNT Drivers SCSI, Disk, Ethernet, Scanner, etc.
drivers/printer	Printer Drivers
drivers/video	
dskutil	
education	

Title	Size	Date	Description
Kihlman's SQL tutorial	11.63MB	02 Mar 01	This program helps you master SQL
English-Polish Tutor	6.54MB	28 Sep 00	English-Polish Talking Tutor
CyberSky	975K	28 Sep 00	Easy-to-use planetarium program
AI-Wheel for Windows	13.56MB	19 Jun 00	Artificial intelligence for task or game environments.
The Presidents	2.19MB	26 Mar 00	Try to identify the Presidents of the USA
MathForKids	727K	18 Mar 00	Teach Kids simple math
Moleculix	2.00MB	22 Feb 00	Manipulate molecules graphically.

Fig. 4.13 *Browsing 'WinSite'*

InfoCard@WinSite

Program Name	Kihlman's SQL tutorial	More Info	Download Now
Description	This program helps you master SQL		
Version/File	1.1.4		SetupSQL.zip
Date	2 Mar 01		
License/Cost	ShareWare		
Runs on	Win NT/2000		
File Size	11.63MB		
Downloads	44		
Author	Dag Kihlman kihlman@algonet.se		1 other program by this author
Company	Dag Kihlman		
User Rating	Waiting for first 5 votes.		Vote Here
User Comments	No Reviews		Submit Review

Fig. 4.14 *Information about files within 'WinSite'*

mation includes the version and filename, license details and the file size, all of which are invaluable to potential users. It is also possible to rate and review the software. The filename ends in **.zip**, indicating that files are compressed, which is likely to reduce the time taken to download the software.

Extensive help information is available, including details about the compression formats used and how to download software. There is a search facility, which has both a simple search interface, where you can type either two keywords describing a file or a filename, and an advanced search interface, where you can search using keywords, authors' names, company names or platforms.

Step 3: An overall impression of the site

An overall impression of this site is that it is likely to be an invaluable source for Windows software, as a range of different materials is available for different platforms. In addition, the site is easy to use and navigate, with invaluable information provided about the files. However, there are some additional considerations. Although details are available for those interested in uploading software, and a contact address is available specifically for 'upload-related comments and questions and inquiries about files', there is no information about virus-checking or other quality-control procedures. This is particularly worrying as it seems that anyone can produce software and make it available via the archive. In addition, there are apparently no mirror sites. However, files are compressed, thereby facilitating the process of downloading software, and the currency of the files would suggest that this site is well maintained. In addition, this site has been available since 1995 – in internet terms, this is a well established service.

CHECKLIST EVALUATING FTP ARCHIVES

✔ what is the purpose of the archive?
✔ what is the coverage of the archive? what software or data are available? in what formats are the software or data? are software or data available for different types of computers and platforms? are upgrades and older versions of data or software available? are trial versions of software available?
✔ is the site easily accessible?
✔ a mirror site available? what is the coverage of the mirror site in

comparison with the original? how frequently is the mirror site updated in comparison with the original?

✔ are files compressed to ensure faster download times? are details available about the software required to decompress files?

✔ what is the reputation of the archive? is it a well-known source for data or software?

✔ are there any quality-control or virus-checking facilities? are they effective?

✔ is the archive well maintained? is there a time delay between software development (or data generation) and its availability via the archive?

✔ is contact information available for a site maintainer?

✔ is information available on file origins, software version numbers, the expiry date for trial versions, and file sizes?

✔ is there a search facility? does the archive allow you to browse or search by filename, platform or type of application?

✔ is the archive easy to use, and are there any user support facilities? is there any help information, a FAQ or README files? Is there any help information for any search facilities? how useful or valuable is the information provided?

✔ how does the archive compare with other similar archives?

✔ what is your overall impression of the quality of the archive?

References

1 Hernández-Borges, A. A., et al., Comparative analysis of pediatric mailing lists on the Internet, *Pediatrics*, 100 (2), 1997, 1–7.

2 Pedersen, R. C., A quantitative approach to the description of internet mailing lists, *Serials Librarian*, 30 (1), 1996, 39–47.

3 Anagnostelis, B. and Cooke, A., Evaluation criteria for different versions of the same database: a comparison of MEDLINE services available via the web. In *Online '97: proceedings of the 21st International Online Information Meeting*, 1997, 165–80.

4 Alexander, J. E. and Tate, M. A., *Web wisdom: how to evaluate and create information quality on the web*, Lawrence Erlbaum, 1999.

5 Using checklists, kitemarks and metadata to indicate 'quality'

Internet resources are generally evaluated using criteria for guidance in the critical appraisal of information. The approach adopted in this book is to describe as many as possible of the available criteria so that you can select those that are relevant to your own needs and the source that you are evaluating. However, additional approaches to indicating resource quality are also either currently in use or under development. This chapter examines checklists and rating tools, kitemarks and other seals of approval, and the potential role of metadata in identifying quality information. Rather than recommending, for example, a particular checklist or seal of approval, the aim of this chapter is to introduce the range of additional instruments and techniques that are available. Throughout the discussion it is notable that many of the examples are drawn from healthcare. While this is in part due to the fact that I work in this field, it is also because quality in relation to the provision of health information via the internet is an area of growing concern, and therefore much work is being undertaken hewre which is not yet being replicated in other fields. If you are interested in using a particular instrument or technique, references and website addresses are included in the text for further information.

Checklists and rating tools

Types of checklists and rating tools

Several different types of checklists and rating tools are available, ranging from a list of evaluative questions requiring a 'yes' or 'no' answer to online tools for assigning a rating score to websites. Below is an overview with some examples of the types of tools that are currently available.

Yes/no checklists

The most commonly available type of checklist is that which simply requires a 'yes' or a 'no' answer indicating the presence or absence of particular features or facilities. One such example is the list of selection criteria produced by the American Library Association (ALA) (**http://www.ala.org/parentspage/greatsites/ criteria.html**). As the sample display in Figure 5.1 shows, this is merely a checklist of points to be used for evaluating websites. The points are similar to those listed throughout the checklists in Chapters 3 and 4 of this book. However, the list is much shorter and there is a lack of explanatory information about how to conduct an evaluation. The function of the ALA checklist is also apparently very similar as it is intended as a guide to the evaluation process – 'every site does not need to meet every one of these criteria to be a great site'. Nevertheless, the ALA stipulates that the more of the criteria that are present in a site, 'the more likely it is to be a worthwhile place to spend time'.

A. Authorship/Sponsorship: Who Put up the Site?

1. The name of the individual or group creating the site should be clearly stated.
2. The creator should give a source for information in the site where necessary.
3. The Web site author or manager should provide a way for users to make comments or ask questions.
4. The Web site author or manager should be responsive to any questions regarding copyright, trademark, or ownership of all material on the site. Sites that knowingly violate copyright statutes or other laws should not be linked, listed, or recommended.

B. Purpose: Every Site Has a Reason for Being There.

1. A site's purpose should be clear and its content should reflect its purpose, be it to entertain, persuade, educate, or sell.
2. Advertising should not overshadow the content.
3. A good site should enrich the user's experience and expand the imagination. Sites promoting social biases (gender, racial, religious, or other types) rather than enlarging the views of the child should not be considered worthwhile sites.

Fig. 5.1 *A simple yes/no checklist for evaluating websites, produced by the American Library Association (ALA)*

Several comparable checklists are available. For example, Kathy Schrock[1] has developed three tools for evaluating educational resources:

- for elementary pupils
  http://school.discovery.com/schrockguide/ evalelem.html
- for middle school pupils
  http://school.discovery.com/schrockguide/ evalmidd.html
- for secondary school pupils
  http://school.discovery.com/schrockguide/ evalhigh.html.

Again, the criteria are listed as questions and students circle either a 'yes' or 'no' answer. For example, elementary students answer the following questions about what they have learnt from a resource:

- Does the title of the page tell you what it is about? YES / NO
- Is there an introduction on the page that tells you what is included? YES / NO
- Are the facts on the page what you were looking for? YES / NO
- Would you have gotten more information from the encyclopedia? YES / NO
- Would the information have been better in the encyclopedia? YES / NO
- Does the author of the page say some things you disagree with? YES / NO
- Does the author of the page include some information you know is wrong? YES / NO
- Do the pictures and photographs on the page help you to learn? YES / NO / NO PICTURES.

Students are also required to summarize their thoughts about the sites that they have been evaluating. For example, the following is included in the tool for elementary students: 'Looking at all of the questions and answers above, write a paragraph telling why this website is helpful (or not helpful) for your project'. The purpose of these checklists is twofold: not only to evaluate websites but also to develop students' skills in thinking critically about internet-based information sources.

Numerical rating tools

Numerical rating tools are very similar to the above, except that scores are allocated according to whether or not different features are present in a site. The *WebSite Investigator* (http://www.motivationmining.com/website_investigator. htm) is also designed for use with school children, both to evaluate websites and to develop students' critical appraisal skills. As displayed in Figure 5.2, the *WebSite Investigator* is an interactive online questionnaire – students complete the questions by selecting one of four faces, and each face corresponds with a score. After completing the questions, the student then answers the two yes/no questions displayed in Figure 5.2: 'Would you like to visit this Web site again sometime?' and 'Do you think other kids your age would like this Web site?' Finally, the option 'Get Web Site Score' is selected.

Scores are allocated as follows:

- 33 or more points = awesome!
- 28–32 points = good
- 23–26 points = average
- 22 and under = needs improvement!

Note: a score of 27 is not included in the results page.

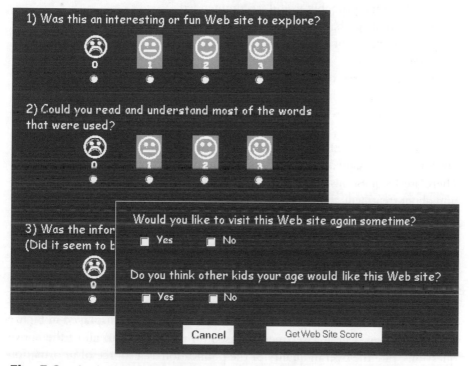

Fig. 5.2 *An interactive questionnaire, the 'WebSite Investigator', for rating websites numerically*

The *WebSite Investigator* lists 12 questions, ranging from 'Was this an interesting or fun Web site to explore?' to 'Was the information on this Web site believable?', thereby covering a range of quality issues.

Other tools focus on specific aspects of evaluation. For example, the *Dermatology Online Journal* (**http://dermatology.cdlib.org/**) contains a guide to quality internet resources. A numerical approach to evaluation has been adopted, using only the following criteria (**http://dermatology.cdlib.org/DOJvol1num1/internet-appraisal.html**):

A   Degree to which material is subject to quality control:
  - 3 points: established and peer-reviewed
  - 2 points: peer-reviewed
  - 1 point: university-based, but not peer-reviewed
  - 0 points: no peer review, no academic affiliation.
B   Relevance or usefulness for the defined target audience:
  - 3 points: must have available
  - 2 points: probably useful, recommended
  - 1 point: perhaps of some use
  - 0 points: probably not useful.
C   Ease of access:
  - 1 point: free to the user
  - 1 point: no obstruction to access
  - 1 point: takes advantage of the medium.

Likewise, the DISCERN tool (**http//www.discern.org.uk/discern_instrument.htm**) has been designed for evaluating patient information on treatment choices. There are 16 questions relating to the reliability and the quality of the information about treatment choices – issues relating to the presentation of information and its accessibility are not covered.

As displayed in Figure 5.3, each question in the *DISCERN* tool is rated on a scale from 1 to 5, indicating whether or not the user answers 'yes', 'no' or 'partially' in response to the question. There are hints on answering each question, and additional information is displayed if you select 'Rating this question'. *DISCERN* is not an interactive tool at present, and users do not total their scores for a final analysis. However, the last question (displayed in Figure 5.3) requires an overall assessment: 'Based on the answers to all of the above questions, rate the overall quality of the publication as a source of information about treatment choices'. Users select from a scale of 1 to 5, which relates to:

- serious or extensive shortcomings
- potentially important but not serious shortcomings
- minimal shortcomings.

SECTION 1. Is the publication reliable?

1. Are the aims clear?

Rating this question

No 1	2	Partially 3	4	Yes 5

HINT   Look for a clear indication at the beginning of the publication of:

- what it is
- what it is
- who migh

If the answer to (

SECTION 3. Overall Rating of the Publication

16. Based on the answers to all of the above questions, rate the overall quality of the publication as a source of information about treatment choices

Rating this question

Low		Moderate		High
Serious or extensive shortcomings		Potentially important but not serious shortcomings		Minimal shortcomings
1	2	3	4	5

Fig. 5.3   *Part of the DISCERN instrument for rating patient information on treatment choices*

Task (The task is the end result of student efforts... not the steps involved in getting there.)

	0 points	3 points	6 points
Cognitive level of the task	Task requires simply comprehending web pages and answering questions.	Task requires analysis of information and/or putting together information from several sources.	Task requires synthesis of multiple sources of information, and/or taking a position, and/or going beyond the data given and making a generalization or creative product.
	0 points	1 point	2 points
Technical sophistication of task	Task requires simple verbal or written response.	Task requires use of word processing or simple presentation software.	Task requires use of multimedia software, video, or conferencing.

Fig. 5.4   *Numerical rating tool with weighted scores*

Certain quality issues will be of increased importance to different users, and for this reason some numerical rating tools weight different criteria according to their perceived importance. For example, 'A draft rubric for evaluating WebQuests' (http://edweb.sdsu.edu/webquest/webquestrubric.html) is a tool for assessing various aspects of web-based teaching resources. As displayed in Figure 5.4, the 'cognitive level of the task' and the 'technical sophistication of the task' are both evaluated. However, while technical aspects are allocated either 0, 1, or 2 points, cognitive aspects are allocated either 0, 3 or 6 points – this is because greater importance is attributed to issues such as the need for synthesis of information, as opposed to the software used for performing the task.

Pros and cons of checklists and rating tools

There are obvious advantages to using checklists and rating tools in resource evaluation. Simply in terms of the amount of effort for the evaluator, users need only answer a limited number of questions to assess the quality of a resource. In addition, it is easy to compare the results for different sites to decide which is the 'better' resource based upon the scores from a numerical rating tool. However, studies suggest that checklists and other similar tools are of questionable usefulness in relation to internet resources because of the lack of structure associated with the available information. In addition, the use of checklists and rating tools is controversial, particularly in terms of whether they evaluate what they claim to evaluate, and whether their use results in an assessment of quality. The discussion below is an overview of some of the main issues and arguments.

Using checklists in resource evaluation

There have been some studies assessing the usefulness of checklists in evaluating information. One checklist not mentioned earlier was published in the *Journal of the American Medical Association (JAMA)*.[2] This checklist was produced as a set of basic standards for the provision of internet-based health and medical information, and has become known as the '*JAMA benchmarks*'. These are:

- authorship: authors, contributors, their affiliations, and relevant credentials should be provided
- attribution: references and sources for all content should be listed clearly, and all relevant copyright information noted
- disclosure: website 'ownership' should be prominently and fully disclosed, as should any sponsorship, advertising, underwriting, commercial funding arrangements or support, or potential conflicts of interest
- currency: dates when content was posted and updated should be indicated.

Hersh, Gorman and Sacherek[3] used the *JAMA* benchmarks to investigate the quality of information available via the web for answering clinical questions.

Information was retrieved using a metasearch tool and 629 pages relating to 50 clinical questions were evaluated using the benchmarks. The findings included the following:

- only one quality measure (site affiliation) was present in the majority of pages
- 69% of pages did not indicate an author
- over 80% of pages gave no authorship credentials
- disclosure of conflicts of interest was present in only 11.1% of pages
- less than 18% of pages gave the date they were posted or updated.

This therefore highlights not only the questionable quality of information available via the internet, but also the inapplicability of a checklist approach to evaluating information – if these benchmarks were used as a method for evaluating resources, no materials would pass the test.

Pandolfini, Impicciatore and Bonati[4] describe three further checklists:

- a technical checklist, which includes the *JAMA* benchmarks, e.g. availability of date, disclosure of potential conflicts of interest
- a completeness checklist to assess whether all information is included on a topic
- a quality of information checklist to compare web-based information with published guidelines.

The checklists were tested by evaluating web-based information on cough management in children. The findings included the following:

- only a few documents displayed a majority of the criteria from the technical checklist
- 3 out of 15 documents fulfilled the completeness criteria
- 10 out of 15 documents provided more incorrect than correct information.

Again, the results highlight not only the questionable quality of information available via the internet, but also the inapplicability of a checklist approach to evaluation. In particular: 'When the three web documents that scored highest in technical aspect were checked for completeness and quality, their content resulted as being generally incomplete and inaccurate'. The authors therefore conclude that there is no relationship between the technical aspects of a site, the completeness of its content and the quality of the information.

These results highlight some of the difficulties of using a checklist approach to evaluation. Silberg, Lundberg and Musaccio[2] suggest that 'in the case of traditional print publishing . . . the rules of engagement have been worked out over five centuries', whereas this is not the situation in a networked environment. Pandolfini, Impicciatore and Bonati[4] argue that the use of checklists is 'difficult because of the lack of structure of the internet'. There are no rules or standards for disseminating information via the internet, and therefore a checklist approach to evaluation is inappropriate because the basic standards are simply not there and therefore cannot be measured. In addition, the results from the Pandolfini study indicate that evaluation using such an approach does not necessarily equate with an assessment of information quality.

Questionable validity of the tools

One of the problems associated with checklists and rating tools is the lack of information about how they have been developed. In particular, there is a general lack of information about which criteria have been used and why, and in the case of numerical rating tools there is a lack of detail about how the scores have been allocated and their perceived importance. It would seem that many of the checklists are simply a list of all possible criteria the authors think are important, and that numerical scores, where applicable, are allocated on an arbitrary basis, with little or no consideration of what the total score will mean in terms of quality.

Jadad and Gagliardi[5] examined 47 instruments used to rate websites providing health information on the internet to establish the degree of validation of the instruments. Of these, 14 provided a description of the criteria used to provide the ratings, and five provided instructions for their use. There was no detail for any of the instruments about their testing and validation, and none gave any indication of whether different people using the tool would provide the same rating for a site. The authors therefore conclude:

> Many incompletely developed instruments to evaluate health information exist on the internet. It is unclear . . . whether they should exist in the first place, whether they measure what they claim to measure, or whether they lead to more harm than good.[5]

However, there is one notable exception – the *DISCERN* tool, which was developed through a process of research and testing.[6] An expert panel generated a list of evaluation criteria by examining patient-based information leaflets on treatment choices. A draft instrument was developed from this analysis, and was subsequently tested on a random sample of new materials. The instrument was then redrafted and tested by both information providers and consumers to assess whether or not different people using the tool would make the same or similar assessments about sources of information. The authors felt:

> The methodology used to develop DISCERN . . . enabled us to identify an agreed set of standards for the content of written information on consumer choices which can be consistently understood and applied by a wide range of users.[6]

In addition, testing meant that:

> DISCERN is a reliable and valid instrument for judging the quality of written consumer health information. While some subjectivity is required for rating certain criteria, the findings demonstrate that the instrument can be applied by experienced users and providers of health information to discriminate between publications of high and low quality.[6]

DISCERN has subsequently been validated using similar techniques for use with treatment information available via the internet. Therefore it would seem that existing tools for numerically rating sites should be used with caution. However, if you are considering developing your own numerical rating tool, it is worth consulting the research methods used in the development of DISCERN for guidance on how to validate such a tool.

An objective assessment of quality?

One of the main arguments for using a checklist or rating tool in evaluation is that ultimately it results in an objective assessment of quality, and it is possible to compare the scores for different sites and decide which is the 'best' to use. For example, using the DISCERN tool described above, it should be possible to evaluate a range of web pages on treatment options in order to consider which is the best available. However, it is questionable whether this is the case with all available tools.

As was mentioned in Chapter 1, any assessment of quality is subjective – one person's quality site is another's dross, and the following factors affect any assessment of quality:

- the nature of the source being evaluated
- the needs of the user
- the context of the information being sought.

In the case of the *DISCERN* tool, the boundaries for these factors are relatively narrowly defined. *DISCERN* is designed for use with information on treatment options; it is designed for use by patients, their friends or their relatives; and it is designed for use when someone has been diagnosed with an illness. In the case of the evaluation of internet-based information sources generally, it becomes much more difficult to define these boundaries – this book, for example, is concerned with the evaluation of any information source which can be accessed via the internet, it is designed for use by any user, and for use in any context where the internet is used to find information. This therefore begins to illustrate some of the complications associated with attempting to develop an 'objective' tool for assessing information quality. Resource evaluation is multidimensional, and it is therefore questionable whether generic tools for rating information result in an objective assessment of quality. Likewise, it is questionable whether rating tools can be used to evaluate a range of resources, or whether the results are indeed comparable.

Kitemarks and seals of approval

Kitemarks and seals of approval, usually taking the form of a badge or logo displayed on internet resources, are designed to indicate third-party approval of information based on a particular set of standards. The standards used depend upon the purpose of the service approving the information. For example, the *Quality Search Engine* or *QSE* (http://www.a1source.com/) awards two badges to indicate that sites are 'QSE Certified Child Safe'. Other examples include the *CIN Seal of Approval* badge (http://www.gocin.com/cin/Seal_Of_Approval.cfm), which is used to indicate sites containing 'no pornography or any type of "questionable" content'. The *Internet Seal of Approval* (http://www.isamember.com/) is 'a membership of businesses who have banded together under one Seal with a mission to give comfort and security to web consumers'. Their 'Internet Seal of Approval Logo' indicates that an organization 'has met rigorous standards of quality, honesty, and customer service, and work[s] hard to establish high standards of integrity for Internet Commerce'.

Of interest here are those kitemarks or seals of approval that have been developed to indicate resource quality. This is an area that has received particular attention in relation to the provision of health and medical information via the internet. For example, the *Health on the Net (HoN) Foundation* (http://www.hon.ch/) was launched in 1996, offering amongst its other services, a gateway to quality health and medical information. In July 1996, *HoN* developed a code of conduct, the *HONcode*, which was subsequently revised in April 1997 (http://www.hon.ch/HONcode/Conduct.html). The *HONcode* is a set of eight ethical principles for the provision of health information relating to authority, complementarity, confidentiality, justifiability, transparency of authorship, transparency of sponsorship, honesty in advertising, and editorial policy. For example, the statement for authority is:

> Any medical or health advice provided and hosted on this site will only be given by medically trained and qualified professionals unless a clear statement is made that a piece of advice offered is from a non-medically qualified individual or organisation.

The code is a self-regulatory scheme. Authors decide whether or not they wish to conform to the principles, and those who do can apply for certification, thereby committing 'strictly to observe all the HONcode principles'. They can then display the HoN logo on their site. However, HoN stipulates: 'It does not seek to rate the medical accuracy, validity or appropriateness of the information itself.' On the contrary: 'Users of the medical internet must themselves develop the knowledge and discernment necessary to avoid dubious Web sites.'

Hi-Ethics (**http://www.hiethics.org/**) and *TRUSTe* (**http://www.truste.org/**) announced in December 2000 the launch of their 'E-Health Seal'. This seal will signify that websites conform to 14 ethical principles relating to privacy, confidentiality, quality of information, advertising and commercial relationships, consumer relations, and best practices for professionals on the internet. The intention is that the 'E-Health Seal will certify that a Web site is in compliance with the 14 *Hi-Ethics* principles', offering 'consumer protection among health oriented Web sites'. The proposed seal will be a 'branded trustmark' that links directly to the statement of practices, and it will be 'click to verify' – consumers will be able to verify that a site is a bona fide participant by clicking on the seal.

MedCERTAIN (**http://www.medcertain.org/**) is a project currently funded by the European Union under its 'Action Plan on promoting safer use of the Internet'. Partly through the use of metadata (discussed below), but also through the use of a trustmark logo (displayed in Figure 5.5), *MedCERTAIN* aims to 'establish a fully functional self- and third-party rating system enabling patients and consumers to filter harmful health information and to positively identify and select high quality information'. *MedCERTAIN* plans to establish a 'Collaboration for Critical Appraisal of Internet Health Information', enabling the rating of health information in a decentralized way:

Fig. 5.5 *The proposed 'MedCERTAIN' trustmark*

In our scenario, doctors, medical societies and associations will critically appraise Internet information and act as decentralised 'label services' to rate the value and trustworthiness of information by putting electronic 'tags' on it.[7]

Pros and cons of kitemarks and seals of approval

In a recent editorial in the journal *He@lth Information on the Internet*, Sue Childs comments:

> Assessing sites against selection and quality criteria and then placing links to these sites on your site is relatively unproblematical. You choose material that is relevant and suitable for your audience. Production of ethical codes that sites can follow voluntarily and that consumers can use to assess sites is also relatively straightforward. However, the use of certification raises a number of issues.[8]

In particular, Childs highlights problems relating to who would regulate any sort of kitemarking. For example, within the health sphere, this could be an international organization, such as the World Health Organization, or a national body, such as the UK Department of Health. However, different countries have different approaches to healthcare – therefore which country would decide on which information is appropriate for kitemarking? Other issues raised relate to the evaluation criteria used and what these might be; who would conduct the evaluations and what their qualifications might be; how kitemarking would be 'policed'; and awareness of any kitemarking schemes by internet users. Tony Delamothe[9] highlights the potential legal complications associated with kitemarking, including whether consumers harmed by their reliance on kitemarked information would have grounds to sue the kite-marking organization, and whether there would be legal implications for resources that did not receive a kitemark.

Kitemarking information, and the use of logos, badges or seals of approval, remains a controversial topic at present. The internet, since its earliest begin-nings, has always been viewed as an anarchic environment where anyone can disseminate almost whatever they like. It is therefore difficult to envisage that widespread 'policing' of any sort is likely to become commonplace in the fore-seeable future. In addition, the vast amount of information poses practical difficulties, as do the potential legal implications. However, it is important to be aware of the existence of such logos, badges or seals of approval, and to understand what they mean.

A word of warning

As mentioned in Chapter 2, during the mid-1990s there was a trend towards pro-viding more effective access to internet materials through the provision of various forms of badges and awards. Many of these services were developed and most have now disappeared, although it is still often possible to see a collection of logos or badges on a site. One such example is the *Philosophy around the Web* guide (http://users.ox.ac.uk/%7Eworc0337/phil_index.html), which includes a link to some of the awards it has received (http://users.ox.ac.uk/%7Eworc0337/reviews.html). However, when you click on any of the eight badges, you are pre-sented with one of the following messages: 'Cannot find server', 'The page cannot be found' or 'The page cannot be displayed'. Two of the badges lead to general search tools – at one time, these tools had included a 'rating' element, but the facility is no longer available. One badge reads 'A1 Quality Directory Award for Excellence', and selecting the button leads to the *Quality Search Engine* men-tioned above. Rather than a guide to quality materials, this site now rates material according to whether it is 'child safe'.

As also discussed in Chapter 2, many of these rating services were of questionable value and usefulness, particularly in terms of finding quality information. Authors within the library profession compared a range of different services in order to consider their effectiveness in guiding users towards high quality materials.[10-13] As further discussed in Chapter 2, the general conclusion was that such services offered little indication of site quality. In particular, the use of badges varied 'so widely in their implementation and interpretation' that it was 'questionable' whether they could 'succeed in guiding the user to the selection of high quality resources.'[13]

With the demise of such services, the use of their badges as an indicator of quality has become even less assured. If you see such a collection of badges, do not assume they offer any indication of resource quality, because the service that rated them may no longer be available – or indeed, if the service still exists, it may be worth investigating how quality has been assessed.

Metadata

Metadata is information about information. It can be compared to the contents of bibliographical records, which are used by libraries throughout the world to describe books in library catalogues or journal articles in databases. The information is written into the 'head' element of the HTML of web pages, which means that the content is not displayed automatically by the web browser to the user. As mentioned in Chapter 2, authors can include descriptive information and keywords for their pages to aid both resource discovery and resource description – keywords included in a document's metadata can be used by search engines for more effective retrieval, and metadata descriptions can be used in search engine results to describe the contents of a site.

The use and development of metadata has been an area of extensive research during recent years. Although general consideration of the various initiatives is outside the scope of this book, there has been some discussion surrounding the potential for using metadata to indicate the quality of information. This is considered below. Readers interested in metadata generally should consult the World Wide Web Consortium (W3C) website (http://www.w3c.org/) or the UK Office for Library Networking (UKOLN) website (http://www.ukoln.ac.uk/).

PICS (Platform for Internet Content Selection)

The Platform for Internet Content Selection (PICS) was originally developed in response to the controversial US Communications Decency Act 1996. Its most common use is for the identification of material with adult content. The resource owner or labeller indicates, for example, the level of violence or nudity on a site according to a scale specified by an external rating service, and software is used to include or exclude material according to the ratings. The rating scheme used and the score allocated are included within the metadata of the site's HTML code – PICS is the platform used rather than a rating scale.

There are a number of services that have developed schemes for rating internet content using the PICS platform. For example, *SafeSurf* (**http://www.safesurf. com/**) provides a scheme for rating internet materials according to: age range; profanity; heterosexual themes; homosexual themes; nudity; violence; sex violence and profanity; intolerance of another person's racial, religious or gender background; glorifying drug use; and other adult themes. The ratings for age range are:

- 'all ages'; value = 1
- 'older children'; value = 2
- 'younger teens'; value = 3
- 'older teens'; value = 4
- 'adult supervision recommended'; value = 5
- 'adults'; value = 6
- 'limited to adults'; value = 7
- 'adults only'; value = 8
- 'explicitly for adults'; value = 9.

Site authors complete a questionnaire by indicating the age range, level of violence, etc. of their site. They can then include the relevant values within the site's metadata. For example, the metadata for the *SafeSurf* homepage contains the following:

```
<META HTTP-EQUIV="PICS-Label" CONTENT='(PICS-1.1
"http://www.classify.org/safesurf/" l gen t for
"http://www.safesurf.com/" r (SS~~000 1))'>
```

This indicates that the site has been rated using the *SafeSurf* scheme (hence the address of the rating system and the address of the rating service). 'SS~~000' denotes the age-range category, and the age-range value that has been assigned is '1', therefore indicating that this site is suitable for all ages.

The *Internet Content Rating Association* (**http://www.icra.org/**), previously the *Recreational Software Advisory Council*, has devised a similar scheme and also uses an online questionnaire to enable authors to rate their materials.

There are questions relating to nudity and sexual material, violence, language, drug and alcohol abuse, and gambling. Once the questionnaire has been completed, a rating is provided and authors are able to label their sites. There are two elements to an ICRA label – the PICS metadata that contains the information about the site, and a logo which authors can select to display on their site to indicate that it has been rated.

PICS and quality indicators

As mentioned above, PICS is the platform that allows materials to be rated, rather than a rating scheme in itself. It therefore follows that the technology can be used to rate material according to any criteria, and there have been some proposals for using PICS to indicate the quality of internet sites. The Centre for Information Quality Management (CIQM) was originally established by the Library Association and the UK Online User Group (UKOLUG) to act as a clearinghouse for database quality issues. It is well known within the information profession for its role in evaluating the quality of electronic databases, and in particular for its work on developing labels designed to provide quality indicators for databases. CIQM has considered the use of PICS to provide similar quality labels for internet-based resources.[14]

As with the proposed CIQM database labels, Armstrong recommends that the PICS labels could contain a similar mix of factual information (e.g. author, length, coverage) as well as qualitative information (e.g. timeliness, accuracy). In particular, he draws on one set of criteria for assessing validity[15] and proposes their translation into rating scales for use within PICS labels. The original criteria are:

- How valid is the content of the information?
- Does the information appear to be well researched?
- What data sources have been used?
- Do the resources fulfil the stated purpose?
- Has the format been derived from another format?
- Does the information claim to be unbiased (when in fact it is biased)?
- Is the information what it appears to be?
- Why is the information there? What was the motivation of the information provider when they made the information available? Do they have an ulterior motive?
- Does the resource point to other sources which could be contacted for confirmation?
- Is the content of the resource verifiable – can you cross-check information?

The proposed scales for use within the PICS labels are:[14]

- Few references ↔ many references
- Data sources are poor ↔ very good
- Bibliography/no bibliography
- Scope statement/no scope statement
- Scope statement supported ↔ not supported by content
- Copy of data available elsewhere; scale: on paper/on CD-ROM/electronically/not a copy
- Information has a geographical/political/other bias
- Site is provided by personal/business/publisher/academic/research institution/other
- Information is incomplete/adequate/complete
- Vanity publishing ↔ refereed article
- Author e-mail contact/postal contact/no contact information.

The proposal is that software would filter out, for example, sites that did not contain an adequate number of references.

MedCERTAIN Project

Unfortunately, the work referred to above by CIQM has not been developed into a tool for evaluating websites. However, one interesting initiative is the *MedCERTAIN* Project discussed in relation to kitemarking. The aims of this project are not only to develop a 'trustmark', but also to use the PICS technology as a platform for rating sites and to devise a metadata rating vocabulary. A workshop was held in September 2000 with the following aims:

- to establish a basic set of reliable consensus-quality criteria for health-related websites, which can be used for assessment by a third party, including the construction of a rating vocabulary (a computer-readable representation of these rating categories and their scales) to be used as evaluative metadata and as standardized, computer-readable evaluative descriptions of health information
- to establish a set of descriptive metadata categories, which will allow health websites to disclose essential information required in the Washington Code of eHealth Ethics in a standardized, computer-readable way
- to discuss a data exchange structure which assures interoperability of rating services.

171

The resulting report provides details about the metadata rating vocabulary for use within PICS labels.[16] Different metadata elements are listed, with an indication of their relevance to the project, sample questions to be asked by an information provider or assessor, and the values to be included in the PICS labels. For example, for the label 'sitespecific_content_currency', assessors would need to answer the question 'Are the dates which indicate when content was created, issued, last reviewed and modified/reviewed, provided as described by the information provider?'. The values to be included in the site metadata would be either 'Dates provided as described by information provider' or 'Dates not provided as described by information provider'. For the label 'sitespecific_content_purpose', assessors answer the question 'What is the aim/purpose of the site?', using one of the following values:

- education information, etc. (balanced, unbiased, evidence-based information), e.g. designed to enable evidence-based choice
- promotional or one-sided information (product information, opinion-based/experience-based information, biased) designed to influence public opinion in one specific direction
- both educational and promotional on the site (requires clear separation)
- support groups (anecdotal information).

Other questions might contain a 'yes' or 'no' value, and others free text descriptions. It is anticipated that users will be able to search for information conforming to particular standards, as well as to view the ratings for a site.

Pros and cons of using metadata to indicate quality

The potential advantages of using metadata to label the quality of internet resources cannot be ignored. We automatically judge books, films and other media using the information found on the dust jacket, but a recurrent problem when we attempt to evaluate any internet resource is the lack of such contextual clues. Eysenbach and Diepgen,[17] for example, highlight the lack of 'clear "markers" . . . to allow patients to easily recognise a document as intended for professionals rather than for patients', and note the ease with which it is possible to read a web page 'without having seen context pages or the "cover" page containing disclaimers'. Therefore the proposed use of metadata to provide this type of contextual evidence could be of obvious benefit.

Furthermore, the use of metadata has an additional advantage over evaluative information provided by the gateways and virtual libraries described in Chapter 2 – users need not seek out an evaluation as well as accessing a resource, because the evaluative information is delivered as part of the same package. As Armstrong argues:

> It is evident that, for internet-based resources at least, there exists the basis of a more direct means of confirming to resource users that they have found an information source that reaches up to an acceptable standard.[14]

Indeed, using the approach proposed by *MedCERTAIN*, a search tool would only retrieve sites if they met specified criteria. To view additional evaluative information, all the user would need to do would be to view the HTML source code (although it is likely they would also need to consult the original rating service to understand how the ratings have been assigned).

However, there are also problems with the use of metadata to indicate resource quality. These relate not only to low levels of use of metadata by site authors, but also to many of the problems already highlighted in relation to the numerical rating of information and the use of kitemarks – these issues are discussed below.

Current use of metadata?

There is a lack of research relating to current levels of use of metadata, although the findings of a study undertaken in 1998 raise some interesting issues associated with its use.[18] The authors examined 1457 public websites and found that 70% contained metadata, with an average of three meta-tags per page. A diverse range of metadata elements were in use, the most common being:

- generator tag – 23%
- keywords tag – 17%
- content-type tag – 16%
- description tag – 15%
- author tag – 6%.

All other tags were present in 3% or less of pages. The authors divide metadata elements into two categories – those that are explicitly provided by the author, and those that are automatically included by the software used to generate web pages. The generator and content-type elements, for example, are automatically supplied when a *Microsoft Word* document is saved in HTML or when material is created using *Netscape Composer*. The authors therefore question the usefulness of this metadata, particularly for document discovery and retrieval.

As part of the study, the authors also examined the use of the keywords tag and whether metadata was used to describe accurately the content of resources – while keywords were usually pertinent in some way to the site's content, they were often 'extremely broad'. The authors therefore suggest that their current use is to cast as wide a net as possible in terms of the site's perceived relevancy, rather than to assist in discovery. They also found that in several cases keywords were repeated several times – this has the potential to increase relevance ranking in search results, although many search engines are able to detect this ploy. However, for the most part, the authors suggest that the use of keywords was not misleading or manipulative.

Of the 1457 public websites examined in the study, only 20 contained the PICS-label element. Of these, 15 referred to the *Recreational Software Advisory Council* and three referred to *SafeSurf*. While only three sites warned against content that might not be suitable for all audiences, the authors found a further 34 public sites that contained sexually explicit content but had not registered with a rating service. They therefore argue that 'sites are using the PICS-label element to indicate that their sites are suitable for all audiences, rather than to warn against potentially inappropriate content'. They also suggest that, while only 1% of sites used the PICS-label element, 'effective use of internet rating services is not possible' because filters permit access to materials containing a rating but the vast majority of sites contained no rating, irrespective of their usefulness.

Further issues

Many of the same questions apply here that have already been raised in relation to the use of numerical tools to rate sites and the use of kitemarking, as the proposals for the use of metadata draw on both of these techniques. A central question relates to the criteria to be used for evaluation. The length of this book alone serves to indicate the complexities involved in attempting to make any qualitative judgement. However, a vast range of different people with different needs and expectations can access internet sites – the criteria used would need to accommodate this wide range of needs and expectations. It would be a daunting task to attempt to convert all the criteria listed here into rating scales that could be used to assign quality values to internet resources. Decisions would need to be made regarding the important and the redundant criteria. If site ratings are to be provided, this again raises questions about whether a rating tool will evaluate what it claims to evaluate, and whether different people using the tool will reach the same conclusions about a resource. Any such tool would need to be tested and validated to ensure its effectiveness.

Additional issues relate to who will undertake the evaluations, and their qualifications and experience. For example, Eysenbach and Diepgen[17] believe that, for the *MedCERTAIN* Project, 'if thousands of doctors continuously took part in a global rating project, we might be able to keep pace with the dynamics of the internet'. While the benefits of this are obvious, it is difficult to envisage how thousands of doctors could be persuaded to participate in a collaborative effort to evaluate materials. It is also difficult to envisage how indeed they might find the time in an already busy schedule to undertake the evaluations. Further issues relate to who would check the raters to assess that they are who they say they are. Related issues include policing any such system and the potential legal implications for those relying on the ratings for a site, or indeed the legal standing of authors whose sites have not been rated.

Conclusions?

> What is needed . . . is a common standard based on the intellectual equivalent of carob beans, with an Honourable Company of . . . Knowledgesmiths to run the assay procedure in an independent and disinterested way so that people can not only distinguish gold from a base metal but also know whether they are reading 24 carat or 18 carat knowledge.[19]

It cannot be denied that, if indeed this were possible, it would be a wonderful thing! However, the above discussion hopefully illustrates that techniques involving the use of rating tools, logos to indicate quality, and metadata to label resources, all have their advantages and disadvantages. The over-riding advantage of rating tools is that they offer a seemingly straightforward method for evaluation; the over-riding advantage of kitemarks, seals of approval and metadata is that internet users can spot high-quality materials both easily and quickly. However, there are also problems associated with the use of all of these approaches. As a discerning internet user, it is important to be aware of the available techniques, but more importantly to be aware of their limitations.

References

1   Schrock, K., *Critical evaluation of a web site: elementary school level*, 1996 [online], available at
    school.discovery.com/schrockguide/evalelem.html
    [2001, March 29].

2   Silberg, W. M., Lundberg, G. D. and Musacchio, R. A., Assessing, controlling and assuring the quality of medical information on the internet: caveant lector et viewor – let the reader and viewer beware, *JAMA*, **277** (15), 1997, 1244–5.

3   Hersh, W. R., Gorman, P. N. and Sacherek, L. S., Applicability and quality of information for answering clinical questions on the web, *JAMA*, **280** (15), 1998, 1307–8.

4   Pandolfini, C., Impicciatore, P. and Bonati, M., Parents on the web: risks for quality management of cough in children, *Pediatrics*, **105** (1), 2000, e1.

5   Jadad, A. R. and Gagliardi, A., Rating health information on the internet: navigating to knowledge or to Babel?, *JAMA*, **279** (8), 1998, 611–14.

6   Charnock, D., et al., DISCERN: an instrument for judging the quality of written consumer health information on treatment choices, *Journal of Epidemiology and Community Health*, **53** (2), 1999, 105–11.

7   Eysenbach, G., *Collaboration for critical appraisal of medical information on the Internet*, 1998 [online], available at
http://www.dermis.net/medpics/
[2001, March 3].

8   Childs, S., Badging health sites as an indicator of quality, *He@lth Information on the Internet*, February, 2001, 1–2.

9   Delamothe, T., Quality of websites: kitemarking the west wind, *BMJ*, **321** (7265), 2000, 843–4.

10 Rettig, J., Beyond 'cool': analog models for reviewing digital resources, *Online*, (September), 1996 [online], available at
http://www.onlineinc.com/onlinemag/SeptOL/rettig9.html
[2001, March 8].

11 Cooke, A., McNab, A. and Anagnostelis, B., The good, the bad and the ugly: internet review sites. In Raitt, D. I. and Jeapes, B. (eds.), *Proceedings of the 20th International Online Information Meeting*, Oxford, Learned Information, **20**, 1996, 33–40.

12 Collins, B. R., Beyond cruising: reviewing, *Library Journal*, **121** (3), 1996, 124.

13 McNab, A., Anagnostelis, B. and Cooke, A., Never mind the quality, check the badge-width, *Ariadne*, **9**, 1997, 6-7 [online], available at
http://www.ariadne.ac.uk/issue9/quality-ratings/
[2001, March 8].

14 Armstrong, C. J., Metadata, PICS and quality, *Online and CD-ROM Review*, **21** (4), 1997, 217–22.

15 Day, M. et al., *Selection criteria for quality controlled information gateways: report for DESIRE*, 1997 [online], available at

http://www.ukoln.ac.uk/metadata/DESIRE/quality/
[2001, March 8].

16 Eysenbach, G., *1st Progress Report, MedCERTAIN Project*, 2001 [online], available at
http://www.medcertain.org/metadata/progress-report1-7-mcdpics.pdf
[2001, March 3].

17 Eysenbach, G. and Diepgen, T. L., Towards quality management of medical information on the internet: evaluation, labelling and filtering of information, *BMJ*, 317 (7171), 1998, 1496–500.

18 O'Neill, E. T., Lavoie, B. F. and McClain, P. D., *Web characterization project: an analysis of metadata usage on the web*, 1998 [online], available at
http://www.oclc.org/oclc/research/publications/review98/oneill_etal/metadata.html
[2001, March 1].

19 Muir Gray, J. A., Hallmarks for quality of information, *BMJ*, 317 (7171), 1998, 1500.

Compilation of evaluation checklists

This compilation draws together all of the checklists from Chapters 2, 3 and 4 of the book. The checklists are designed to provide a reminder of what to look for when attempting to evaluate an aspect of quality or a particular type of source.

The checklists are:

1 What to look for in a search tool
2 Identifying the purpose of a source
3 Assessing coverage
4 Assessing authority and reputation
5 Assessing accuracy
6 Assessing the currency and maintenance of a source
7 Considering the accessibility of a source
8 Evaluating the presentation and arrangement of information
9 Assessing how easy a source is to use
10 Making a comparison with other sources
11 Assessing the overall quality of a source
12 Evaluating organizational sites, personal home pages and other websites
13 Evaluating mailing lists, newsgroups and other forms of communication via the internet
14 Evaluating full-text documents
15 Evaluating databases
16 Evaluating electronic journals and magazines
17 Evaluating sources of news information

CHECKLIST 1 WHAT TO LOOK FOR IN A SEARCH TOOL

If you are interested in identifying a search tool to find high-quality information, the main questions to consider are:

✔ what subject areas does the search tool cover?
✔ who are the intended users of the tool?
✔ are resources selected and evaluated prior to their inclusion in the database?
✔ are resources awarded a rating according to their perceived quality?
✔ are explicit evaluation criteria available which explain how resources are evaluated and on what basis?
✔ are descriptions provided about each resource, and do the resource descriptions provide sufficient information to enable you to assess their relevance?
✔ are the resource descriptions evaluative? i.e. do they indicate the likely value and usefulness of materials?
✔ how frequently are materials revisited to ensure their continuing value and usefulness?
✔ what is the knowledge and expertise of those involved in selecting, evaluating and describing materials?
✔ what types of materials does the search tool cover? does it only include information available via the web, or are other materials also covered?

It is also worth considering:

✔ what search options are available?
✔ are there facilities to narrow and broaden searches?
✔ is it possible to browse by subject categories, and are the subject headings or categories meaningful?
✔ are there any additional options available for using the tool to find information?
✔ are the different options effective, easy to use and useful?
✔ is any help information available which provides guidelines on using the tool? is the help information clear and understandable? is it useful?

CHECKLIST 2 IDENTIFYING THE PURPOSE OF A SOURCE

✔ is there a statement of the intended purpose of the source?
✔ is there a statement of the aims, objectives and intended coverage?
✔ what are the aims and objectives of the source?
✔ what is the intended coverage, and are there any limitations to it?
✔ who are the intended audience?

CHECKLIST 3 ASSESSING COVERAGE

✔ what subject areas and types of materials are covered by the source?
✔ what range of different subjects is covered?
✔ are the subject areas covered comprehensively?
✔ what are the limitations in terms of coverage?
✔ what is the retrospective coverage of the source?
✔ what level of detail is provided, and is the level of detail sufficient for the audience? is the information pitched at an appropriate level?
✔ are there any links to further sources of information? is any descriptive information available for any links? are the links selected, and if so on what basis? are the links valuable and useful?
✔ is the site an original or a mirror site? does the mirror site cover the same materials as the original? what are the advantages and disadvantages of accessing the mirror versus the original site?

CHECKLIST 4 ASSESSING AUTHORITY AND REPUTATION

✔ what is the reputation and experience of the author or institution responsible for the information? is the source written by a subject expert or produced by an institution with recognized knowledge and expertise in the field? are details available of the author's credentials?
✔ what is the reputation and experience of any other organizations involved in the production of the information, such as publishers, sponsors or funding agencies?
✔ what is the reputation of the source? is the source well known?
✔ what is the address of the site? does the address indicate an authoritative institution?
✔ are there any reviews available discussing the source? do they indicate that the site is reputable and authoritative? are the reviews themselves authoritative?

✔ is there a counter on the site? does the number of visits to the site suggest that it is popular?

CHECKLIST 5 ASSESSING ACCURACY

✔ is the information contained in the source factually accurate?
✔ does the information have a research basis? what is the quality of the research?
✔ are there any references to published sources of information?
✔ has the information been through any quality-control processes, such as refereeing or editing?
✔ is the information likely to be biased by any individuals or organizations involved in its production? what is the motivation of those involved in the production of the source?
✔ is the information professionally produced? are there any typographical, spelling or grammatical errors? is there a facility to send corrections to inaccurate information?

CHECKLIST 6 ASSESSING THE CURRENCY AND MAINTENANCE OF A SOURCE

✔ is there an explicit date for the information? when was the source originally produced, either in printed form or on the internet?
✔ is the information up-to-date? when was the information last updated? when will the information next be updated? how frequently is the information updated?
✔ is there a statement of policy regarding the frequency of updating and the updating process?
✔ is the site generally well maintained? are any links to external sources live?
✔ is there a maintenance policy?
✔ is there an individual or group responsible for maintenance? do they maintain the site voluntarily? what is their knowledge and expertise?
✔ are contact details available for a site maintainer?
✔ does the source need to be monitored or reassessed at a later date to ensure continued currency and maintenance?

CHECKLIST 7 CONSIDERING THE ACCESSIBILITY OF A SOURCE

✔ is the source fast to access? does the location affect the speed of access? have thumbnail images been used to improve access speeds? is there a local mirror site?

✔ is it possible to view a text-only version of the information? is the meaning of the information lost by not viewing graphics? is there a meaningful description of any images in the ALT-TEXT tag of the HTML source code?

✔ what software is required to view the information? do you need the latest version of *Netscape Navigator* or *Internet Explorer*?

✔ is it possible to view a non-frames version of the information?

✔ is any additional software or hardware required? is any additional software easily accessible? are instructions available from the original source for downloading and use of the software?

✔ are there any restrictions to access, such as the need to prove eligibility or membership of an organization?

✔ do you need to register to use the site, and is registration straightforward?

✔ is it possible to bookmark an internal page, or have cookies been used, to avoid the need to re-enter passwords? is there a route for users who have forgotten their passwords?

✔ what language is the information in?

✔ does it cost anything to access the source? what charging schemes are available? is some information available for free? how useful and valuable is the free information in comparison with what is charged for?

✔ is there a statement of copyright ownership? are there details of how materials should be cited in a publication or attributed to an author? is contact information available?

✔ is the source reliably accessible, or is it frequently unavailable? are the times specified when the site is unavailable?

✔ is the site stable, or does it frequently move location? if the site moves, is forwarding information provided?

CHECKLIST 8 EVALUATING THE PRESENTATION AND
ARRANGEMENT OF INFORMATION

✔ is the source clearly presented and arranged? is each screen clearly laid out and aesthetically pleasing? is the text easy to read and do the headings stand out?

✔ is the presentation and arrangement of each page consistent throughout the source?

✔ is there a site map, contents list, index, menu system or search facility? are any such facilities effective?

✔ is the source logically presented and arranged? is the information categorized, and has it been appropriately organized?

✔ are individual pages within a site appropriately divided up? are there too few long pages or too many short pages?

✔ how many 'clicks' does it take to find what you want? are steps unnecessarily repeated? are shortcuts available to access information in as few clicks as possible?

✔ how are hypertext links defined? are they meaningful? do they interrupt the flow of the text?

✔ are there any graphics or moving images? are they necessary? have they been used appropriately? do they add value to the text? are they logically presented in relation to the text?

✔ have frames been used? are they necessary? have they been used appropriately? do they add value to the text?

✔ are there any advertisements? have they been used appropriately, or do they distract the user from the information or the main purpose of the page?

CHECKLIST 9 ASSESSING HOW EASY A SOURCE IS TO USE

✔ is the source generally easy to use?

✔ is the source easy to access?

✔ is the source user-friendly and intuitive, or is training and/or experience required in order to use the source effectively?

✔ is it easy to move around the source and locate information?

✔ are any searching or browsing facilities straightforward and easy to use?

✔ is any help information available? is the help information clear? is the help information context-sensitive? is the help information useful?

✔ are any system messages meaningful and useful?

✔ are any training courses or training documentation available?

✔ is there a telephone helpline, e-mail address or any other user support service available? do you receive a response to e-mails or telephone messages, and is the response time acceptable?

CHECKLIST 10 MAKING A COMPARISON WITH OTHER SOURCES

✔ is the source unique in terms of its content or format, or does the source offer any unique features or facilities?
✔ what is the purpose of the source compared with others?
✔ what is the coverage of the source compared with others?
✔ how authoritative and reputable is the source compared with others?
✔ how accurate is the source compared with others?
✔ how current and well maintained is the source compared with others?
✔ how accessible is the source compared with others?
✔ is the information contained in the source well presented and arranged compared with others?
✔ how easy is the source to use compared with others?
✔ what are the benefits of accessing this information via the internet compared with other formats?
✔ what is the cost of the source and its value for money in comparison with others?

CHECKLIST 11 ASSESSING THE OVERALL QUALITY OF A SOURCE

✔ what is your overall assessment of the source? what conclusions can you draw after having considered the other evaluation issues? is the source valuable and useful, and is the information contained in it valuable and useful?
✔ are any reviews available or is the site included in any databases of high-quality materials?
✔ is it possible to elicit comments from someone who has used the source or who uses it regularly? what is their overall impression of the source?

CHECKLIST 12 EVALUATING ORGANIZATIONAL SITES, PERSONAL HOME PAGES AND OTHER WEBSITES

✔ what is the purpose of the site?
✔ are contact details for the person or the organization concerned readily available? is it easy to locate contact information within the site?
✔ what is the coverage of the site? does the site provide basic information about an individual or an organization, or are additional

materials provided? does the site cover a particular area comprehensively? what subject areas and materials are covered? are there
any pointers to further information and do they enhance the coverage of the site? if the site links to other materials, are the links
valuable and useful? what materials are covered by the links? is
descriptive information provided about the links? is the descriptive
information useful?

✔ what is the reputation and expertise of the individual or the institution responsible for the information? is there any sponsorship for
the site, and does the sponsorship suggest a good reputation? is
there a counter for the site, and does it indicate that the site is
popular? are there any reviews for the site, or has the site been
included in any gateways or virtual libraries?

✔ what is the likely accuracy of the information?

✔ is the information current and is the site well maintained? is there
an update date for each page of information, or is it otherwise possible to ascertain its currency?

✔ is the site easily accessible?

✔ is the information well presented and arranged? is the information
clearly, consistently and logically presented and arranged? are there
any features such as a site map, an index or a search facility? how
effective are they in assisting users to find information?

✔ is the site easy to use, and are there any user support facilities?

✔ how does the site compare with other similar sites? is the site
unique?

✔ what is your overall impression of the quality of the site?

CHECKLIST 13 EVALUATING MAILING LISTS, NEWSGROUPS AND OTHER FORMS OF COMMUNICATION VIA THE INTERNET

✔ what is the purpose of the mailing list or newsgroup?

✔ what is the coverage of the mailing list or newsgroup?

✔ does real exchange and discussion take place via the mailing list or
newsgroup, or does it largely consist of one-off messages?

✔ is the mailing list or newsgroup moderated?

✔ what is the reputation of the mailing list or newsgroup?

✔ is there a list of group members or participants? who are the
participants in the group? how many participants are there? is the
group local, national or international? what is the likely knowledge

and expertise of the participants? are there any restrictions to accessing or subscribing to the group? does the group have a closed membership?

✔ for individual messages: what is the likely accuracy of the information? what is the reputation and expertise of the author? what is the date of the message? is an original source of information cited in the message?

✔ what is the average volume of traffic? is the volume manageable?

✔ is it possible to receive messages in a digest? how frequently is the digest distributed?

✔ has the group adopted conventions for labelling messages?

✔ is an archive available? are files of discussion downloadable from an FTP site? what is the retrospective coverage of the archive? is there a facility for searching the archive? is the archive browsable by date, author and subject thread? is help information available for searching the archive?

✔ is an individual responsible for the group administration? is any administrative or help information available? is the information periodically posted to the group? how useful is the information? are details of subscription, withdrawal of subscription and posting messages included?

✔ how does the mailing list or newsgroup compare with others?

✔ what is your overall impression of the quality of the mailing list or newsgroup?

CHECKLIST 14 EVALUATING FULL-TEXT DOCUMENTS

✔ what is the purpose of the document?

✔ what is the coverage of the document? is the subject covered comprehensively? are there any pointers to further information?

✔ who has produced the document? what is the reputation and expertise of any individuals or organizations involved in the production of the document? is this an authoritative source of information? what is the address of the site, and does it indicate an authoritative institution?

✔ what is the likely accuracy of the information?

✔ does the information have a research basis? what is the quality of the research?

✔ are there any references to published sources of information?

✔ has the information been through any quality-control processes, such as editing or refereeing?

✔ what is the motivation of those involved in the production of the information? is the information likely to be biased by any individuals or organizations involved in its production?

✔ is there a last update date for the document and is the information current?

✔ is the information well presented and arranged?

✔ how does the document compare with others that cover a similar subject?

✔ what is your overall impression of the quality of the document?

CHECKLIST 15 EVALUATING DATABASES

✔ what is the intended purpose, coverage and audience of the database? is this information available from any introductory information or help files?

✔ what is the coverage of the database? what subject areas and materials are covered? is the database comprehensive within a particular area? what is the retrospective coverage of the database? is information available about the material which is included in the database?

✔ does the database contain links to further sources of information?

✔ are different versions of the same database available? are there any differences in coverage?

✔ how much information is provided in each record of the database? is the amount of information useful, and sufficient for the needs of the user?

✔ in the case of bibliographical databases: do they consist of references only or are abstracts available? for what percentage of the records are abstracts provided? have the abstracts been truncated by word length?

✔ is it possible to identify the authors responsible for the information in the database? what are their knowledge and expertise?

✔ what is the reputation of the database? is the database included in any guides to reference works, such as *Walford*'s, or in a gateway or virtual library?

✔ are there any typographical or spelling errors? are there any errors in bibliographical citations? are there any quality-control procedures in place?

✔ is the database current and well maintained? how frequently is the database updated? is there a time delay between the publication of materials and their appearance in the database?

✔ what searching and browsing facilities are available? are any searching and browsing facilities useful, effective and easy to use? what outputting and downloading options are available? is it easy to output and download data from the database? can data be exported to other packages? is this easy to do?

✔ in relation to bibliographical databases: is it possible to search by author, title or subject keyword? can searches be limited by publication type and date range? are there any additional searching or browsing features? are the search and browse facilities effective, easy to use and useful?

✔ is it possible to order material directly from the database?

✔ is contact information available?

✔ is the database easily accessible? are there any restrictions to access? is there a charge for accessing the database or downloading records?

✔ is the database easy to use and are there any user support facilities?

✔ how does the database compare with other similar databases?

✔ what is your overall impression of the quality of the database?

CHECKLIST 16 EVALUATING ELECTRONIC JOURNALS AND MAGAZINES

✔ what is the coverage of the site? what are the aims and objectives of the site providing access to the journal or magazine? is the whole journal or magazine available? if only parts are available, how are those parts selected? is the site intended simply for advertising purposes?

✔ what is the purpose of the journal or magazine?

✔ what is the coverage of the journal or magazine?

✔ is there an archive for accessing back issues of the journal or magazine? what is the retrospective coverage of the archive? is the archive searchable by subject, author, volume and/or issue number? is it possible to limit searches by date range? how useful and effective is the search facility?

✔ what is the reputation of the journal or magazine? is it an authoritative journal or magazine? what are the reputation and experience of the editorial board? what are the reputation and experience of any other organizations involved in the production of the journal or magazine?

✔ in relation to academic journals: what is the impact factor of the journal? what is the genealogy of the journal? how long has it been available? is there a paper-based equivalent? is the journal refereed, and how stringent is the refereeing process? is the journal indexed in any appropriate bibliographical databases?

✔ is the site well maintained? is there a time delay between article acceptance and publication in the journal? what is the time delay? is there a time difference between production of the printed and electronic publications? is there a facility for updating articles? are details provided of any updating procedures?

✔ is the site easily accessible?

✔ is the information well presented and arranged? is there a site index? how easy is it to locate individual issues within the site? is there a contents list for each issue? is it easy to locate individual articles? are there links between citations and the main body of the text in each article?

✔ are there any additional features, such as an option to e-mail comments on articles or to link directly into other electronic sources? can you receive the contents pages of each issue of a journal as it is published? do these facilities add value to the journal or magazine?

✔ can articles be displayed in PDF? is it easy to download the necessary software and access the article concerned?

✔ is the site easy to use, and are there any user support facilities?

✔ how does the site, journal or magazine compare with other similar sites, journals or magazines?

✔ what is your overall impression of the quality of the site, journal or magazine?

CHECKLIST 17 EVALUATING SOURCES OF NEWS INFORMATION

✔ what is the purpose of the site?

✔ what is the coverage of the site? what topics are covered, and are they covered comprehensively?

✔ is the site an electronic version of a printed publication, or is it the site for a television or radio station? does the site provide access to the whole content, and if not how has the information been selected?

✔ what is the reputation and expertise of any individuals or organizations involved in the production of the site? is this an authoritative source of information?

✔ what is the likely accuracy of the information? has the information been through any quality-control processes, such as refereeing?

✔ is the information likely to be biased by any individuals involved in its production?

✔ is there an explicit date for the information? is the information up-to-date? when was the information last updated? when will the information next be updated? how frequently is the information updated? is there a statement of policy regarding the frequency of updating and the updating process? does the source need to be monitored or reassessed at a later date to ensure continued currency and maintenance?

✔ is the site easily accessible?

✔ is the information well presented and arranged?

✔ is the site easy to use and are there any user support facilities?

✔ how does the site compare with other similar sites?

✔ what is your overall impression of the quality of the site?

CHECKLIST 18 EVALUATING ADVERTISING, SPONSORSHIP AND OTHER COMMERCIAL INFORMATION

✔ what is the purpose of the site? is the site designed purely to advertise a product, or to advertise the products and services of a particular company? is it easy to distinguish between advertisements and other information?

✔ who is responsible for producing the information? what is the motivation of any individuals or organizations in making this information available? is the information likely to be biased by any individuals or organizations involved in its production?

✔ what is the coverage of the site?

✔ is the information current, and is the site well maintained?

✔ is the site easily accessible?

✔ is the information well presented and arranged?

✔ is the site easy to use and are there any user support facilities?

✔ how does the site compare with other similar sites?

✔ what is your overall impression of the quality of the site?

CHECKLIST 19 EVALUATING IMAGE-BASED AND MULTIMEDIA SOURCES

✔ what is the purpose of the site?

✔ what is the coverage of the site? what topics are covered by individual images, video or sound clips? what is the range of different subjects covered as a whole? is the site comprehensive within an area?

✔ is explanatory text available? what level of detail is provided in any explanatory text? is the explanatory text sufficient for the needs of the user concerned? does the explanatory text enhance the value of the images or other non-textual materials? is the balance of text and images or other non-textual materials appropriate?

✔ are there any pointers to further information which enhance the coverage of the site?

✔ what is the reputation of the source? is it an authoritative source? for teaching materials: is the material provided commercially or by an academic institution?

✔ is the information current, and is the site well maintained? is there a date of production for any images or other non-textual materials? are there any details of updating? what is the motivation and expertise of those responsible for maintaining the materials?

✔ is the site easily accessible?

✔ is there a mirror site?

✔ have thumbnail images been used?

✔ is copyright information available?

✔ are contact details available?

✔ for teaching materials: is it possible to download a self-contained package using FTP for local use, or are materials accessed via a website? does the mode of access affect the speed?

✔ what is the file format that is used? what is the size of the files?

✔ is the information well presented and arranged? is it easy to navigate between different images or materials? are images or other non-textual materials clear? what is the image resolution?

✔ are images in colour or black-and-white? are images two-dimensional, three-dimensional or video clips?

✔ are there any features or facilities which take advantage of the multimedia format? do any such features or facilities add value to the content of the site?

✔ is the site easy to use and are there any user support facilities?

✔ how does the site compare with other similar sites?

✔ what is your overall impression of the quality of the site?

CHECKLIST 20 EVALUATING CURRENT AWARENESS AND ALERTING SERVICES

✔ what is the purpose of the service?
✔ what is the coverage of the service? is it possible to submit a profile to the service in order to limit the information received to particular subject areas?
✔ what is the reputation and expertise of any organizations involved in the production of the service?
✔ what is the likely accuracy of the information?
✔ is the information current? how frequently is the service updated or the mailing list distributed? is the information provided by the service timely – i.e. is the information provided when it is most needed?
✔ is the service available as a mailing list, a website or both?
✔ is the service easily accessible?
✔ is the information well presented and arranged? is it easy to identify the subjects covered by individual postings for mailing lists?
✔ is the service easy to use and are there any user support facilities?
✔ how does the service compare with other similar services?
✔ what is your overall impression of the quality of the service?

CHECKLIST 21 EVALUATING FTP ARCHIVES

✔ what is the purpose of the archive?
✔ what is the coverage of the archive? what software or data are available? in what formats are the software or data? are software or data available for different types of computers and platforms? are upgrades and older versions of data or software available? are trial versions of software available?
✔ is the site easily accessible?
✔ is a mirror site available? what is the coverage of the mirror site in comparison with the original? how frequently is the mirror site updated in comparison with the original?
✔ are files compressed to ensure faster download times? are details available about the software required to decompress files?
✔ what is the reputation of the archive? is it a well-known source for data or software?
✔ are there any quality-control or virus-checking facilities? are they effective?

✔ is the archive well maintained? is there a time delay between software development (or data generation) and its availability via the archive?
✔ is contact information available for a site maintainer?
✔ is information available on file origins, software version numbers, the expiry date for trial versions, and file sizes?
✔ is there a search facility? does the archive allow you to browse or search by filename, platform or type of application?
✔ is the archive easy to use, and are there any user support facilities? is there any help information, a FAQ or README files? is there any help information for any search facilities? how useful or valuable is the information provided?
✔ how does the archive compare with other similar archives?
✔ what is your overall impression of the quality of the archive?

List of websites

Abortion: some medical facts
http://www.nrlc.org/abortion/ASMF/asmf.html

alldomains.com
http://www.alldomains.com/

AltaVista
http:// www.altavista.com/

AltaVista Australia
http://au.altavista.com/

AltaVista Canada
http://in.altavistacanada.com/

AltaVista India
http://in.altavista.com/

AltaVista UK
http://uk.altavista.com/

American Library Association (ALA) criteria
http://www.ala.org/parentspage/greatsites/criteria.html

Argus Clearinghouse
http://www.clearinghouse.net/

Argus Clearinghouse ratings system
http://www.clearinghouse.net/ratings.html

Ariadne
http://www.ariadne.ac.uk/

Barnsley Chronicle Online
http://www.barnsley-chronicle.co.uk/

BBC News
http://news.bbc.co.uk/

BigHub.com
http://www.isleuth.com/

BIOME
http://biome.ac.uk/

Bristol BioMed Image Archive
http://www.brisbio.ac.uk/

Britannica.com
http://www.britannica.com/

British Library
http://www.bl.uk/

British Medical Journal (BMJ)
http://www.bmj.com/

BUBL Information Service
http://bubl.ac.uk/

BUBL Link / 5:15
http://bubl.ac.uk/link/

CIN Seal of Approval
http://www.gocin.com/cin/Seal_Of_Approval.cfm

CNN
http://www.cnn.com/

CompletePlanet
http://www.completeplanet.com/

Corbis
http://store.corbis.com/

Department of Health
http://www.doh.gov.uk/

Dermatology Online Journal
http://dermatology.cdlib.org/

Dermatology Online Journal evaluation criteria
http://dermatology.cdlib.org/DOJvol1num1/internet-appraisal.html

DISCERN
http//www.discern.org.uk/

DISCERN tool
http//www.discern.org.uk/discern_instrument.htm

Dr Hulda R. Clark
http://members.aol.com/sidskids1/health/cancerbk.htm

EEVL
http://www.eevl.ac.uk/

eLib
http://ukoln.ac.uk/services/elib/

Elsevier Science
http://www.elsevier.nl/

Excite
http://www.excite.com/

Excite search voyeur
http://www.excite.com/search/voyeur/

Excite UK
http://www.excite.co.uk/

FindIt
http://www.rdn.ac.uk/findit/

Foot and Mouth FAQ
http://www.maff.gov.uk/animalh/diseases/fmd/qa1.htm

Galaxy
http://www.galaxy.com/

Genome Database
http://www.gdb.org/

Google
http://www.google.com/

Google newsgroups
http://groups.google.com/

GU sports nutrition for athletes
http://www.gusports.com/

The Guardian
http://www.guardian.co.uk/

Health on the Net (HoN) Foundation
http://www.hon.ch/

Hi-Ethics
http://www.hiethics.org/
HONcode
http://www.hon.ch/HONcode/Conduct.html

Humbul
http://www.humbul.ac.uk/

Infomine: scholarly internet resource collections
http://infomine.ucr.edu/

Internet Content Rating Association
http://www.icra.org/

Internet Movie Database (IMDb)
http://www.imdb.com/

Internet Public Library
http://www.ipl.org/

Internet Seal of Approval
http://www.isamember.com/

InvisibleWeb.com
http://www.invisibleweb.com/

JISCmail
http://www.jiscmail.ac.uk/

jobs.ac.uk
http://www.jobs.ac.uk/

Journal Citation Reports
http://jcrweb.com/

Journal of Theoretics
http://www.journaloftheoretics.com/Editorials/Editorial%201-4.html

Kathy Schrock's criteria (elementary)
http://school.discovery.com/schrockguide/evalelem.html

Kathy Schrock's criteria (middle school)
http://school.discovery.com/schrockguide/evalmidd.html

Kathy Schrock's criteria (secondary school)
http://school.discovery.com/schrockguide/

The Lancet
http://www.thelancet.com/

Librarians' Index to the Internet
http://lii.org/

Librarians' Index to the Internet selection criteria
http://lii.org/search/file/pubcriteria/

LifePlus Health Benefits
http://www.staywellvitamins.com/lifep.htm

list UNIVERSE.COM
http://list-universe.com/

Liszt
http://www.liszt.com/

LookSmart
http://www.looksmart.com/

Lycos
http://www.lycos.com/

MAFF home page
http://www.maff.gov.uk/

Mailbase
http://www.mailbase.ac.uk/

MedCERTAIN
http://www.medcertain.org/

Medical Matrix
http://www.medmatrix.org/index.asp

National Institutes for Health
http://www.nih.gov/

National Right to Life Committee
http://www.nrlc.org/

NBCi.com
http://www.nbci.com/

NISS Vacancies
http://www.vacancies.ac.uk/

Northern Light
http://www.northernlight.com/

Nutrition advice for athletes
http://www.hhdev.psu.edu/research/athletes.htm

Nutrition for athletes
http://www.ausport.gov.au/nut.html

OMNI
http://omni.ac.uk/

pchelp mailing list
http://groups.yahoo.com/group/pchelp/

Pet emails
http://www.petemails.com/

Phil Bradley's home page
http://www.philb.com/

Philosophy around the Web
http://users.ox.ac.uk/%7Eworc0337/phil_index.html

PIER
http://www.sussex.ac.uk/library/pier/subjects/general/gateways.html

PINAKES
http://www.hw.ac.uk/libWWW/irn/pinakes/pinakes.html

PSIgate
http://www.psigate.ac.uk

PubMed
http://www.ncbi.nlm.nih.gov/PubMed/

Quality Search Engine (QSE)
http://www.a1source.com/

Resource Discovery Network (RDN)
http://www.rdn.ac.uk/

Rubric for evaluating WebQuests
http://edweb.sdsu.edu/webquest/webquestrubric.html

SafeSurf
http://www.safesurf.com/

SCOUT Report selection criteria
http://scout.cs.wisc.edu/report/sr/criteria.html

SCOUT Report Signpost
http://www.signpost.org/

Search Adobe PDF Online
http://searchpdf.adobe.com/

Search Engine Watch
http://www.searchenginewatch.com/

SoccerAge
http://www.soccerage.com/

Sonia Baur's home page
http://www.unc.edu/~bauer/

SOSIG
http://www.sosig.ac.uk/

SOSIG evaluation criteria
http://sosig.ac.uk/desire/ecrit.html

Southern Trekking and Mountaineering Club
http://www.st-mc.org.uk/

Star Trek FAQ
http://www.ee.surrey.ac.uk/Contrib/SciFi/StarTrek/FAQ.html

The Telegraph
http://www.telegraph.co.uk/

The Times
http://www.thetimes.co.uk/

topica
http://www.topica.com/

TRUSTe
http://www.truste.org/

Ugly People of the Internet
http://www.tqci.net/~tvc15/ugly/main.html

UK Office for Library Networking (UKOLN)
http://www.ukoln.ac.uk/

Useless Pages
http://www.go2net.com/useless/

Van Gogh Museum
http://www.vangoghmuseum.nl/

viewimages
http://www.viewimages.com/

Vincent Van Gogh Gallery
http://www.vangoghgallery.com/

Web of Science
http://wos.mimas.ac.uk/

WebSite Investigator
http://www.motivationmining.com/website_investigator.htm

WinSite
http://www.winsite.com/

World Health Organisation (WHO)
http://www.who.int/

World Wide Web Consortium (W3C)
http://www.w3c.org/

Yahoo!
http://www.yahoo.com/

Yahooligans!
http://www.yahooligans.com/

Glossary

Acrobat Reader
: The software required for displaying or printing documents in portable document format (PDF)

bibliographical database
: A database of references to journal articles, books, conference proceedings, etc.

bookmark
: A website address stored on a user's computer as a menu item so that he or she can easily return to it without having to retype the address – referred to as a 'favorite' in *Internet Explorer*

Boolean operators
: 'AND', 'OR' and 'NOT', commonly used to combine more than one term in a search query to ensure more effective retrieval

browser
: A piece of software which is used to view information available via networks; examples are *Netscape Navigator* and *Internet Explorer*, which are browsers used for accessing information available via the web

CAL materials *see* computer-assisted learning materials

CAS *see* current awareness service

citation searching
: Traditionally refers to using the *Citation Indexes* to find papers which have cited a particular author; used within the internet environment to refer to searching for web pages which link to a particular site

client

Refers to a local computer, and also the software which resides on a local computer; the user inputs data into the client software which then interprets any information which is received from a remote computer (the server)

command-line interface (CLI)

An interface which generally appears as a prompt on the screen which users must type in predefined commands in order to run a program

computer-assisted learning (CAL) materials

Multimedia materials which are designed to aid teaching and learning through the use of computing technology

cookies

Facilities which allow users to specify preferences for viewing particular web pages; the preferences are saved as a cookie on the user's machine, and each time the user views a site, the browser checks to see if the user has any preferences (or cookies) for the page; an example of their use is for storing usernames and passwords

counter

Used to indicate how many people have visited a site during a specified time period, and thus to indicate a site's popularity

current awareness service (CAS)

A service designed to alert users to new developments in a particular topic or issue; an example is a service that distributes the contents listings of journals

database

A collection of records, each with details of a different data item, whether numeric, textual or image-based; usually searchable

deep web *see* invisible web

directory service *see* subject catalogue

discussion list *see* mailing list

distributed client-server computing

The technology whereby data is located on a remote computer, the server, which is accessible via a network; the software for accessing the data is located on the user's own machine, the client

electronic journals

Also sometimes called e-journals, electronic journals are journals that have been produced in an electronic format; sometimes the electronic equivalent of a paper-based journal, although an increasing number of journals are produced entirely in an electronic format

eLib

The *Electronic Libraries Programme*, a programme of nationally funded research projects in the UK which are concerned with the development, implementation and evaluation of the electronic library

e-mail

Electronic mail – software which enables messages to be sent from one person's computer to another across a network or the internet

FAQ *see* frequently asked questions

favorite

A website address stored on a user's computer as a menu item so that he or she can easily return to it without having to retype the address – referred to as a 'bookmark' in *Netscape Navigator*

File Transfer Protocol (FTP)

The protocol that enables users to transfer files from one computer to another across the internet

frames

A facility which is used to divide an HTML page into two or more pages, so that more than one page can be viewed at the same time; commonly used to display the contents listing for sites in one frame, with the site itself in a second frame

frequently asked questions (FAQ)

A file of commonly asked questions, with answers, about a particular topic or issue; these are often used to summarize the most frequently asked questions to a Usenet newsgroup or discussion list, but are also commonly used as a source of help information about websites and pages

FTP *see* File Transfer Protocol

FTP archive

A collection of files, such as software, textual materials or numerical data, which can be accessed and retrieved across the internet using the FTP protocol

gateways

A collection of searchable (and usually browsable) resource descriptions which have been developed by library professionals and/or subject experts with the explicit aim of providing access to high-quality sources of information within a particular subject area

Gopher

An early example of a distributed client-server tool which presented information available via the internet through a browsable system of menus; a Gopher browser was required to access the information

graphical user interface (GUI)

An interface that includes images as well as text which the user can select in order to access information

GUI *see* graphical user interface

harvester

Another name for a search engine

home page

The opening page of any site on the web is generally referred to as the 'home page'; for example, the first page of an organization's site is the 'home page'; an individual's personal site or page is also referred to as a 'personal home page'

HTML *see* HyperText Mark-up Language

HTTP *see* HyperText Transfer Protocol

hypertext

Text which contains cross-references or links (hypertext links) to different parts of the same page or to different pages; information can be browsed by simply clicking on the links

HyperText Mark-up Language (HTML)

The language used to produce information in a format suitable for dissemination via the web

HyperText Transfer Protocol (HTTP)

One of the protocols used to transfer information via the web

internet

A world-wide network of interconnected networks, connected together using recognized standards or protocols to enable electronic communication and the exchange of information

Internet Explorer

A multimedia browser for accessing information available via the web that is supplied as part of the *Microsoft Office* suite of software products

invisible web

Sometimes also referred to as the 'deep web' – the information that cannot be accessed by search engines because it is hidden behind a log-in screen or a search interface

Java

A programming language which allows authors to create applets – small programs that run within a web page

kitemarks

A logo or badge displayed on a website which is used to indicate that it has been evaluated and approved by a third-party rating service

Listserv *see* mailing list

mailing list
Also sometimes called a 'discussion list' or 'listserv', a mailing list is a group of e-mail users who are interested in a particular topic area; e-mail users subscribe to the list and they can then post to it and receive all the messages which are posted

metadata
Data about data, similar to a bibliographical record, which is written into the 'header' part of the HTML of a web page but is not displayed automatically to the user; metadata can be used to specify information about a page, such as a description or subject keywords which represent the contents of a site

metasearch engines
Also sometimes called 'meta-crawlers' and 'multisearch engines', these allow users to search several search facilities all at once

meta tag
The group of tags containing the metadata for a web page; located within the 'header' part of the page so that the information is not displayed automatically to the user by the browser

mirror site
A copy of an original site which is located elsewhere; usually contains the same or similar information as the original site and is often used to improve access speeds to heavily used sites

Mosaic
One of the earliest multimedia browsers for accessing the web; now largely superseded by *Netscape Navigator* and *Internet Explorer*

multimedia
Something which encompasses a range of different media, such as images, sound and video clips, as well as text

multimedia browser
A browser which allows the user to view text, graphics, moving images, etc.

Netscape Navigator
A multimedia browser for accessing information which is available via the web

newsgroups *see* Usenet newsgroups

organizational website
A collection of web pages that are created and maintained by a particular organization; the opening page is generally referred to as the 'home page'

password
> A secret and unique identifier which individuals use, in conjunction with their username, and that allows them to log onto a machine or to log into a particular service

PDF *see* Portable Document Format

personal home page
> A web page (or collection of pages) which is maintained by an individual and relates to his or her personal interests

PICS *see* Platform for Internet Content Selection

Platform for Internet Content Selection (PICS)
> The metadata tags of a web page which can be used for ratings supplied by the author or by a third-party rating service; commonly used to rate adult content and filter materials; PICS is the platform used, not a rating scheme in itself

Portable Document Format (PDF)
> A file format created by Adobe Systems, which allows the display or printing of materials in a format which is virtually identical to an original paper-based publication; commonly used to display journal articles as they appear on paper; requires the use of *Acrobat Reader* to view or print materials

protocol
> A set of data-exchange rules which specify how computers transmit data between different computers and across networks

publicly indexable web
> The part of the web which can be indexed by search engines because the information is not hidden behind a log-in screen or a search interface

RDN *see* Resource Discovery Network

Resource Discovery Network
> A free internet service funded by the UK government to enable access to high-quality internet-based resources through the development of gateways

seal of approval
> A logo or badge displayed on a website which is used to indicate that it has been evaluated and approved by a third-party rating service

search engines
> Also called 'spiders', 'crawlers', 'robots' and 'harvesters', search engines are automatically generated databases of web materials; software searches the web, creating a searchable index or database of materials

server
> A remote computer which is accessed by a client via a network

subject catalogue

Subject catalogues and directories are search services which involve human input in identifying relevant resources and allocating them to particular subject categories; the tools are usually searchable and browsable via the subject categories; resources are not evaluated in terms of their quality prior to inclusion in the catalogue or directory

TCP/IP *see* Transmission Control Protocol/Internet Protocol

telnet

A protocol and application which allows users to log onto and access or search a remote computer

text-based browser

A browser which only allows the user to view text; different software must be used to access graphics, moving images or sound

thumbnail image

A small-scale image which can be selected in order to view a much larger version of the same image

tilde

The character '~', which appears in the address of some web pages

Transmission Control Protocol/Internet Protocol (TCP/IP)

A set of computer networking standards upon which the running of the Internet is based

Uniform Resource Locator (URL)

The full address of a resource on the internet; every site or page on the internet has a unique URL, which consists of the protocol (e.g. http), the server name, the domain name and the pathname of the resource

URL *see* Uniform Resource Locator

Usenet newsgroups

A world-wide distributed system of bulletin boards which are hierarchically arranged into topic areas; these are similar to discussion lists in that users can discuss a particular area of interest, but users do not have to subscribe, and anyone can view the messages

username

The name which individuals use to log onto a machine or to log into a particular service; usually individuals will also have a password which is used in conjunction with the username

virtual libraries

Collections of resources which have been selected, evaluated and described by library professionals and/or subject experts with the explicit aim of providing access to high-quality sources of information

web

The part of the internet based around documents written in HTML; hypertext links enable users to move between different parts of the same document, as well as to different documents in different locations

world wide web *see* web

WWW *see* web

web page

An individual HTML page which is available via the web; a collection of related pages is usually referred to as a website

website

A collection of linked HTML pages available via the web, generally owned or produced by a single institution or individual

Index